19.50

MALAYSIAN NATURE HANDBOOKS
General Editor
M. W. F. TWEEDIE

The aim of the Malaysian Nature Handbooks is to provide a series of handy, well-illustrated guides to the fauna and flora of Malaysia and Singapore. They can, of course, be no more than introductory; the animal and plant life of Malaysia is on such a lavish scale that comprehensive accounts of the groups described in each of the Handbooks must be either severely technical or voluminous and correspondingly costly. The selection of species described in each one has been carefully made, however, to illustrate those most likely to be the first encountered by reasonably observant people residing in or visiting Malaysia and Singapore; reference to rarities or species confined to inaccessible country has been avoided, except where such species are of special interest.

It is the Editor's belief that interest in animals and plants is best aroused by providing the means of identifying and naming them. The emphasis of the Handbooks is therefore firstly on identification, but as much information on habits and biology is included as space will allow. It is hoped that they may be of use to schools in supplementing courses in nature study and biology, and a source of pleasure to that quite numerous assemblage of people whose complaint has been that they would gladly be naturalists if someone would show them the way.

OTHER TITLES IN THE SERIES

M. R. Henderson COMMON MALAYAN WILDFLOWERS

R. Morrell COMMON MALAYAN BUTTERFLIES

M. W. F. Tweedie COMMON BIRDS OF THE MALAY PENINSULA

B. M. Allen COMMON MALAYSIAN FRUITS

M. W. F. Tweedie MAMMALS OF MALAYSIA

L. J. Henrey CORAL REEFS OF MALAYSIA AND SINGAPORE

MALAYSIAN NATURE HANDBOOKS

Common Malaysian Beetles

VINCENT WENG-YEW TUNG

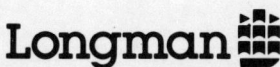

LONGMAN MALAYSIA SDN. BERHAD
Wisma Damansara, Jalan Semantan, Kuala Lumpur

Associated companies, branches and representatives throughout the world

© Vincent Weng-Yew Tung 1983

All rights reserved. No part of this publication may be reproduced, stored in a retrieval system, or transmitted in any form or by any means, electronic, mechanical, photo-copying, recording, or otherwise, without the prior permission of the Copyright owner.

First published 1983

ISBN 0 582 72427 9

Printed by Art Printing Works Sdn. Bhd., Kuala Lumpur.

TO
ELAINE (HOO-KIAN)
MY PARENTS, BROTHERS AND SISTERS
AND ALL MY FAMILY AND FRIENDS

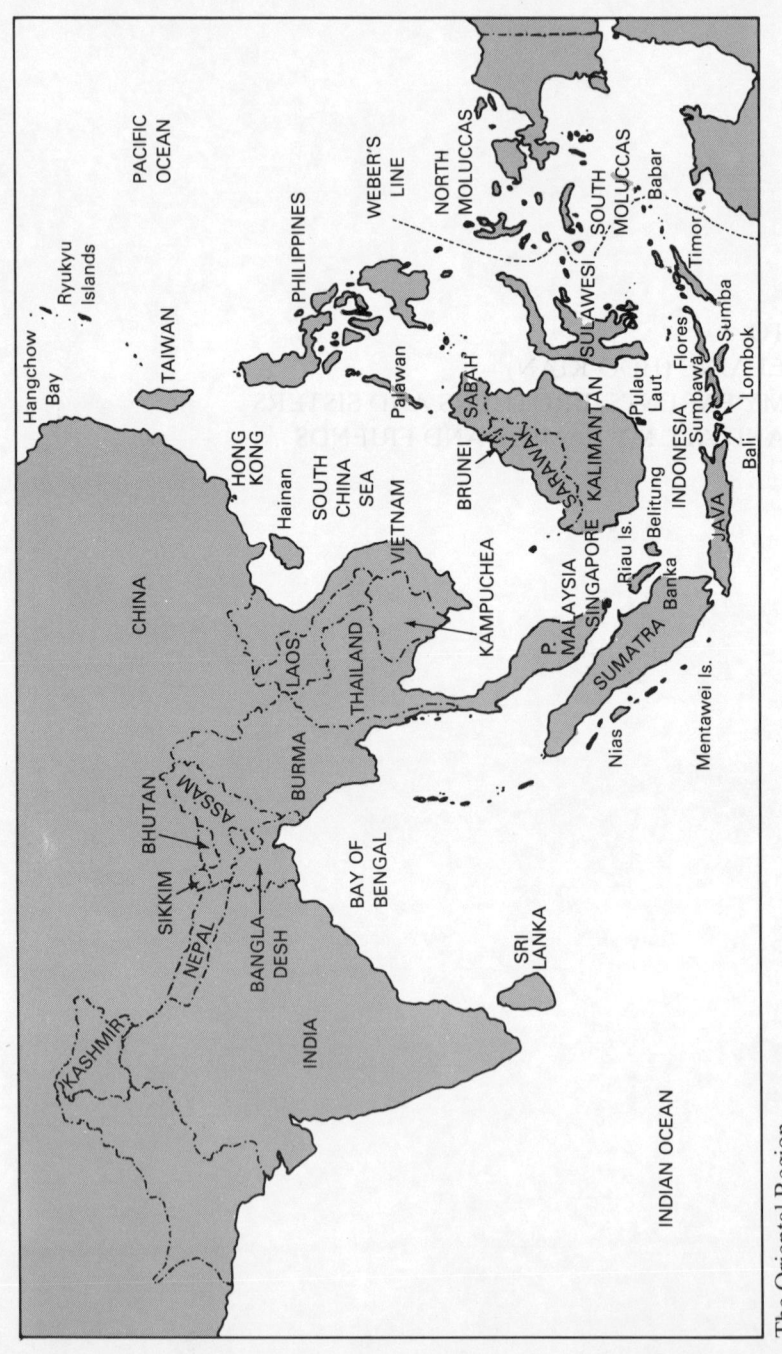

The Oriental Region

CONTENTS

Preface	viii
Acknowledgements	x
List of Plates	xii
Introduction	1
The Beetle	3
Making a Collection	20
Description of Species	32
CICINDELIDAE (Tiger Beetles)	34
CARABIDAE (Ground Beetles)	36
DYTISCIDAE (Predaceous Diving Beetles)	39
SILPHIDAE (Carrion Beetles)	40
LUCANIDAE (Stag Beetles or Pinching Bugs)	41
PASSALIDAE (Sugar Beetles or Bessbugs)	54
SCARABAEIDAE (Scarab Beetles and Chafers)	57
BUPRESTIDAE (Splendour or Metallic Wood-boring Beetles)	69
ELATERIDAE (Click Beetles or Skipjacks)	76
LAMPYRIDAE (Fireflies)	78
LYCIDAE (Net-winged Beetles)	80
EROTYLIDAE (Pleasing Fungus Beetles)	81
COCCINELLIDAE (Ladybirds)	82
TRICTENOTOMIDAE (False Longhorn Beetles)	84
CERAMBYCIDAE (Longhorn, Longicorn or Timber Beetles)	85
CHRYSOMELIDAE (Leaf Beetles and Tortoise Beetles)	99
CURCULIONIDAE (Weevils or Snout Beetles)	103
Beetles and Man	109
Integrated Pest Control	114
Glossary	119
Bibliography	129
Food Plant Index	135
General Index	137

PREFACE

This book is intended to provide a brief introduction to common beetles occurring in Malaysia. It is hoped that it will prove informative and of assistance to students of natural history and agriculture, making possible the identification of a number of the commoner Malaysian beetles, with the help of illustrations.

To most people, beetles are pests on the food we grow and eat. Man himself is always endeavouring to invent better and more insecticides for the purpose of controlling them. Man has achieved to a certain degree his aim of getting rid of many of the commoner beetles. But we must take into consideration that not all Coleopteran (beetle) species are harmful. From time immemorial these insects have also been extremely beneficial to mankind; many serve as important pollinators, others do good service by destroying aphids, scale insects, plant lice, and other bugs which are injurious to cultivated crops and the valuable timber of our tropical rain forest. In addition, carrion beetles (SILPHIDAE) and dung beetles (SCARABAEINAE) break down and digest vegetable and animal debris and carrion; they also insert these into the soil, as food for their broods, which, in turn, enriches the earth. Species of PASSALIDAE and LUCANIDAE are also agriculturally important, as they help to break down aged, fallen, and dead trees. This not only enriches the soil but also clears away unwanted vegetation so that it is not a barrier to human activity.

Artificial insecticides, habitat destruction (e.g. by clearing forest), and insect trade are among the greatest threats to these small creatures. Such activities will eventually mean the extinction of countless species, a great loss ecologically, not to mention the loss to entomologists.

Over-collecting (mainly for sale) of insects can be seen to be going on in many parts of the world, Africa and South America as well as our own country. Amateur collectors should not be tempted to sell their specimens, for this can endanger the survival of the species. Near the Cameron Highlands the collector is liable to find himself in competition with dozens of aborigines who are collecting insects for dealers.

It is sad that there are only a handful of Malaysians who are really interested in the study of beetles and very few records have been made. But it is not too late to take a look at the natural history of Malaysia and learn something about the mysterious life habits, the diverse coloration and the economic importance of these insects. Malaysia is still a paradise for collecting and studying beetles, for hundreds of these small creatures are waiting to be discovered and classified. Perhaps one day, a new species may be named after you as the person who first collected it.

Finally, this book is written to encourage more people to start collections of beetles and keep detailed records so as to help in solving the vast number of entomological and ecological questions which still need to be answered.

ACKNOWLEDGEMENTS

To Mr H.S. Barlow, I offer my utmost gratitude and thanks for his kind assistance, his interest in my work on our beetle fauna, his many generous gifts of books which enabled me to carry on this work, and for reading the drafts.

My thanks are due to Ms Avril Fox who kindly volunteered to correct the English of the manuscript of the book.

I should like to thank Elaine who has helped, with much persuasion as well as encouragement, to make this dream into a reality.

And to Mr Michael K.P. Yeh, the person who first suggested that such a book should be written, I am greatly indebted for his invaluable co-operation and for the most up-to-date information he constantly provided me with.

I also owe deep gratitude to Mr Leow Kon Fah; Mr and Mrs Chong Chin Phuan and especially their son, Mr Chong Kia Kwang, who have collected many interesting and unusual specimens for me; Dr Michael Cox of the Commonwealth Institute of Entomology, British Museum Natural History, England; and Mrs Bernadette Choe of Longman Malaysia Sendirian Berhad. Mr and Mrs Choo Chiew Chin and my sister Corina have also given help and encouragement.

Additionally I would like to acknowledge the help and assistance, in various ways, of the following: Mr S. Chan, Dr D.H. Murphy, Mr Shoji Soman, Mr Mana Sukkit, Mr A.S. Tan, Mr K.C. Thong, Mr and Mrs James and Regina Too, Misses Joanna, Selina and Sook-Kiew, Messrs Francis and Patrick Tung, Mr and Mrs Stephen and Kathryn Tung, Mr and Mrs S. Wong, Mr T.H. Wong, the Most Honourable Datuk Seri Y.L. Yuen, and Encik Syed Zafri Zin.

Special thanks are due to my parents who have given me much valued guidance.

Last but not least, I would like to acknowledge the assistance of the Director-General of Museums Department, Dato' Shahrum bin Yub, the Deputy Director-General, Encik Mohd. Zulkifli bin Haji Abdul Aziz, the Curator of Natural History, Mr S.H. Heah and the staff of the Entomology Section, Mr Roy D. Lourdes and Encik Shaiful Bahkri bin Basri for providing several specimens for photography. The editorial board and staff of Longman Malaysia have been extremely helpful, particularly Mr M.W.F. Tweedie, general editor of the Malaysian Nature Handbooks.

V.W.Y. Tung

LIST OF PLATES

PLATE 1 A *Cicindela aurulenta* ♂
B *Cicindela sumatrensis* ♂
C *Cicindela versicolor* ♂
D *Collyris bonelli* ♂
E *Therates basalis* ♂
F *Casnoidea interstitialis* ♂
G *Mormolyce phyllodes* ♂
H *Mormolyce castelnaudi* ♂
I *Mormolyce castelnaudi* ♀

PLATE 2 A *Aegus acuminatus* ♂
B *Aegus capitatus* ♂
C *Aegus falcifer* ♂
D *Aegus capitatus* ♀
E *Allotopus moseri* ♂
F *Allotopus moseri* ♀
G *Allotopus rosenbergi* ♂
H *Allotopus fruhstorferi* ♂

PLATE 3 A *Cladognathus giraffa* ♂
B *Cyclommatus albersi* ♂
C *Cyclommatus canaliculatus* ♂
D *Cyclommatus lunifer* ♂
E *Cyclommatus terandus* ♂
F *Dorcus antaeus* ♂
G *Dorcus curvidens* ♂

PLATE 4 A *Dorcus gypaetus* ♂
B *Dorcus reichei* ♂
C *Hexarthrius deyrollei* ♀
D *Dorcus titanus* ♂

E *Hexarthrius deyrollei* ♂
F *Odontolabis aerata* ♂-form *mesodonta*
G *Odontolabis aerata* ♂-form *amphiodonta*
H *Odontolabis aerata* ♀

PLATE 5 A *Odontolabis castelnaudi* ♂
B *Odontolabis dalmani* ♂
C *Odontolabis castelnaudi* ♀
D *Odontolabis femoralis* ♂-form *amphiodonta*
E *Odontolabis femoralis* ♂-form *telodonta*
F *Odontolabis femoralis* ♀

PLATE 6 A *Odontolabis gazella* ♂
B *Odontolabis latipennis* ♂
C *Odontolabis bellicosus* ♂
D *Odontolabis sommeri* ♂-form *mesodonta*
E *Odontolabis sommeri* ♂-form *amphiomesodonta*
F *Odontolabis wallastoni* ♂-form *amphiodonta*
G *Odontolabis wallastoni* ♂-form *telodonta*
H *Odontolabis wallastoni* ♀

PLATE 7 A *Hexarthrius mandibularis* ♂
B *Odontolabis brookeana* ♂
C *Odontolabis brookeana* ♀
D *Duliticola* sp ♀

PLATE 8 A *Prosopocoilus cinnamoeus* ♂
B *Prosopocoilus elaphus* ♂
C *Prosopocoilus cinnamoeus* ♀
D *Prosopocoilus feai* ♂
E *Prosopocoilus forceps* ♂
F *Prosopocoilus forcifer* ♂
G *Prosopocoilus occipitalis* ♂-form *amphiodonta*
H *Prosopocoilus occipitalis* ♂-form *mesodonta*
I *Prosopocoilus occipitalis* ♀
J *Prosopocoilus zebra* ♂-form *telodonta*

PLATE 9 A *Prosopocoilus zebra* ♂-form *amphiodonta*
B *Prosopocoilus zebra* ♀
C *Aceraulis grandius* ♂
D *Agestrata orichalcea* ♂

   E *Rhaetulus didieri* ♂
   F *Passalus tridens* ♂
   G *Heliocopris bucephalus* ♂
   H *Adoretus compressus* ♂
   I *Anomala viridis* ♂
   J *Catharsius molossus* ♂

PLATE 10 A *Heliocopris dominus* ♂
   B *Chalcosoma atlas* ♂-form *mesodonta*
   C *Chalcosoma atlas* ♂-form *amphiodonta*
   D *Chalcosoma atlas* ♀

PLATE 11 A *Chalcosoma atlas* ♂-form *telodonta*

PLATE 12 A *Chalcosoma caucasus* ♂
   B *Chalcosoma causasus* ♀

PLATE 13 A *Chalcosoma moellenkampi* ♂
   B *Chalcosoma moellenkampi* ♀

PLATE 14 A *Cheirotonus parryi* ♂-form *mesodonta* (dwarf-form)
   B *Cheirotonus parryi* ♂-form *telodonta* (giant-form)
   C *Cheirotonus parryi* ♀

PLATE 15 A *Eupatorus gracilicornis* ♂
   B *Eupatorus gracilicornis* ♀
   C *Lepidiota stigma* ♂
   D *Euselatus sponsa* ♂
   E *Fruhstorferia sexmaculata* ♂
   F *Apogonia destructor* ♂
   G *Oryctes rhinoceros* ♂
   H *Exopholis hypoleuca* ♂
   I *Fruhstorferia sexmaculata* ♀
   J *Holotrichia leucophthalma* ♂

PLATE 16 A *Trichogomphus lunicollis* ♂
   B *Oryctes rhinoceros* ♀
   C *Xylotrupes gideon* ♂-form *mesodonta*
   D *Xylotrupes gideon* ♂-form *telodonta*
   E *Oryctes trituberculatus* ♂

PLATE 17 A *Callopistus castelnaudi* ♂
   B *Callopistus castelnaudi* ♀
   C *Catoxantha opulenta* ♂

D *Catoxantha opulenta* ♀
E *Chrysochroa buqueti* ♂
F *Chrysochroa buqueti* ♀
G *Chrysochroa castelnaudii* ♂
H *Chrysochroa castelnaudii* ♀
I *Chrysochroa ephippigera* ♂
J *Chrysochroa ephippigera* ♀
K *Chrysochroa fulgidissima* ♂
L *Belionota prasina* ♂

PLATE 18 A *Chrysochroa fulminans* ♂
B *Chrysochroa fulminans* ♀
C *Chrysochroa wallacei* ♂
D *Chrysochroa wallacei* ♀
E *Demochroa gratiosa* ♂
F *Chrysochroa weyersii* ♂
G *Chrysochroa weyersii* ♀
H *Iridotaenia sumptuosa* ♂
I *Iridotaenia chrisostome* ♂
J *Megaloxantha daleni* ♂
K *Megaloxantha hemixantha* ♂
L *Megaloxantha hemixantha* ♀
M *Megaloxantha nigricornis* ♂
N *Megaloxantha nigricornis* ♀
O *Chrysobothris militaris* ♂

PLATE 19 A *Megaloxantha purpurascens* ♂
B *Oxyropterus audoniwi* ♂
C *Cibister roeselii* ♂
D *Calais lacteus* ♂
E *Anisolema* sp ♂
F *Coccinella arcuata* ♂
G *Epilachna indica* ♂
H *Campsosternus leachei* ♂
I *Encaustes* sp ♂
J *Encaustes verticalis* ♂
K *Diamesus osculans* ♂
L *Hemiops nigripes* ♂
M *Pteroptyx* sp ♂
N *Chalchromus* sp ♂

xv

PLATE 20 A *Autocrates aeneus* ♀
B *Anhammus deleni* ♂
C *Anhammus deleni* ♀
D *Trictenotoma davidi* ♀
E *Anoplophora medembachi* ♀
F *Anoplophora medembachi* ♂
G *Anoplophora longehirsuta* ♀

PLATE 21 A *Anoplophora zonatrix* ♀
B *Aethalodes verrucosus* ♂
C *Aristobia approximator* ♂
D *Batocera albofasciata* ♂
E *Batocera davidis* ♂
F *Combe brianus* ♂
G *Combe brianus* ♀
H *Cyriopalus wallacei* ♂
I *Cyriopalus wallacei* ♀

PLATE 22 A *Diastocera wallichi* ♂
B *Dorysthenes planicollis* ♂
C *Epepeotes luscus* ♂
D *Euryphagus lundi* ♂
E *Glenea elegans* ♂
F *Eurybatus lesnei* ♂
G *Leprodera elongata* ♂
H *Leprodera elongata* ♀
I *Epepeotes lateralis* ♂
J *Epepeotes lateralis* ♀

PLATE 23 A *Rhaphipodus hopei* ♂

PLATE 24 A *Neocerambyx grandis* ♂
B *Neocerambyx grandis* ♀

PLATE 25 A *Neocerambyx gigas* ♂
B *Neocerambyx gigas* ♀
C *Omocyrius jansoni* ♂
D *Pachyteria dimidiata* ♀

PLATE 26 A *Pachyteria equestria* ♂
B *Pachyteria virescens* ♂
C *Pachyteria imitans* ♂

xvi

D *Pachyteria lambi* ♂
E *Euryorthrum carinatum* ♂
F *Paraleprodera diophthalma* ♂
G *Pseudomyagrus waterhousei* ♂
H *Parepicedia fimbriata* ♂
I *Pseudomyagrus waterhousei* ♀
J *Macroioma fisheri* ♂

PLATE 27 A *Batocera parryi* ♀
B *Batocera hector* ♂
C *Epicedia maculatrix* ♂
D *Zonopterus consanguineus* ♂
E *Celosterna sulphurea* ♂
F *Joesse sanguinolenta* ♂

PLATE 28 A *Trirachys orientalis* ♂
B *Trirachys orientalis* ♀
C *Xylorhiza adusta* ♂
D *Xylorhiza adusta* ♀
E *Xystrocera festiva* ♂
F *Xystrocera festiva* ♀
G *Aspidomorpho inquinata* ♂
H *Aspidomorpho miliaris* ♂
I *Laccoptera tredecimpunctata* ♂
J *Prioptera decempunctata* ♂
K *Aulacophora coffeae* ♂
L *Aulacophora flavomarginata* ♂
M *Hispa armigera* ♂
N *Nisotra gemella* ♂
O *Sagra borneensis* ♂
P *Xystrocera globosa* ♂
Q *Sagra buqueti* ♂
R *Sagra buqueti* ♀

PLATE 29 A *Alurnus* sp ♂
B *Polyphylla fullo* ♂
C *Plectrone nigrocoerulea* ♂
D *Rhomborrhina splendida* ♂
E *Macronota abdominalis* ♂
F *Arcyphorus conformis* ♂

            G *Xylotrechus affinis* ♂
            H *Mimistena biplagiata* ♂
            I *Macrochenus melanospilus* ♂
            J *Macrochenus melanospilus* ♀

PLATE 30 A *Cyrtotrachelus buqueti* ♂
            B *Macrochirus praetor* ♀
            C *Protocerius colossus* ♀
            D *Rhynchophorus schachi* ♂
            E *Rhynchophorus ferrugineus* ♂
            F *Rhynchophorus ferrugineus* ♀

PLATE 31 A *Alcides cinchonae* ♂
            B *Cryptorhynchus gravis* ♂
            C *Lophobaris serratipes* ♂
            D *Sitophilus granaria* ♂
            E *Sitophilus oryzae* ♂
            F *Sphenophorus sordidus* ♂

PLATE 32 A *Rhynchophorus palmarum* ♂
            B *Rhynchophorus palmarum* ♀
            C *Brachycerus congestus* ♂
            D *Jumnos ruckeri pfanneri* ♂
            E *Jumnos ruckeri pfanneri* ♀
            F *Jumnos ruckeri ruckeri* ♂
            G *Jumnos ruckeri ruckeri* ♀
            H *Diceros dives* ♂
            I *Diceros dives* ♀

INTRODUCTION

The Order COLEOPTERA is by far the largest insect order with almost a quarter of a million species described and classified. Beetles are generally characterized by their hardened forewings (the elytra) with the membranous hind wings folded neatly beneath them, and by their biting mouth-parts. They are found in almost every conceivable situation, living on almost every possible kind of food. Beetles are most numerous and diverse in the tropical regions and our country, Malaysia, lies entirely within this zone.

The study of entomology aims to produce as much information as possible on the life histories, habits and habitats of insects, especially those of economic and agricultural importance, but our knowledge of insects is still very far from complete.

The study of Malaysian beetles has suffered from apathy and neglect. Many of the local beetles are little more than names to scientists of foreign countries and some are practically unknown to local entomologists. Most of the type-specimens are in overseas museums and inaccessible to local students and there is no checklist of Malaysian species. This book is intended to serve as a text for beginners and has been designed as a guide to the common beetles which are likely to be seen or taken during field trips. The text describes over 180 species of beetles under seventeen different families. These provide no more than a representative sample of the more typical forms found within the region. The families HYDROPHILIDAE, STAPHYLINIDAE, TENEBRIONIDAE, CLERIDAE, HISTERIDAE, RHIPIPHORIDAE, MORDELLIDAE and MELOIDAE are mentioned but have not been described in detail in the text.

The first section of this book deals with classification with a brief discussion of morphology and physiology. The explanation of the principles of classification and of the technical terms used has been kept to a minimum. Key technical words are defined in the Glossary at the end of the text.

Unfortunately very few beetles have common English names, so Latinized scientific names cannot be avoided, and have been used in this book.

When comparing specimens with the illustrations, bear in mind that both pattern and colour are subject to variation and the colours are brightest in fresh specimens. Habitats also may vary and it has only been possible to give general indications of the kind of terrain in which the beetle is normally found. Wherever possible, names of food plants or food materials of the larvae are also given.

A brief description on setting traps, methods of collecting, preserving, storing and breeding is included.

Little is as yet known of the life histories and metamorphosis of Malaysian beetles, and of such matters as pigmentation, luminescence (the emission of visible light) and of the significance of many structural features. There must also be many species yet to be discovered, and the author hopes that this book will stimulate interest and lead to such discoveries being made.

THE BEETLE

CLASSIFICATION AND NOMENCLATURE

The system of zoological classification and nomenclature using Latin names was first devised by a Swedish naturalist, Carolus Linnaeus in his famous work *Systema Naturae* published in 1758. It is at present used internationally by zoologists and taxonomists throughout the animal and vegetable kingdoms, and now follows a code of rules issued by the International Code of Zoological Nomenclature.

The principal categories in this classification are Phylum, Class, Order, Family, Genus and Species. Beetles belong to the order COLEOPTERA of the class INSECTA. Insects are included in the phylum ARTHROPODA which includes other invertebrate animals with jointed limbs, such as spiders, centipedes and crustaceans.

The order COLEOPTERA is divided into families, which are the main subdivisions under which beetles will be arranged in the following pages. Each kind of beetle is placed in a genus and given a specific name, and the two are used together to define the species, for example, *Cicindela sumatrensis*, a tiger beetle first discovered in Sumatra. These names are printed in a distinctive type, usually italics, and the generic name, but not the specific name, has an initial capital letter. The word 'genus' has 'genera' as its plural; 'species' is the same in singular and plural.

The Latin name may be descriptive, as in *Glenea elegans*; it may honour the name of a collector or authority, as in *Chrysochroa wallacei*, or refer to a locality, as in *C. sumatrensis*, mentioned above.

The word 'COLEOPTERA' is of Greek derivation and means 'sheath-wing', the reference being to the condition of the forewings in beetles, which are nearly always represented by a pair of hard, rigid structures that form a sheath covering the membranous hind wings and the hinder part of the body. Beetles are also characterized by having strong biting mouth-parts and by undergoing complete metamorphosis; that is to say they pass through larva and pupa stages just as a butterfly does.

The table that follows is a classified list of the families of beetles found commonly in Malaysia. It will be noted that some intermediate categories have been used, such as 'suborder' and 'superfamily'; these are self-explanatory.

Order:	**COLEOPTERA** (beetles)
Suborder:	**ADEPHAGA** (which are all carnivorous)
Superfamily:	CARABOIDEA
Families:	CICINDELIDAE (tiger beetles)
	CARABIDAE (ground beetles)
	DYTISCIDAE (predaceous diving beetles)
Suborder:	**POLYPHAGA** (which are omnivorous)
Superfamily:	STAPHYLINOIDEA
Family:	SILPHIDAE (carrion beetles)
Superfamily:	SCARABAEOIDEA
Families:	LUCANIDAE (stag beetles, pinching bugs)
	PASSALIDAE (sugar beetles, bess bugs)
	SCARABAEIDAE (scarab beetles, dung beetles, chafers)
Superfamily:	BUPRESTOIDEA
Family:	BUPRESTIDAE (splendour beetles, metallic wood-boring beetles)
Superfamily:	ELATEROIDEA
Family:	ELATERIDAE (click beetles, skipjacks)
Superfamily:	CANTHAROIDEA
Families:	LAMPYRIDAE (fireflies)
	LYCIDAE (net-winged beetles)
Superfamily:	CUCUJOIDEA
Families:	EROTYLIDAE (pleasing fungus beetles)
	COCCINELLIDAE (ladybirds)
	TRICTENOTOMIDAE (false longhorn beetles)
Superfamily:	CHRYSOMELOIDEA
Families:	CERAMBYCIDAE (longhorn beetles)
	CHRYSOMELIDAE (leaf beetles, tortoise beetles)
Superfamily:	CURCULIONOIDEA
Family:	CURCULIONIDAE (weevils, snout beetles)

According to the list of families of the order COLEOPTERA occurring in West Malaysia, issued by the Commonwealth Institute of Entomology in England, there are at least ninety-three families known to occur here. Of these only seventeen are included in this short introduction to the subject.

LIFE HISTORY OF BEETLES

The knowledge of the life history of this group of insects is very scanty and much effort is required to fill up the gaps for those beetles whose life history is still unknown. In this book, where life histories are known, they are mentioned in the text; otherwise it may be assumed that life histories are not known.

All Coleopteran species undergo a complete metamorphosis, that is, their young hatch from eggs into larvae, they then pupate and emerge as adults. The wings (if any) are developed internally during the immature stages. The following is a brief discussion of the various stages in the life cycle of the beetles.

Fertilization

Most male beetles are attracted to their mates by the scent or pheromone which the female beetles produce. Such scent glands are highly complex and are found in the antennae, legs and abdominal segments which are often invisible to the human eye. The usual method of mating is the male resting completely or partially on top of the body of the female (depending on the size of the male). Using all its legs as support, the male bends its notched *aedeagus* to meet the *ostium bursae* at the posterior surface on the anal end of the abdomen of its mate. Capsules containing sperms (spermatophores) are then introduced.

Ova (Eggs)

The eggs of COLEOPTERA are very diverse in shape, size and colour. Many eggs are provided with characteristic spines and tubercles which distinguish them from one another. As is the case with most insects, the eggs are laid in a situation where the conditions are suitable for their development and protection. Often they are laid in holes and burrows in the soil, compost, heaps of leaves, dead wood, trees, on vegetation or even on pieces of old clothes; they are deposited in clusters or rows of ten to a hundred eggs varying according to the species. Different species deposit their eggs in different localities which provide a suitable food plant or food material for their young. Often a beetle will lay clusters of eggs in holes or on leaves. Female weevils tend to cover their eggs with a special protective layer to prevent predators from destroying them. A female rhinoceros beetle deposits her eggs on animal refuse or rotting tree trunks, preferably palms, whereas stag and sugar beetles prefer to oviposit in the core of rotted fallen trees found in primary and secondary forests. Generally large numbers are laid and there is a tremendous loss of individuals at all stages mainly due to human activities, parasites, and unfavourable conditions for survival like rainy weather which washes away the eggs from their food plant or food material, or even 'drowns' them.

Larvae
The duration of each stage is dependent on the climate and the species. Thus after varying lengths of time, the minute worm-like larvae emerge from the eggs, showing at this stage no resemblance to the adults at all. Each species feeds on a particular type of food plant or food material using its strong chewing jaws.

Typically, larvae are sluggish with a well-developed head and three pairs of thoracic legs but without abdominal prolegs. Adjoining the head are the three thoracic segments, called the prothorax, mesothorax, and metathorax; and each bears a pair of jointed legs (Fig. 1). There are ten abdominal segments which are often fur-

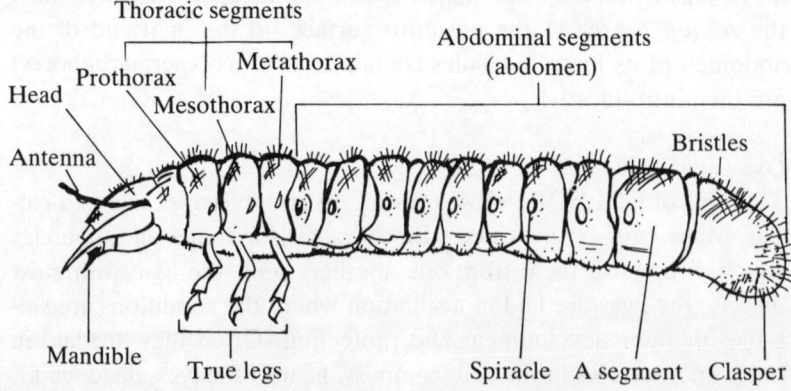

FIGURE 1 Lateral view of a typical Coleopterous larva

nished with bristles, soft spines and tubercles, and these are useful in the determination and classification of scarabaeiform larvae. The development in a young larva includes casting off the hard outer skin which is inelastic and does not grow in proportion to the fleshy body of the larva. Most larvae undergo five to six moults before pupation can take place. The stage between successive moults is termed an instar, and the process of shedding the exoskeleton is known as ecdysis. During larval instars, the wings (if any in the adult stage) are developed internally but not everted until the end of the last larval instar.

Larvae vary widely according to families. Many are *aphytophagous*, feeding on vegetable debris, animal materials and/or larvae of other insects; and others are *phytophagous*, feeding on foliage of plants.

Pupae

The fully grown larvae frequently spin silken cocoons in which they pupate. The larval skin splits, leaving the fully formed soft whitish pupa underneath. This hardens and darkens in a few days. This represents a dormant stage. The pupae do not feed but complete their transformation into adults. This process can take from one week to several years. Malaysian aborigines have recorded that they once kept a pupa of a Cerambycid species and it took seven years before the insect emerged.

Many pupae are white and pale yellow with a translucent body, and usually resemble the adults. Pupation often takes place in the deeper layers of the soil, within a cocoon made of earth or earth combined with dung or vegetable matter.

In other families, for example, COCCINELLIDAE and the subfamily CASSIDINAE, the pupae are more or less naked and are often protected by the remains of the last larval skin which harden and form an integument.

Adults

At the end of the pupal stage, the adults emerge from the pupae. They are usually pale in colour when they first emerge and their wings, particularly the elytra, are short, soft and wrinkled. They then open their elytra (Fig. 2) and spread their well-protected membranous hind wings out to dry in the sun for a few days, or a week,

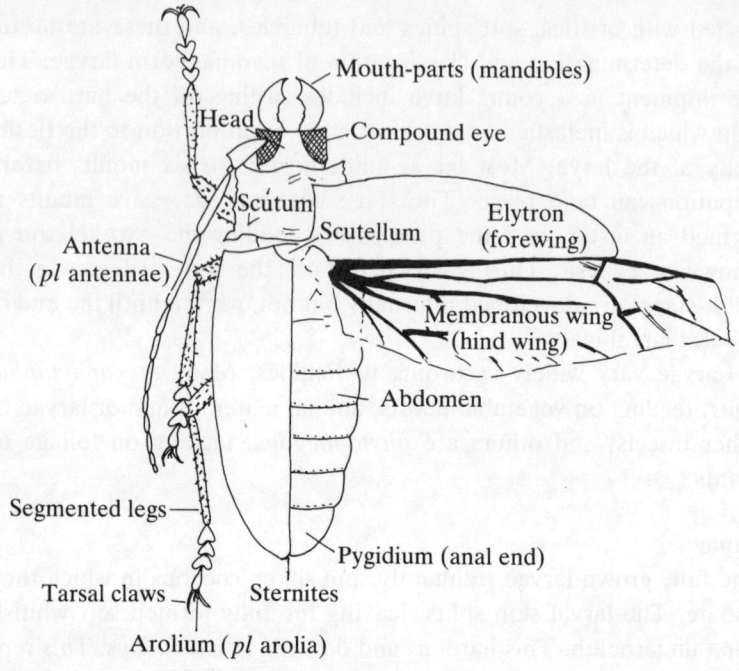

FIGURE 2 Dorsal view of a longhorn beetle

or more, depending on the species. Eventually, the wings dry, the elytra harden, and the adults prepare for their new lives. Within minutes, they fly off and find food for their survival. A number of species complete the life cycle only once or twice a year, spending much of their time in hibernation, for example, BUPRESTIDAE and the subfamily DYNASTINAE. The adults will spend their new life in a different habitat. Many adults feed on types of food which are entirely different from those they ate as larvae. Most remain alive for a few months to several years.

SEXUAL DIMORPHISM

As in the order LEPIDOPTERA (butterflies and moths), sexual dimorphism is very common among beetles, that is, there is often a considerable difference between the male and the female. Often the males have wings whereas the females are frequently wingless. Other dimorphic aspects can be observed from antennae of different proportions and lengths (click beetles, longhorn beetles); legs of different structures (water beetles); mandibles and labia with different biting or cutting edges, sizes and lengths (stag beetles, false longhorn beetles); horns and knobs of different lengths, sizes and structures (rhinoceros and atlas beetles); pronota, heads, thoraxes and abdomens with different numbers of segments (longhorn beetles); differences in colouring and size (click beetles, metallic wood-boring beetles).

In the absence of clear external differences between the sexes, the abdomens of the specimens must be dissected to show clearly the internal features of their genitalia. This is a complicated and time-consuming operation, usually undertaken by taxonomists in museums.

STRUCTURE AND SENSES

Of the twenty-four orders of the INSECTA, beetles have the largest number of species, amounting to about half a million. In West Malaysia, it is believed that there are more than twenty thousand beetle species. Most beetles have a hard external skeleton, and they vary greatly in size and shape. The majority of the better known Malaysian beetles are robust, measuring between ten and one hundred millimetres (0.4 to 4 inches) in length.

The structure of the adult beetle may be considered under three main headings: head, thorax and abdomen.

Head

The head bears the eyes and antennae, the mouth-parts and the mentum and submentum (if any). The heads of many male scarab beetles belonging to the subfamily DYNASTINAE, such as the male atlas beetle, *Chalcosoma atlas*, have horns and knobs jutting out at the mentum and pronotum. These prominent growths are used to pierce holes in the trunks of trees and palms, for example, the undergrowth palm, *Johannesteijsmannia altifrons*, to feed on the sap. The tropical male rhinoceros beetle, *Oryctes rhinoceros*, bears a horn on the mentum which is used as a lever to gain access to the growing points of palms (e.g. oil and coconut palms). Likewise, Japanese rhinoceros beetles, *Xylotrupes gideon*, have been observed to use their pincer-like growths to girdle branches of rubber trees so as to feed on the latex.

The heads of male stag beetles bear elongated antler-like mandibles, developed for protection as well as to attract their mates. In the family CURCULIONIDAE (the weevils), there is a long snout or beak called the *rostrum* on the head. At the tip of this snout are the mouth-parts (mandibles) usually reduced in size (Fig. 3). This

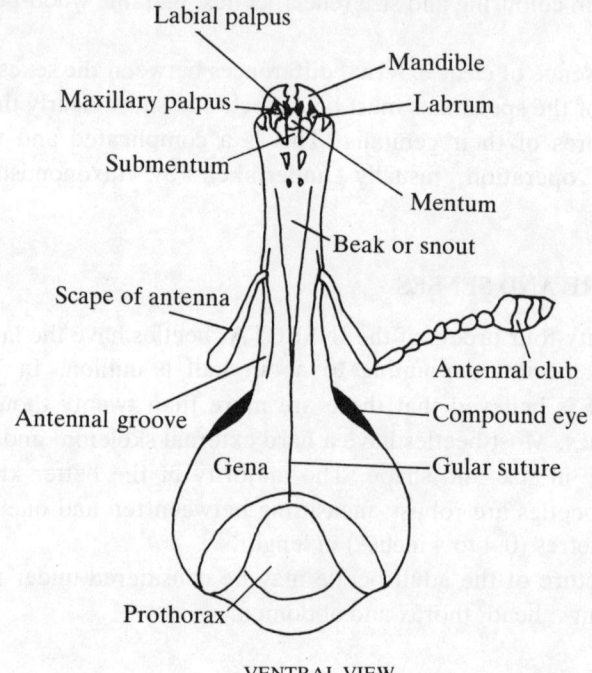

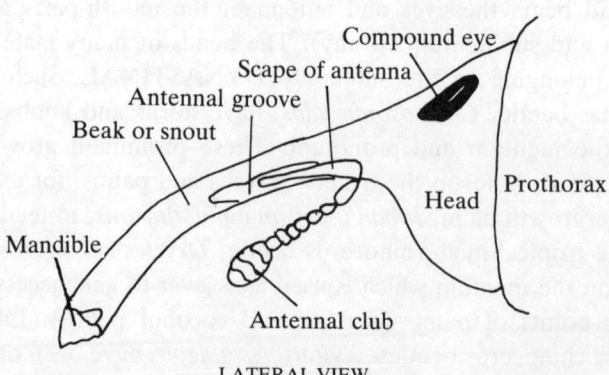

FIGURE 3 The aspect of a weevil's head including the mouth-parts

10

arrangement of the mandibles is used mainly to drill deep holes in fruits, nuts, buds, seeds, stems and other plant tissues to devour the sap. Female weevils drill deeper and larger holes in which they deposit their eggs. Figure 4 shows the structure of the heads of species of different families.

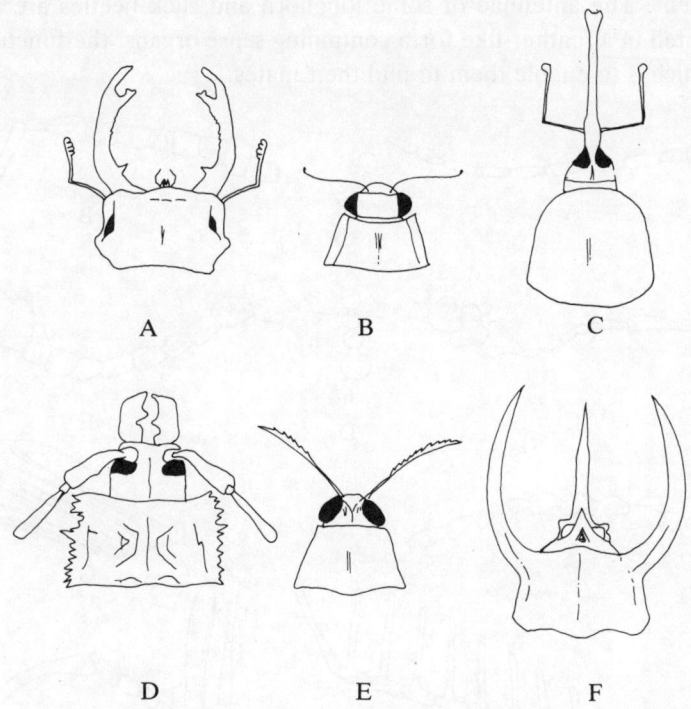

A. A stag beetle, *Odontolabis castelnaudi*, LUCANIDAE, with a pair of antler-like mandibles.
B. A water beetle, *Cibister roeselii*, DYTISCIDAE, with a somewhat flattened mentum.
C. A weevil, *Macrochirus praetor*, CURCULIONIDAE, with a long and slender snout or beak.
D. A longhorn beetle, *Rhaphipodus hopei*, CERAMBYCIDAE, with its blade-like mandibles.
E. A jewel beetle, *Chrysochroa fulminans*, BUPRESTIDAE, with its rounded mentum and big eyes.
F. An atlas beetle, *Chalcosoma atlas*, SCARABAEIDAE, with its prominent growths on the head and pronotum.

FIGURE 4 Dorsal view of heads and pronota of beetles

Antennae In front of the compound eyes lie a pair of antennae which play an important role in the life of beetles and other insects. They function as highly developed sensory organs. They exhibit marked diversity of shape, form and length. Some of these forms are shown in Figure 5. Most beetles have long antennae which are divided into ten or eleven segments bearing bristles or hairs on each segment. The antennae of some longhorn and click beetles are articulated in a feather-like form containing sense organs, the function of which is to enable them to find their mates.

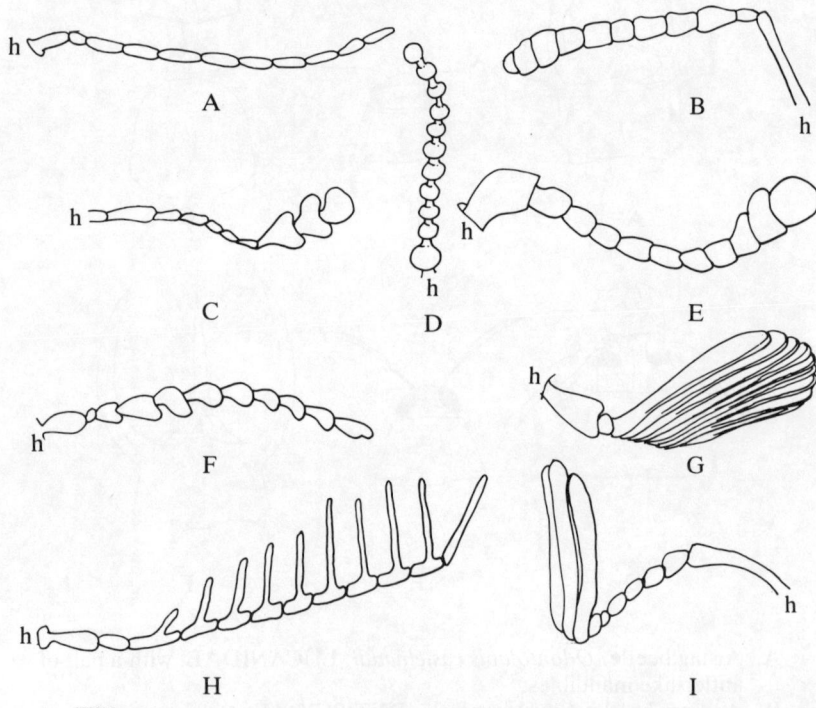

A. Filiform
B. Geniculate
C. Capitate
D. Moniliform
E. Clavate
F. Serrate
G. Flabellate
H. Pectinate
I. Lamellate
h. The head of the insect

FIGURE 5 Types of antennae

Mouth-parts (mandibles, labium and labrum) The mouth-parts are located at the front of the head and are adapted for cutting, biting, chewing and boring. Many types of tropical beetles have remarkably strong mandibles with two or three teeth. The mandibles, which are attached to the mentum and the gular sutures of the insect's head, are saw-like blades used mainly for cutting and biting (Fig. 6). Stag beetles use their gigantic antler-like mandibles for protection and as an instrument to attract females as well as to excavate homes in rotted logs.

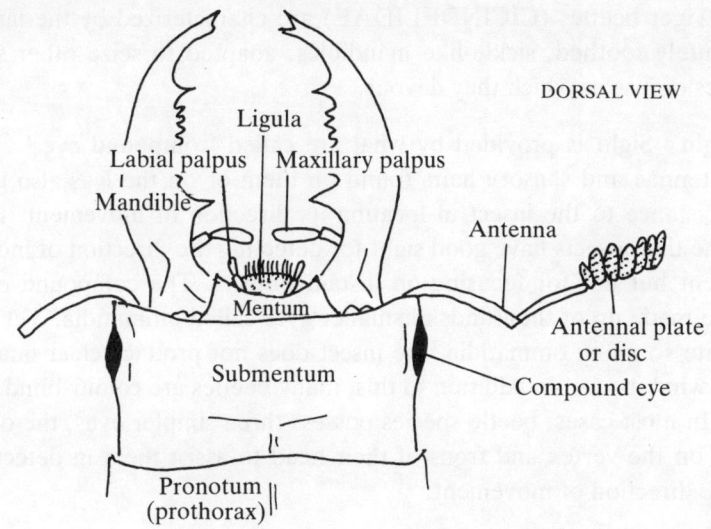

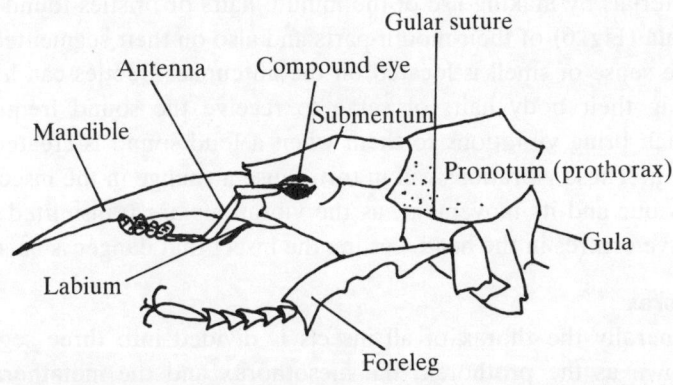

FIGURE 6 The aspect of a stag beetle's head including the mouth-parts

Covering the mouth opening (the ligula) on the mentum are the labium (the upper lip) and the labrum (lower lip) which are usually covered with minute hairs or pilosities (Fig. 6). On each side of the labium are two short segmented parts jutting out like two pairs of small feelers, known as the labial palpi (singular labial palpus) which are nearer to the labium and shorter than the other maxillary palpi (Fig. 6) which have more segments. Day-flying beetles and weevils use this apparatus to obtain nectar from fragrant flowering plants.

Tiger beetles (CICINDELIDAE) are characterized by the large, acutely toothed, sickle-like mandibles, adapted to seize other species of insects which they devour.

Sight Sight is provided by what are called 'compound eyes'. The antennae and sensory hairs found on them or on the legs also give assistance to the insect in locating its direction of movement. It is true that insects have good sight for detecting the direction of movement but not for focusing on distant objects. The compound eyes are made up of thousands of smaller eyes called ommatidia. Yet despite so many ommatidia, the insect does not produce clear images of what it sees. In addition to this, many beetles are colour-blind.

In most cases, beetle species possess three simpler eyes, the ocelli, on the vertex and frons of their head to assist them in detecting the direction of movement.

Other sense organs COLEOPTERA taste their food plants or food materials by making use of the minute hairs or bristles found at the ligula (Fig. 6) of their mouth-parts and also on their segmented legs. The sense of smell is located on the antennae. Beetles can hear by using their body hairs or setae to receive the sound frequencies which bring vibrations to them when a loud sound is created near them. These vibrations will in turn cause a change in the insect's behaviour and its movement, as the vibrations are transmitted to the nerve centres in the head alerting the insect that danger is near.

Thorax
Generally the thorax of all insects is divided into three segments known as the prothorax, the mesothorax and the metathorax. In beetles, the scutum covers only the first thoracic segment (the prothorax) of the insect.

Legs All beetles have three pairs of strong legs, one pair each on the prothorax, mesothorax and metathorax. They are subject to considerable variation in different families of COLEOPTERA. Each leg is divided into the coxa (the proximal segment which joins the body), trochanter, femur, tibia, tarsus, tarsal claws and arolia (Fig. 7). The number and shape of the tarsal segments are important characteristics for the identification of beetles. Land beetles have tarsal

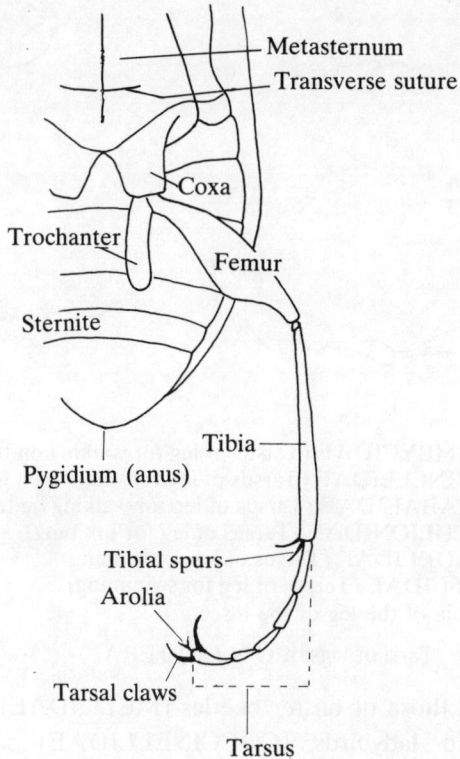

FIGURE 7 The ventral view of the abdomen and the hind limb of a beetle

claws with well-developed arolia for walking and running, whereas aquatic beetles have straight, hairy tarsi for swimming. Legs which are typically adapted for running are slender, but strong, and of equal length with claws and arolia. Most beetles have legs with well-developed claws and arolia which exude a sticky fluid adapted for walking in an inverted position and on slippery surfaces (Fig. 8). Among the most typical characteristics in the development of tarsal

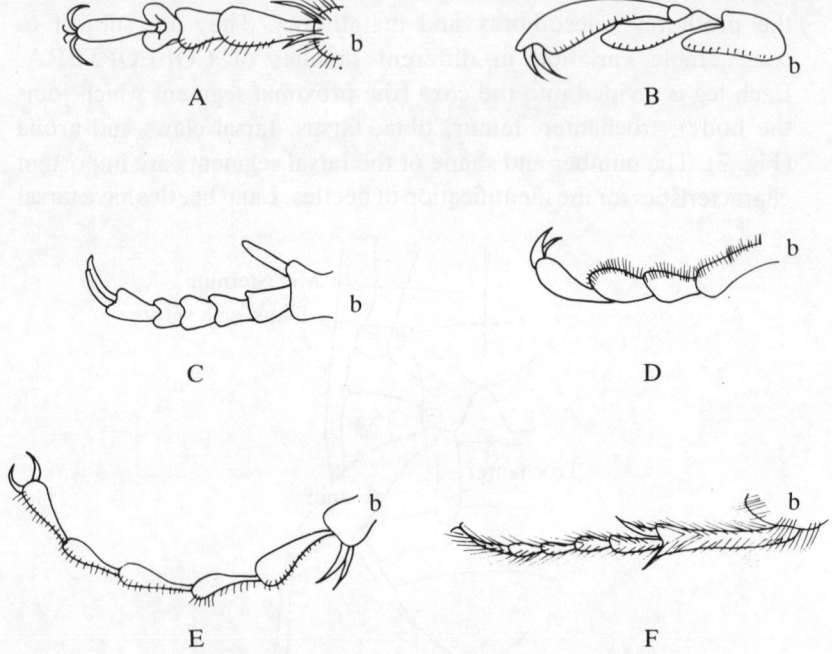

A. CERAMBYCIDAE (Tarsus of leg for walking on bark of trees)
B. COCCINELLIDAE (Tarsus of leg for walking on foliage)
C. SCARABAEIDAE (Tarsus of leg for walking on trees and ground)
D. CURCULIONIDAE (Tarsus of leg for jumping)
E. CICINDELIDAE (Tarsus of leg for running)
F. DYTISCIDAE (Tarsus of leg for swimming)
b The tibia of the leg of the insect

FIGURE 8   Tarsi of legs of COLEOPTERA

claws are those of blister beetles (MELOIDAE) which are deeply cleft, and ladybirds (COCCINELLIDAE) which are greatly toothed.

In weevils, the hind limb is considerably larger than the others with a long and thickened femur mainly adapted for jumping. Another fine example of long thickened hind legs is the Tropical Leaf Beetle, *Sagra buqueti*, which uses them to gather strength as it kicks up towards the air in search for food or escape from enemies. These hind legs are strong, as the musculature of their coxa, femur and tibia shows. Using the tarsal claws and arolia, these beetles are thus able to grip any surface and move swiftly across it.

Wings (including the elytra) Beetles have two pairs of wings, the forewings and the hind wings attached to the prothorax and mesothorax respectively. The forewings consist of the hard and thickened elytra covering and protecting the fragile membranous hind wings which fold neatly beneath the protective sheaths (Fig. 2). The hind wings are longer than the elytra and are the sole organs of flight.

The V-shaped scutellum (Fig. 2) bordering the edge of the scutum forms a natural divider between the scutum and the elytra. The hard pair of elytra covers the mesothorax, metathorax and all the eleven abdominal segments of the beetles, with some exceptions in the families STAPHYLINIDAE, SILPHIDAE and CURCULIONIDAE, in which the abdominal sternites are left uncovered or partially uncovered. The elytra are generally smooth, well-polished and hairless, but they may be variously sculptured or ridged. The elytra are frequently black or metallic green in colour. They are usually thickened and rigid and extend back to cover the last abdominal tergite, the pygidium (Fig. 2), of the insect. Often the meeting of the right and left elytron forms a very straight line running along the top of the abdomen.

Only the membranous hind wings are ordinarily used for flying, the wings thrust forward and backward, vibrating vigorously in a systematic up and down movement. The elytra may serve as rudders and aerofoils. Movement of the elytra is sometimes noisy. Certain non-flying beetles have long legs adapted for running (ground beetles) or fringed with hair for swimming (water beetles) (Fig. 8).

Abdomen
The structure of the first abdominal segment is used to separate the two suborders of beetles. In the ADEPHAGA, the hind coxae cover the entire central part of the first abdominal segment, leaving only the part near the edges exposed, whereas in the POLYPHAGA, the hind coxae are very much reduced in size and shape, so that almost the whole area of the abdominal sternites is exposed (Fig. 9).

The number of visible abdominal sternites varies in different groups and it is of great taxonomic importance. In the ELATERIDAE, there are six, but in the case of BUPRESTIDAE, only two

ADEPHAGA
(Tiger beetle)

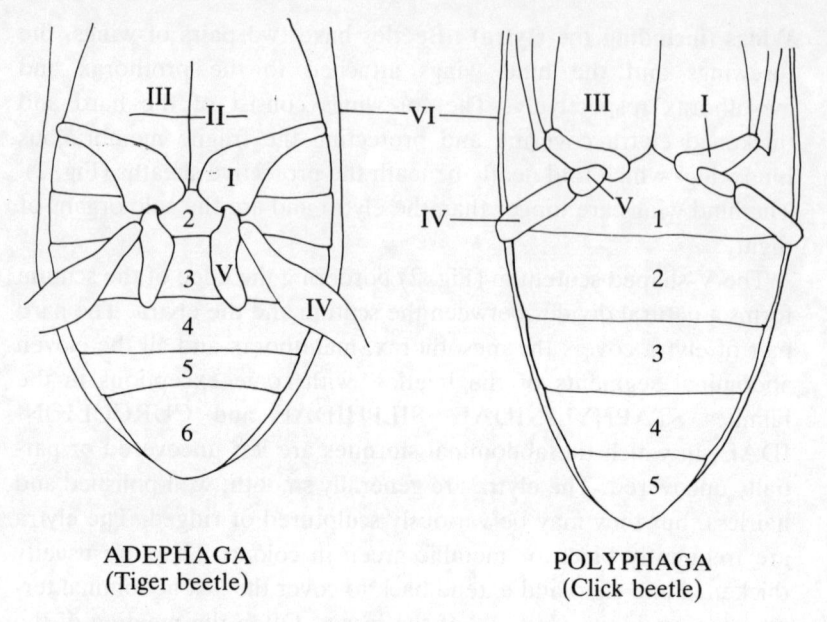

POLYPHAGA
(Click beetle)

    I Hind coxa
   II Suture in the metasternum
  III Metasternum
  IV Hind femur
   V Hind trochanter
  VI Elytra
1–6 are visible abdominal sternites

FIGURE 9 Ventral view of the abdominal segments showing the difference between ADEPHAGA and POLYPHAGA

are evident, as the others are more or less fused together and the sutures between them are hardly visible.

The last abdominal tergite (the pygidium) is sometimes exposed beyond the tips of the elytra. There are no appendages at the hind end of the abdomen of the adult beetles as found in some more primitive insects.

Reproductive organs These differ dramatically from one species to another. The male reproductive apparatus is the intromittent organ called the *aedeagus* (functionally a penis) which lies at the bottom end of the pygidium. The *ostium bursae* (corresponding to the vagina) of the female is found at the rear end of the eighth abdominal tergite.

During the act of copulation, the *aedeagus* of the male is locked together with the *ostium bursae* of its mate for one or two days. Sperm is then introduced in the form of sticky capsules, or spermatophores, usually on the second day.

HABITS, ENVIRONMENT AND FEEDING

Habits and environment

Detailed data on the habits and habitats of Malaysian species are few because very little work on this has been carried out in the past It is a pity that most collectors do not bother to try to breed what they catch, or to keep a record of all the circumstances of capture, vegetation and surroundings, or note down the habits of the insects they seek.

Many beetles are aquatic and semi-aquatic in habit, some are subterranean, and a few live as commensals in the nests of social insects.

Food plants and food materials

There is vast variation in the types of food plants or food materials on which beetles feed. In general very little work has been done in discovering the specific food plant or food material. In cases where these are known the names of food plants and/or food materials are given for the beetles described and illustrated.

The majority of beetles are *phytophagous*, many are predaceous, some are scavengers, others feed on mould or fungi, and a few are parasitic. *Phytophagous* species feed on foliage, or bore into wood, fruit and other tissues of plants. A few species of weevils feed on stored grains, and plant and animal products. The beetles of some families, including SILPHIDAE and SCARABAEIDAE, mostly live on animal dung and other decomposing materials; details are found in the discussion on each species.

MAKING A COLLECTION

COLLECTING

Collecting beetles in Malaysia is becoming an increasingly popular pastime and this is one of the best ways to learn more about their life history, habits and habitat. Today, many people find that collecting insects is an extremely interesting hobby, and there is no doubt that it is a worthwhile pursuit.

Since this book aims to assist beginners, it is essential to discuss briefly the various methods of collecting and the equipment required to start a collection.

Equipment

Net A net is a necessity when catching beetles, especially dayfliers. It should be strong, large and light. The simplest way to make a net is to buy two pieces of rattan stick from a local rattan shop. One must be about 1.5 to 1.8 metres (5 to 6 feet) long with a diameter of 25 millimetres (1 inch), while the other is between 1.37 to 1.8 metres (4.6 to 6 feet) long with a diameter of 10 millimetres (0.4 inch). Heat the latter stick carefully over a bunsen flame, curving, bending and shaping it until it forms a circle. This is the rim.

Then attach the rim securely to the other rattan stick by means of nails and wires. Nails used are 20 millimetres (0.8 inch) long, with a thickness of one millimetre. Hammer two nails at each side and at different spots. Fasten a coil of wires round this joint (Fig. 10).

The bag should be made from black or white muslin cloth or better still silk (though this is expensive) about 840 millimetres (33 inches) deep.

The net must be used with care and should be kept away from thorns of tropical plants, spikes and sharp edges of broken twigs or branches, and should always be kept dry.

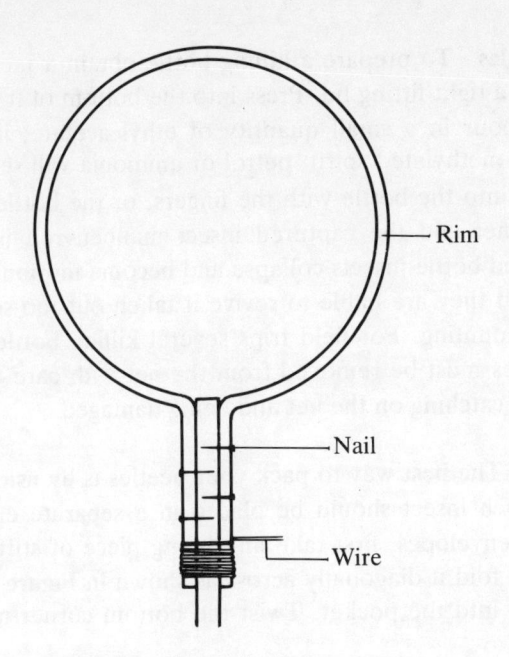

FIGURE 10 The joint of a home-made beetle net

Nowadays modern collapsible entomological nets are made by the Japanese in which the handle can be removed and disjointed from the stainless steel rim, and the rim itself can be folded by hinged joints. The bag is made of fine silk and can be taken out of the rim. The handle of the net is made of strong fibre glass and is approximately 1.52 metres (5 feet) long. These nets are necessarily light and the diameter of the rim generous for collecting insects. Extending nets are also available and are useful for tropical collecting; their handles can be extended to 4.6 metres (15 feet) and 15.2 metres (50 feet) in length.

A sweeping net is required when collecting the very small beetles found in grassland or patches of low vegetation. Since such a net will receive rough usage, the rim must be very strong. The method of making it is similar to that outlined above; but the rim must be made of stiff wire with a thickness of 10 millimetres (0.4 inch). This rim should have a diameter of about 300 millimetres (12 inches). The bag must be made of a tough material, such as canvas. This sort of net is heavy, and it is only used for sweeping through low vegetation.

Killing bottles To prepare a killing bottle obtain a jar with a wide mouth and a tight-fitting lid. Press into the bottom of it some cotton wool and pour in a small quantity of ethyl acetate; if this is unobtainable, methylated spirit, petrol or ammonia will serve. Beetles can be put into the bottle with the fingers, or the bottle can be put inside the net and the captured insect manoeuvred into it. In a tightly closed bottle insects collapse and become motionless in a few minutes, but they are liable to revive if taken out too soon for pinning and mounting. For field trips several killing bottles are desirable. Beetles must be removed from the net with care to avoid the tarsal claws catching on the net and being damaged.

Envelopes The best way to pack your beetles is by using paper envelopes. Each insect should be placed in a separate envelope. To make such envelopes, first take an oblong piece of stiff paper (not cardboard), fold it diagonally across as shown in Figure 11, and put a forefinger into the pocket. Twist the bottom corner neatly and a

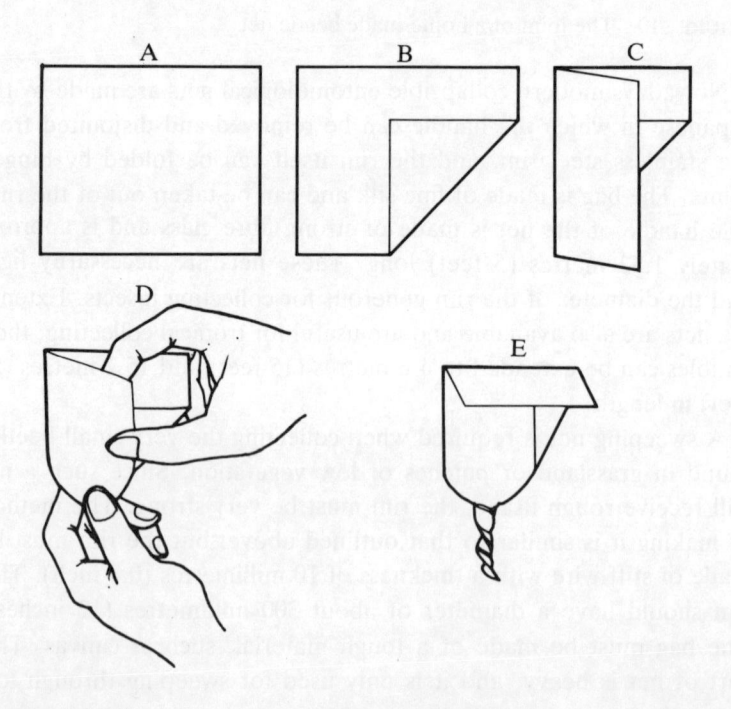

FIGURE 11 How to make an entomological envelope

firm pocket is formed. The size of the pocket is made according to the size of the insect's body. Fold the upper edge to close the pocket.

Dead beetles from the killing bottle can be placed into envelopes. When inserting an insect such as a longhorn beetle make sure the antennae are carefully folded backwards towards the abdomen to avoid breaking or spoiling them. On the upper edge of each envelope, a brief description should be written including the place and date of capture. Details of such descriptions will be discussed later.

The filled envelopes must be dried in the sun for at least six hours before they are packed in a box tightly enough to prevent them from being shaken and to protect the body of the insect from attacks of ants and cockroaches. It is advisable to drop a few paradichlorobenzene crystals into the box to prevent minute insect mites from destroying the specimens.

Methods There are many basic methods of collecting beetles according to their habits and habitats. Day-flying beetles such as the common metallic wood-boring beetles (BUPRESTIDAE) can be captured with a net. Such insects favour large showy flowers with a strong attractive odour.

After the capture of an insect the net should be twisted sideways to prevent its escape. Beetles on rocks or on the ground can be captured either by a sideways sweep or by carefully placing the net over them. Unlike butterflies, beetles can be removed from the net with your fingers and dropped into a killing bottle or injected with alcohol in a hypodermic syringe. Make the injection through the suture of the pronotum, that is, through the insect's neck.

Many tropical beetles feign death by dropping off the foliage when it is jarred slightly, for example, click beetles (ELATERIDAE) and ladybirds (COCCINELLIDAE). The best device for capturing these is the beating tray, for which an umbrella or your net is a good substitute. Put the tray or inverted umbrella underneath a plant and then jar the plant or branch with a stick; insects that fall into the tray can easily be taken.

Natural food baits Animal excrement of all kinds, and the soil underneath it, is worth searching for beetles, and also decomposing bodies of animals; dung beetles, carrion beetles and burying beetles can be found in this way. Stag beetles are attracted by overripe fruit and other decomposing matter.

Traps and baits A baited trap is often effective in capturing nocturnal beetles and can be constructed as follows:

A big tin is sunk into the ground and an attap roof is made to keep out the rain. A piece of meat or fruit, preferably overripe

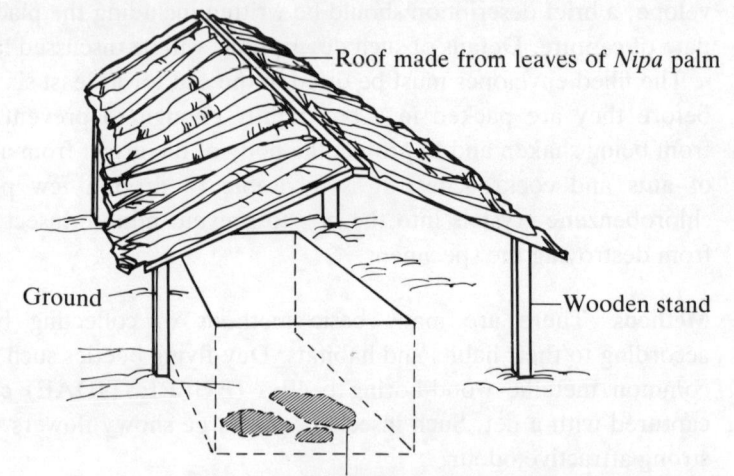

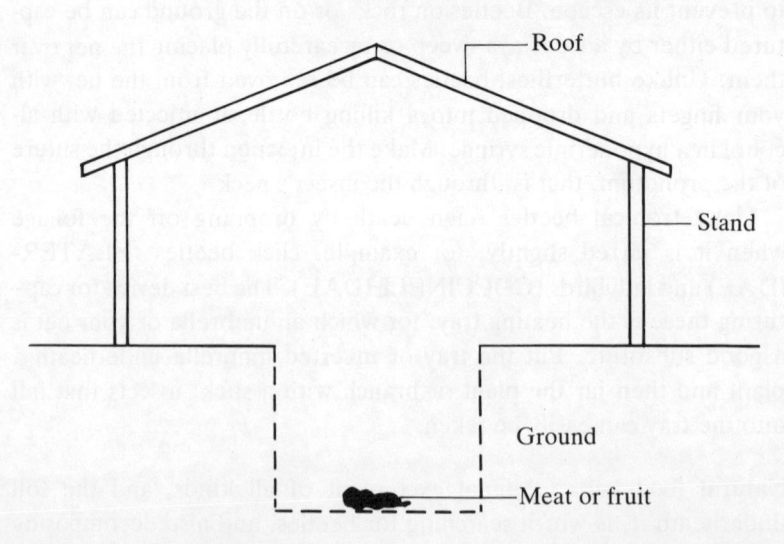

FIGURE 12   A 'pitfall' insect trap

pineapple or banana, is placed in the bottom of the tin. Many beetles feed on these and once they have found their way in they will not be able to get out (Fig. 12). This method is commonly called the pitfall trap. If the bait is dispensed with and a little dilute formaldehyde is put in the tin, insects walking about at night in search of food will often fall into it and be killed.

Many insects are attracted to light and this is the most productive method of collecting beetles at night. Hang a lamp or electric light bulb directly over a container with a wide mouth. Put in it a piece of rag soaked with alcohol or petrol. The container can be sunk into the ground, but this is not necessary. The best results of all are obtained with an ultra-violet lamp with a piece of white cloth hung behind it (Fig. 13). A variation of this method is to take advantage of street lamps. In the Cameron Highlands, it is possible to collect at the foot of lighted lampposts at night those beetles which usually settle down on the ground. The best results are obtained when there is no moon and the sky is overcast.

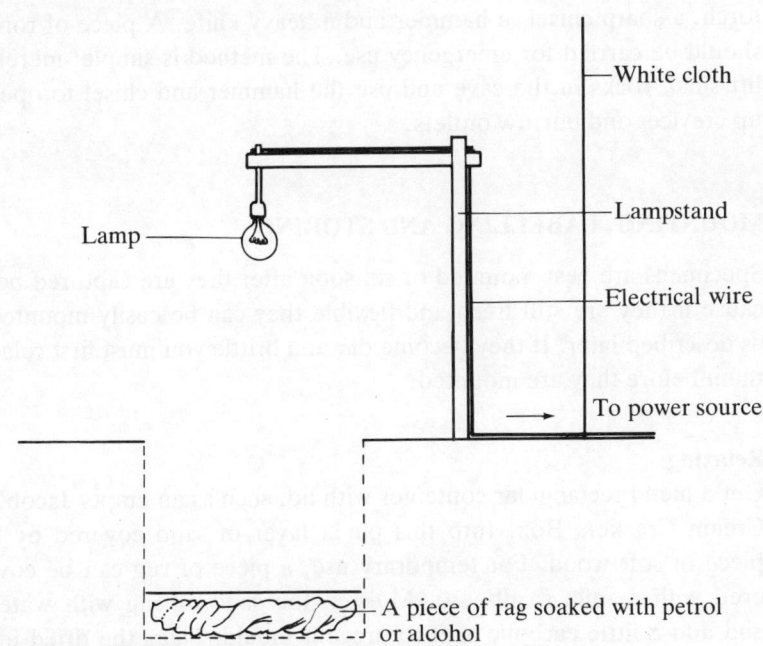

A pressure lamp may be used if electric power is not available.

FIGURE 13 A simple light-trap

Stag beetles (LUCANIDAE), longhorn beetles (CERAMBYCIDAE) and sugar beetles (PASSALIDAE) are commonly found in fallen trees and logs in both primary and secondary forests. A hammer and chisel is needed in searching for these, and a killing bottle is needed for all types of collecting. Chisel down any decaying fallen trees and logs you come across in the forest. Always chisel carefully and responsibly, avoiding unnecessary injury to hidden creatures and looking out for active beetles that disappear quickly. Remember that you may encounter dangerous animals such as the poisonous spider, *Selenocosmia crassipes*, the black scorpion, *Palamnaeus fulvipes*, centipedes and snakes.

For collecting aquatic beetles, a dip net is needed with a strong metal rim between 6.4 to 19.1 millimetres (0.25 to 0.75 inch) thick, and shaped like the letter 'D'. The bag may be made of tough marquisette material. A heavy steel knife is useful at the side of the river or ponds for searching for hidden beetles.

To collect cave-dwellers, one requires a head lamp or a hand torch, a sharp chisel, a hammer and a heavy knife. A piece of rope should be carried for emergency use. The method is simple: merely lift small rocks in the cave and use the hammer and chisel to open up crevices and burrow outlets.

MOUNTING, LABELLING AND STORING

Specimens are best mounted or set soon after they are captured because if they are still fresh and flexible they can be easily mounted as described later. If they become dry and brittle you must first relax them before they are mounted.

Relaxing

Get a metal rectangular container with lid, such as an empty Jacob's Cream Crackers Box. Into this put a layer of sand covered by a piece of soft wood. For temporary use, a piece of rug can be covered with manila cardboard. Moisten the sand or rug with water and add a little carbolic acid to prevent mould. Place the dried insects on the surface of the dry soft wood or cardboard and close the lid. After thirty-six hours specimens are usually sufficiently relaxed to be mounted. An alternative method is to place the specimen in boiling hot water for twenty to thirty seconds; when withdrawn it is flexible enough to be mounted.

Equipment
To mount or set an insect correctly, the collector must equip himself with a box of entomological pins[1], a piece of soft board or cork, a pair of forceps with sharp edges, a small brush and a good hand lens.

Mounting
First, insert an entomological pin into the right elytron of the dead insect, just behind the metathorax and perpendicular to its body; then place the pinned insect on the surface of the soft board. Press down the pin into the soft board — deep enough to hold the weight and the balance of the insect (Fig. 14). Use short pins or normal dressmaker's pins, not necessarily entomological pins at this stage, to spread out its legs to the position in which you wish to set them. A few short pins must be affixed to secure each leg so as to maintain its mounted position. There is a disadvantage in using long pins as they often get entangled with other pins. Manipulation with the fingers spoils the colour of some beetles, so use forceps as far as possible.

For beetles with long antennae, use a pair of forceps with pointed ends to carefully set the antennae backwards, making a semicircle towards the abdomen of the insect, gently and slowly to avoid breaking them. If the antennae are very long and slender, use a brush with moistened hairs to spread them out instead of forceps.

Leave the insect on the setting board for a week or more until it is thoroughly dry. Dryness is indicated by the stiffness of the body and the brittleness of the legs and antennae of the insect. Slowly withdraw all pins from the setting board except the one through the insect's body. You can then transfer the specimen into a storage box or a specially made glass case, using forceps to hold the pin.

Be careful of ants, cockroaches and lizards which will attack and eat mounted insects set aside to dry. Two small bags of naphthalene

---

[1] Entomological pins are stainless, usually nickel-plated, steel pins. They are not available in the local market but can be obtained from entomological dealers in Europe, Australia and America.

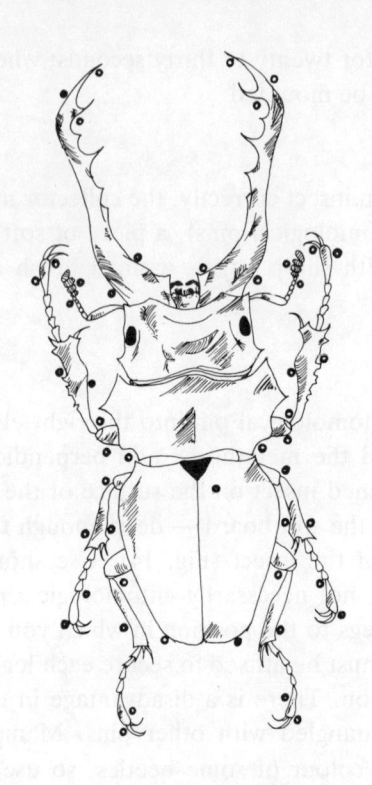

• Denotes the
position of
a pin.

DORSAL VIEW

FIGURE 14   How to mount a beetle

should be placed at the edges of the setting board, and the board should be placed in a cool, dry place away from direct sunlight, preferably inside an airtight entomological box.

Labelling
To be of any scientific value, each mounted insect must bear a small data-label with locality, date of capture, and the collector's name, and the label is impaled on the pin below the specimen. Wherever possible, record the scientific name and sex of the insect, the name of the plant or type of material where it was collected, the exact time it was taken, and a brief description of the environment with the habits and habitat of the insect.

Storing

Mount the properly labelled insects in special entomological storage boxes. These boxes have tight-fitting lids to prevent the entry of pests, dust and direct rays of the sun which tend to destroy the colours. The bottom of these airtight boxes is covered with a piece of cork or soft board. Local carpenters currently charge M$18.00 to M$25.00 for a box of dimensions 381 millimetres (18 inches) in length, 300 millimetres (12 inches) in breadth, and 107 millimetres (4.2 inches) in width.

You should fix a small bag containing naphthalene or paradichlorobenzene crystals at the right-hand bottom edge of the interior of the box. This will discourage pests and mites inside the box. The crystals will need replacing from time to time.

Preserving

Fresh specimens of fully dried and well-mounted beetles do not require much in the way of preservatives; but because of the warm humid climate of Malaysia there is a possibility that mould may form and grow on the outside of the specimens, destroying the chitin. Creosote should be applied to remove this, by painting it on the affected area(s) with a small brush. A small packet of silica gel should also be placed inside to absorb moisture, and replaced when the blue crystals turn pink, showing that they have become saturated.

Arranging

The simplest arrangement of an insect collection for a beginner is to have the specimens arranged in families. They should be laid out in straight rows with the male on the left-hand side and the female on the right-hand side. A label with the scientific name is pinned behind the nearest insect in each row. Labels indicating the sex of specimens should bear the symbols ♂ (male) or ♀ (female).

BREEDING AND REARING BEETLES

Beetle larvae can be reared in a breeding cage of which the four sides are frames covered with perforated zinc for ventilation. Food plants can be kept fresh by putting the stems in a small vessel of water; they must be renewed as soon as they are withered or eaten. A breeding cage of this kind is shown in Figure 15.

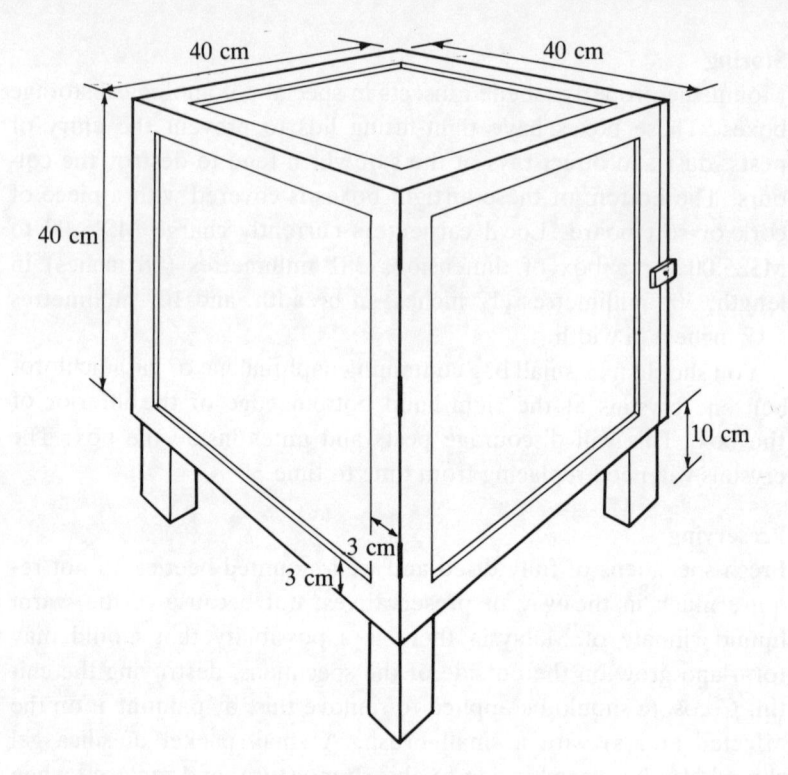

FIGURE 15   A common breeding case

Aquatic beetles are reared in a glass aquarium with a netted lid to prevent the insects from escaping. Proper food plants must be inserted in the layer of sand at the bottom of the aquarium. During their breeding season, you will observe the presence of larvae in your aquarium, followed by the pupae and the emergence of a new generation.

For beetles such as the stag and sugar beetles, which live in decaying wood, a big wooden box with a lid made of muslin cloth is used. Fill the bottom of the box with a layer of soil about 75 to 100 millimetres (3 to 4 inches) deep. Cut off the part of the log in which the larvae are living, lay it on the soil and close the lid. Sprinkle some water with a 10 per cent mixture of sugar onto the log and the soil every six hours so that they are always kept slightly damp. If you want to observe the development of the larvae, the log must first be split into halves and replaced inside the box. Gently replace any larva that has fallen out. By reopening the log slightly, you can see the larvae. Do this slowly and carefully to avoid destroying the habitat or killing any young.

When rearing beetles which devour food materials such as carrion and cowpats, make a wooden box as above but place it at the furthest end in the compound around your house so as to avoid the unpleasant smell of the contents. A piece of decaying carcass or cowpat with eggs and larvae, depending on the species, is put into the box in place of a log, then covered with a lid.

It is interesting and absorbing to observe the full life history. A detailed journal about the course of the life history is scientifically valuable and should be kept. Such a record should include the number of moults, the name of the food plants or food materials, the season (the month and date), the number of eggs laid at the time, the name of the species, the lifespan, length of pupation, date of emergence of the adult beetles and sketches of the egg, larva (early and late stages), pupa and the adult beetle.

DESCRIPTION OF SPECIES

The text gives details of the scientific name, the structure, colour, habits, habitat, evidence of occurrence and range of distribution of every insect which is illustrated on the plates. Wherever possible, the life history, the natural food and the economic importance, if any, of the beetle are described.

The nomenclature and classification of Malaysian beetles is at present incomplete, and the author has encountered many difficulties in getting his collection classified. Even museums abroad could not provide him with a list of beetles which occur in Malaysia. All the names given in the text are from the numerous articles issued by Japanese museums or from private collectors and agricultural departments. In case of error, the author would be happy to accept correction and criticism

Since most COLEOPTERA have marked sexual dimorphism externally, the separation of the sexes is not a problem. Sex is indicated by symbols after the scientific name of each beetle specimen illustrated.

It is important to note the total length of a beetle by measuring from the longest part of the mouth-parts, or any other prominent growths on the prothorax or head, to the tip of the abdomen of the insect. Figure 16 shows how to take measurements of some typical specimens. In the text, the measurement of each insect is given immediately after its Latin name.

Where the black and white illustrations are enlarged for better reference, a line representing the actual length of each specimen is shown next to the drawing. All colourplates shown are actual-size except for Plate 31 where the specimens illustrated are greatly magnified.

Other abbreviations used in the text are as follows:
sp   denotes species (singular)
spp   denotes species (plural)
mm   denotes millimetre(s)
m   denotes metre(s)
P. Malaysia denotes Peninsular or West Malaysia

The symbols ♂ and ♀ denote male and female respectively and are used only for plate references.

The word 'complex' after the specific name indicates that several species, which have not yet been separated, are probably confused under the name.

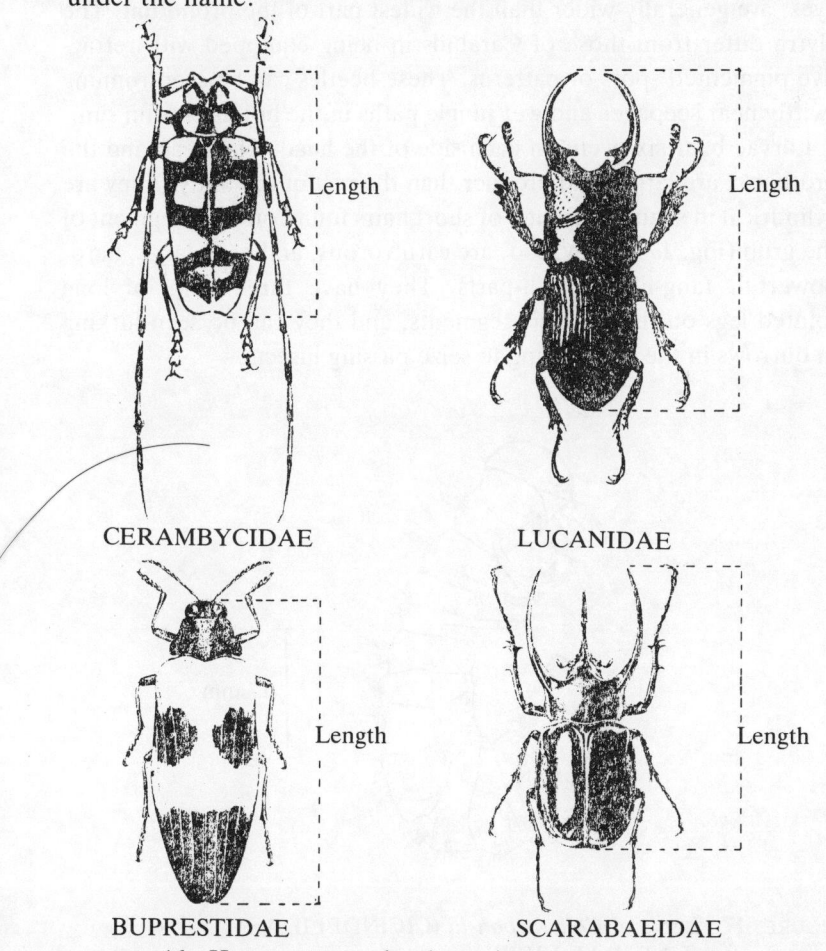

CERAMBYCIDAE   LUCANIDAE

BUPRESTIDAE   SCARABAEIDAE

FIGURE 16   How to measure beetle specimens

CICINDELIDAE (TIGER BEETLES)

Beetles of this family are perhaps the most ferocious of all insect predators on other insects. They possess formidable enlarged, sharply toothed and sickle-shaped mandibles. When not in use, these mandibles overlap each other. Antennae are long and slender, thread-like and glabrous.

All species are predatory and active, and they fly at the least alarm. They have long, powerful legs adapted for running extremely fast. The majority of tiger beetles are greenish or brown in colour.

The heads of CICINDELIDAE species, including the compound eyes, are generally wider than the widest part of the pronotum. The elytra differ from those of Carabids in being equipped with refractive pigmented spots or patterns. These beetles can be seen running swiftly near seepages and wet jungle paths in the hot afternoon sun.

Larvae bear six ocelli on each side of the head. The head and the prothorax are larger and broader than the rest of the body. They are cylindrical in shape with tufts of short hairs found on each segment of the grub (Fig. 17). They, too, are carnivorous, and have large, hard, powerful, fang-like mouth-parts. They have three pairs of long jointed legs on the thoracic segments, and they can be seen lurking in burrows in the soil waiting to seize passing insects.

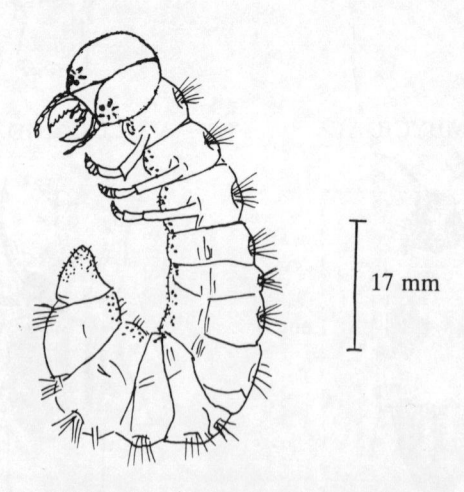

FIGURE 17   Larva of *Collyris bonelli* (CICINDELIDAE) (LATERAL VIEW)

Cicindela aurulenta (14–20 mm) PLATE 1A♂
One of the commonest of all tiger beetles, found mostly running about on wet jungle roads and watery sandy banks of streams, making brief flights. The females are quite similar to the males but they have the abdomen broadened and usually lengthened. They prefer running on leaves of low shrubs. Adults are cuprous greenish blue with three yellow spots at the edge of each elytron. Though true carnivorous insects, they do some harm to trees by boring in stems and branches. Their young prey on other insects.
Range: Himalaya to Indo-China and Taiwan, south to Java, Borneo and P. Malaysia.

Cicindela sumatrensis (12–18 mm) PLATE 1B♂
This species lives generally in sandy habitats including salty beaches. Occasionally seen running very fast, chasing one another, or hunting for food. Life history unknown.

The head is bronze with a green reflection. The ventral side is metallic dark green with white labrum, light brown eyes and bronze pronotum. The elytra are dark bronze coloured with white or testaceous markings.
Range: India to P. Malaysia and Sumatra.

Another distinctive insect which resembles *C. sumatrensis* is *C. sexpunctata* (13–18 mm). It is not uncommon in paddy fields during the dry season. Adults are recorded as preying upon paddy flies, *Leptocorisa varicornis*, and rice borers, *Scirpophaga innotata*. Both the larvae and adults are insectivorous.
Range: India to P. Malaysia, southern Thailand and Sumatra.

C. versicolor (8–10 mm) (PLATE 1C♂) is another species which has extra yellow spots on the elytra and is commoner in open woodlands.
Range: Thailand, P. Malaysia to Java.

Collyris bonelli (10–12 mm) Plate 1D♂
This insect is glossy blue in colour with brownish-red legs. It is slender and found abundantly in coffee plantations. The darting movements of these insects render them difficult to capture with a net.

The female beetle deposits eggs in burrows on stems and thick

branches of coffee plants. The larva (Fig. 17) eats ants and small caterpillars. It uses its strong mandibles and hard chitinized head to burrow into flowering twigs of cocoa, kapok and *Loranthus*, and stays inside the tunnel to wait for its prey. Pupation usually takes place in one of the many tunnels it has made.
Range: Java, Sumatra and P. Malaysia.

C. tuberculata, which is larger in size (14–18 mm) than the above species, is another common beetle in thick secondary forest. The author has observed numbers of this species moving about in old rubber plantations in Selangor.
Range: P. Malaysia to Borneo and the Philippines.

Therates basalis (10–13 mm)   PLATE 1E ♂
A beautiful tiger beetle with long thread-like antennae and swollen eyes. The biting mouth-parts are red in colour. The head and pronotum are green. Legs are, as usual in this group, long and slender, brown in colour. The hind pair of legs are very much lengthened. The wing sheaths are purplish-indigo, red at the top and highly reflective. They are found on jungle paths partially covered with vegetation, making darting movements.
Range: Throughout Sundaland.

CARABIDAE (GROUND BEETLES)

Few species are known from the Malaysian region; in the temperate zone this family comprises over a thousand species.

The habits and habitats of this family are similar to those of the CICINDELIDAE. They feed on insects, small animals and sometimes on carrion and other decomposing matter. They are shy insects, hiding by day under thick undergrowth, logs and rocks.

Mandibles are short and crescent-like, with strong biting edges. Antennae are long and thread-like. The body is usually dull black or matt blue.

Though most Carabids are very good fliers, they are found more on the ground than in the air, and prefer to stalk and run down their prey in shady areas.

Larvae of CARABIDAE look quite like those of the CICINDELIDAE but have shorter legs, smaller mouth-parts and are not so

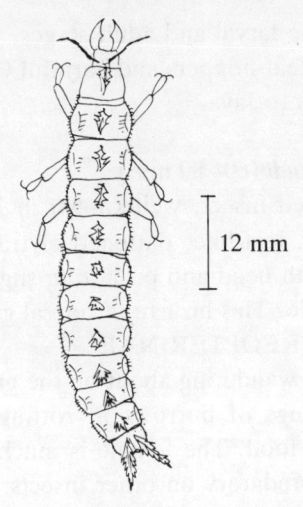

FIGURE 18 Larva of *Casnoidea interstitialis* (CARABIDAE) (DORSAL VIEW)

densely covered with hairs (Fig. 18). Larvae are predatory and attack their prey with sickle-like biting jaws.

From the ecologist's point of view, both CICINDELIDAE and CARABIDAE species are beneficial insects of great economic importance, because they are *aphytophagous*, feeding on insect larvae as well as on the adults of various species which are harmful to agriculture.

Casnoidea interstitialis (8–10 mm) PLATE 1F♂

The beetle is brown with golden-greenish elytra. A string of bronze spots is present at the extremity of the wing covers. The prothorax has bright yellow margins.

The larva is yellowish-white with black markings and tufts of bristles or setae on the dorsal side of the body. Usually it grows to a length of 10 to 12 mm (Fig. 18). Like those of CICINDELIDAE species, it lives mainly on insects.

Range: India to South-east Asia.

In rice-growing areas, a genus closely related but smaller, *Ophionea interstitialis* (6–8 mm), is also found abundantly. Its body is brownish-red, flat and slender with black head and elongated prothorax. The base of the elytra and the broad cross-band, running through the middle, are bluish-black. It is attracted by the lights of

houses. At both the larval and adult stages, the insect feeds on the eggs and young of leaf-hoppers and harmful Chrysomelids.
Range: P. Malaysia to Java.

Mormolyce castelnaudi (60–80 mm) PLATE 1H♂ 1♀
This easily identified insect, well-known in English as the 'Fiddle Beetle', has broad, leaf-like, flattened elytra. Its wing sheaths are coloured brown with head and pronotum slightly darker. Antennae are long and flexible. This bizarre, arboreal genus is classified under the subfamily THYREOPTERINAE.

It is usually seen wandering about on the ground or jutting out its head at the openings of burrows in rotting trees of the tropical forest, hunting for food. The female is much smaller in size. In its early stages, it is predatory on other insects. The larva lives in the core of dead logs.
Range: Sumatra to P. Malaysia.

Mormolyce phyllodes (60–80 mm) PLATE 1G♂
This fiddle-shaped species differs from *M. castelnaudi* in the less sharply edged pronotum, not so pointed, and drawn backwards. Antennae are much longer, about 70 mm. It has much the same way of life as the above species and is commonly found near logging camps.

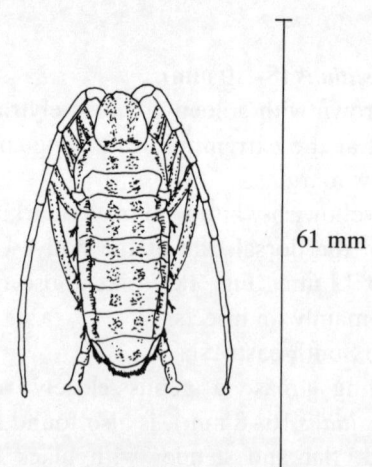

FIGURE 19 Larva of *Mormolyce phyllodes* (CARABIDAE) (DORSAL VIEW)

The larva (Fig. 19) is an ugly-looking grub with long and slender legs and antennae. The body is broad and cylindrical, and measures about 62 mm. The mouth-parts include a pair of sharp cutting mandibles used to prey on aphids and other scale insects. It can be found on freshly felled trees in logging sites.
Range: Indo-China, Thailand to P. Malaysia and islands of Sumatra, Java and Borneo.

DYTISCIDAE (PREDACEOUS DIVING BEETLES)

This group of insects is commonly found in ponds and quiet streams.

The scutellum of the insect is usually visible and the hind coxae are large, characteristics which differentiate these from other water beetles. The body is smooth, oval and hard, with flattened hind legs fringed with long hairs, generally used for swimming (Fig. 8). There are six visible sterna in the abdomen. The front coxae open behind and the hind coxae are quite big and muscularly built. Dytiscids differ from HYDROPHILIDAE in having long filiform antennae and very short maxillary palpi.

Both adults and larvae of the DYTISCIDAE are predaceous and feed on various small aquatic creatures. Larvae have long, hollow, sickle-like mandibles and when they attack they suck out the body fluids of their prey through these. These larvae are extremely voracious and even prey upon small fishes (Fig. 20).

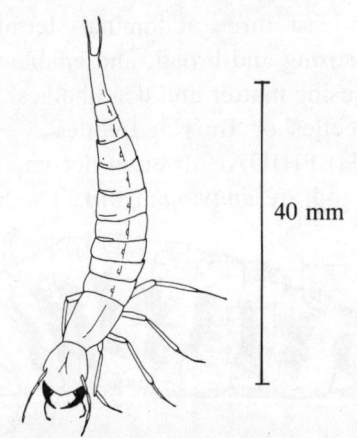

FIGURE 20   Larva of *Cibister roeselii* (DYTISCIDAE) (LATERAL VIEW)

Cibister roeselii (28–30 mm)   PLATE 19C♂

The whole insect is brown in colour with a yellow marginal edge on the pronotum and elytra, forming a yellow horseshoe marking. The fore and middle legs are short and slender whereas the hind legs are strong, muscular, fringed with long brownish-yellow hairs, and are efficient oars.

This beetle is found in freshwater lakes, ponds and streams in forested areas. A strong dip-net is used to collect such water beetles.

Like most typical DYTISCIDAE larvae, the larvae of this species are found in freshwater ponds and lakes. They have a broad head bearing strong mandibles and are sluggish with three pairs of long legs adapted for swimming. There is also a pair of fork-like appendages at the anal end and the entire body is covered with fine, soft, minute hairs (Fig. 20). They prey upon various aquatic animals, including molluscs, worms and tadpoles, with their long sickle-like jaws.

Range: Europe to Asia Minor and probably South-east Asia.

SILPHIDAE (CARRION BEETLES)

These beetles are commonly captured on the bodies of dead animals and at traps with baits.

Their bodies are soft and flattened. The antennae are capitate and the tarsi are five-segmented. The elytra are usually rounded and short, leaving at least three abdominal sternites uncovered. The hind femora are strong and broad, and enable the beetles to move pieces of decomposing matter and dead bodies. They are commonly called 'Carrion Beetles' or 'Burying Beetles'.

The larvae of SILPHIDAE dwell in decomposing vegetable matter or carcasses, and are *aphytophagous*. The head is small and so

FIGURE 21   Larva of *Diamesus osculans* (SILPHIDAE) (DORSAL VIEW)

are the mouth-parts. The thoracic segments are broad but legs are usually short. There are ten abdominal segments with bristles on each segment (Fig. 21).

Diamesus osculans (30–32 mm)   PLATE 19K ♂
A completely dull black or sometimes dark brown beetle which is easily obtained at bait-traps and in carrion.

The elytra are short with two or four pink spots (which usually fade away in time), and a few abdominal segments are often left uncovered. The body is somewhat flattened. The hind legs are strong and muscular; they play an important role in moving pieces of decaying material and the bodies of dead creatures.

The female is duller brown and smaller in size. It is much commoner than the male, and lays eggs in decayed matter or dead bodies. The larva (Fig. 21) resembles a giant maggot and bears thick black coloured setae on the back of the body. The side of the body is covered with very short bristles, thickened around each spiracle. Development to the pupal stage takes place within decayed matter or a carcass.

Range: India to South-east Asia and Australia; north to Taiwan and southern Japan.

LUCANIDAE (STAG BEETLES OR PINCHING BUGS)

The well-known stag beetles or pinching bugs have a broad rectangular prothorax and a pair of long protruding jaws, taking various forms. The males of this family are distinguished by their large mouth-parts exhibiting the pair of antler-like mandibles which in some cases are thought to be used to impress their mates so as to attract them during the mating season; each male has to battle for its mate and probably those with larger and longer mandibles will tend to be the privileged ones. Mandibles of females are normally developed and are very much shorter. Thus the separation of the sexes is clearly evident.

The antennae of these insects are geniculate with the first antennal segment greatly lengthened, elbowed and bearing plates fixed to the loose clubs as shown in Figure 22. The mentum is entire and the pronotum does not have a median groove as it does in Passalids. The elytra are usually black, chestnut or yellow in colour, and the

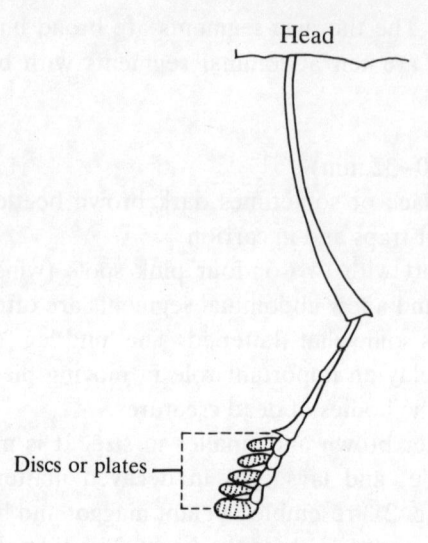

FIGURE 22 A geniculate antenna of a stag beetle

majority have smooth, polished surfaces; some resemble those of the Passalids in being deeply striated longitudinally.

There are five visible sternites on the ventral side of the abdominal segment, and when in flight the elytra of the adult insect frequently produce a castanet-like sound.

The larvae of stag beetles dwell and develop together with the adults in dead or partly decayed fallen trees found in both primary and secondary forest. The blackened, enormous, denticulate mandibles of these grubs are very powerful and are used to chew the rotting wood. Larvae have three pairs of true legs attached to the thoracic segments which help them to move from place to place. These grubs are creamy white in colour and normally measure between 30 and 70 mm in length. The body cuticle is soft with soft nongeniculated antennae (Fig. 23). After dwelling in the decayed treedust for a long period, they change to a hard cradle-like pupa showing the full body shape of the adult. A further considerable length of time (from a few weeks to a few months, depending on each species) is taken for the insect to emerge from the pupa.

Agriculturalists and entomologists have recorded damage done by some species of this family, viz. *Dorcus titanus* and *Odontolabis latipennis*, on flowers and flower stalks of oil palms, coconuts and coffee plants.

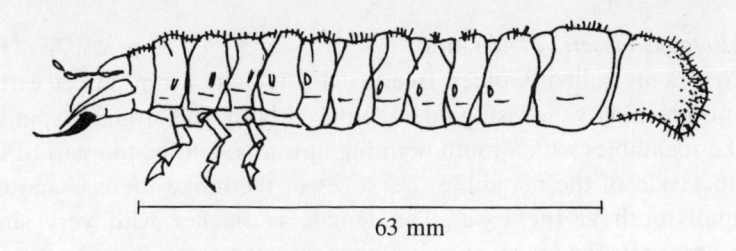

FIGURE 23   Larva of *Rhaetulus didieri* (LUCANIDAE)
(LATERAL VIEW)

Aegus acuminatus (20–30 mm)   PLATE 2A♂
Both sexes are black with deeply striated elytra. The head and prothorax of the adult are broad and as long as the elytra. Mandibles are curved inwards, and forked at the tips. A small tooth is found at the inner base of each mandible. The female has short, developed mandibles.

Records from Agricultural Stations show damage done by this species on the flowers of coffee and cocoa.
Range: Sumatra and P. Malaysia.

Aegus capitatus (30–42 mm)   PLATE 2B♂ D♀
This is quite a common species in open forest. It much resembles the above species but has a broader prothorax, and the mandibles have a large tooth at the mid-length. A smaller one is seen near the base. Both point inwards. The female is smaller, measuring a little over 30 mm and is commoner than the male.
Range: P. Malaysia.

Aegus falcifer (30–35 mm)   PLATE 2C♂
The body is slender, narrow and long. Elytra with longitudinal grooves or depressed line-markings. The entire insect is black in colour. Mandibles of the male are sabre-shaped and sharp, having pointed ends with saw-like inner edges. A long hard tooth is present at the rear base. At the front of the head are two pointed V-shaped growths. The female measures 25 to 30 mm in length and has smaller mandibles than the male. A depression is clearly evident in the prothorax.
Range: P. Malaysia to Sumatra.

Allotopus moseri (70–80 mm)   PLATE 2E♂ F♀
Commonly called 'Golden Beetle', this is quite a rare insect with a smooth shiny yellowish-golden coloured body and straight, spindle-like mandibles with a tooth pointing upwards. On the top part of the inner side of the mandibles lies a set of teeth and there is another small tooth at the base. The female is smaller with very short mouth-parts, and is much commoner than the male. Usually seen on the bark of trees.
  Both sexes can be captured at light-traps.
Range: Sumatra and P. Malaysia.

  A commoner species, *A. rosenbergi* (60–70 mm), shown in PLATE 2G♂, is slightly smaller and has a golden colouring tinted greyish-blue. Its habits and habitat are similar to those of *A. moseri*.
Range: Sumatra and P. Malaysia.

  Another species, *A. fruhstorferi* (50–55 mm) (PLATE 2H♂) which was recorded from Sabah, has been found in the highlands of Peninsular Malaysia at an altitude of about 760 m above sea-level. The body, head, pronotum, elytra and legs are smooth and polished greyish-golden in males, and black in females. Both sexes have short triangular mandibulate jaws with inner edges that are dentate, though these are smaller in females.
Range: Borneo and P. Malaysia.

  All the above species live on the sap of wounded trees of the tropical lower montane evergreen rain forest. All these three species of *Allotopus* are taken at light-traps during the months of May to August, but none of them are common.

Cladognathus (Cyclommatus) giraffa complex
(70–95 mm)   PLATE 3A♂
A very large beetle with conspicuously antler-like mandibles. The body is entirely black, and the elongated smooth elytra are somewhat convex. The legs are long and slender.
  The mandibles are divaricate with the fifth tooth from the tip enlarged and sharp, ending the strong beautiful curvature on the tip. Another huge tooth juts out at the base of the mandibles. When at rest, the mandibles overlap one another. Though sex attraction nor-

mally depends on pheromonal secretions, it is believed that these jaws are also of great attraction to the opposite sex. They are often found dwelling in rotting tree trunks and under decayed trees in lowland forests.

A number of forms with smaller mandibles are found but are still unclassified. Smaller forms of this insect are commoner than the largest form that is described above, for example, form *telodonta*, measuring between 85 and 95 mm.

Range: Southern China and northern India, Thailand to P. Malaysia, Sumatra and Java.

Cyclommatus albersi (40–43 mm)   PLATE 3B ♂

The head, pronotum and legs are reddish-brown with a greenish lustre. The central part of the scutellum is entirely black. There is a strong broad median line on the elytra. The body is rather slender. The mandibles are thick, arcuate and forked at the tips with two smaller teeth at the inner edges.

It is usually found in numbers in the cores of freshly fallen trees and logs in logging sites.

Range: Assam, northward to Taiwan, and south to northern P. Malaysia.

Cyclommatus canaliculatus (45–50 mm)   PLATE 3C ♂

The rough broad head has a pair of curved mandibles and is larger than the prothorax. The tip of each mandible is irregular with four tooth-like structures. Another big thorn-like tooth is clearly visible jutting out near the base. The head, mandibles and prothorax are coloured dark greyish-brown, whereas the body is plain brown.

This insect inhabits lowland forests and dwells in decomposing tree trunks.

Range: P. Malaysia.

Cyclommatus lunifer (45–50 mm)   PLATE 3D ♂

This species is less common than *C. canaliculatus* and is dull dirty brown in colour. It has fork-tipped arcuate mandibles with a tooth near the middle, pointing inwards. The tip is dentate with four or five teeth. The legs are slender and brown.

The habits and habitat of this insect are similar to those of the species above.

Range: P. Malaysia.

In Borneo, *C. montanellus* (60–70 mm), which is related to the above species, is commonly found. Specimens have been collected near the base of Mount Kinabalu using light-traps. The pronotum, scutellum, mandibles and legs are lustrous green tinted light brownish-red. The elytra and the setae on the tarsi of the legs are bright brownish-orange.

Observation suggests that variations are numerous. It can be distinguished from the mainland species by the much broader and longer mandibles, which have more small teeth at the bifurcated tip and another five or six teeth near the base of the inner edge. Generally it is much bigger than *C. lunifer*.
Range: Borneo.

Cyclommatus terandus (45–50 mm)   PLATE 3E♂
This species dwells deep in the primary forest. Its body is slender and purplish-brown. The mandibles are divaricate and deflexed. At the rear end of the mandibles lies a set of small tooth-like structures. Legs are slender and long. Antennae are geniculate.

The male frequents bleeding wounded trees of the genera *Shorea* and *Swietenia*.
Range: Borneo to P. Malaysia.

Dorcus antaeus (70–76 mm)   PLATE 3F♂
Quite a large beetle with a shining black body, including stout, curved, deflexed and forked mouth-parts. An acute tooth is sharply outcurved from the base to the middle, pointing inwards. The centre of the dorsal part of the head is deeply depressed. The head is rectangular and as broad as the prothorax. Both these and the elytra are entirely polished black.

It has been found living in the fallen trunks of kapok trees in lowland dipterocarp forest.
Range: Assam to Burma, Thailand and P. Malaysia.

Dorcus curvidens (68–72 mm)   PLATE 3G♂
This beetle is commonly found on trees, mostly kapok and red meranti, sometimes also wild durians. It is totally polished black in colour and is seen on the wing in twilight, making loud creaking noises by the movements of the hind wings against the hard elytra.

Its mandibles are strong, thick and black. They have an arrow-

headed tip with an acute tooth pointing deeply inwards.
Range: India to Indo-China and P. Malaysia.

In Borneo and the surrounding islands in the south a very closely related species, *D. parryi* (60–65 mm), occurs. Its habitat is similar. It can be distinguished from the mainland form by its mandibles, of which the tips are more sharply pointed, the tooth in the middle of each mandible is larger and more pointed; and the curvature between the tip and the middle tooth is slightly longer and more curving.
Range: Sumatra to Java and Celebes, Borneo.

Dorcus gypaetus (50–60 mm)   PLATE 4A ♂
This beetle occcurs only on the hills between 300 and 750 m, but it is not very common.

Males are large, conspicuous insects with straight jaws which differ from those of most stag beetles in having a brush of short orange-brown setaceous pubescence at the middle edges of the mandibles. They are seen mostly under fallen and badly rotted trees such as *Shorea curtisii*, feeding on decaying organic matter, and are easily captured. The females are smaller, about 30 mm long.
Range: P. Malaysia southward to Java. Also the Philippines but not recorded from Borneo.

Dorcus reichei (55–60 mm)   PLATE 4B ♂
Closely resembles *D. gypaetus* with the head and prothorax black and elytra chestnut. The only visible differences are the frontal edge of the head which is almost a straight line. The mandibles are bifurcated at the tip and a recurved bifid tooth arises from the base of the dorsal area of each mandible.

It is found rarely in secondary forest between 300 and 750 m above sea-level and lives on decayed tree stumps and fallen trees especially kapok trees, together with its young. Both sexes are nocturnal, and are sometimes taken at light-traps.
Range: Northern India, Indo-China, Thailand and P. Malaysia.

Dorcus (*Serrognathus*) *titanus* complex (45–85 mm)   PLATE 4D ♂
Species of this handsome group come from the lower dipterocarp

forest of Peninsular Malaysia. They vary greatly in size. Some are as small as 45 mm while others grow to a length of 85 mm. Their long, broad, straight decumbent mandibles which usually curve inwards at their extremity, are black. The inner edge of each jaw is saw-like. These beetles have the body entirely black, with elytra sometimes castaneous and the head as big as the prothorax.

The females are smaller, being at the most 50 mm long. The heads are not as big as the pronota. The mouth-parts are small. The larvae drill their way through decomposing tree trunks and the adults attack clusters of flowering coffee and cocoa twigs.
Range: Throughout Sundaland.

The only species related to *D. (S.) titanus*, from Borneo is *D. (S.) thoracicus* (70–85 mm). Its remarkably straight mandibulate jaws are different from those of *D. (S.) bucephalus* (70–80 mm) of the neighbouring islands of Java and Sumatra, in being longer and less curved. The jaws have a bifurcated tip and two large teeth are seen jutting inwards, between the tip and the mid-length of each mandible, forming another raised curvature. Both the head and pronotum are rectangular and broader than the elytra. The entire insect is polished black.

There is evidence of damage to flowering branches of coffee and cocoa plants by this species.
Range: Borneo.

Hexarthrius deyrollei (75–90 mm) PLATE 4E♂ C♀
Another handsome Malaysian insect which feeds on sweet fermenting juices oozing from wounded trees. It occurs in August, when several beetles can frequently be captured at one spot.

It, too, has marked sexual dimorphism. The male has distinct recurved mouth-parts, whereas those of the female are small and crescent-shaped. The female is entirely black and much smaller in size, about 65 mm in length.

Rather common, with very well-developed, strong, thick mandibles, truly forked. When at rest, the forked tips form a big complete circle. The head and pronotum is black and the wing covers are yellowish-chestnut and black at the apex. Two or three longitudinal striae can be seen on the elytra.
Range: Thailand to P. Malaysia.

Hexarthrius mandibularis (70.–80 mm)   PLATE 7A♂
Dull black with deep brick-red elytra. Mandibles are long, slender, straight and decumbent, with two pointed teeth, excluding the one which forms the tip. The whole length of the inner edges of the mandibles is denticulate. The body and legs are slender, long and black. The head is broader and bigger than the rectangular prothorax.

This Bornean race is rarely obtained unless baited with decomposing meat.
Range: Borneo.

Odontolabis aerata complex (30–40 mm)   PLATE 4F♂ G♂ H♀
According to some Japanese authorities, there are two distinct forms of this species, and the difference is marked by the shape of the mandibles. The one illustrated in the plate (G) is form *amphiodonta*, which has crescent-like mandibles with small conical teeth at the inner edges, while the other (F) has mandibles shaped like a semi-circle with rough inner edges. These two forms occur during development within the pupae, when some develop long mandibles and others develop short ones. The insect is lustrous deep green and is not uncommon in the trunks of dead trees in forests of northern mainland Malaysia. The active larvae make numerous burrows in which they later pupate.
Range: P. Malaysia and neighbouring islands.

Odontolabis brookeana (50–55 mm)   PLATE 7B♂ C♀
The elytra are smooth and marked with bright yellow. The head is dull dark brown, and the pronotum has two depressions marked dirty orange-brown. The mandibles are very well-developed, crescent-shaped, with huge teeth like the cutting blade of a saw. Legs are long, narrow and brown in colour. The ventral side of the body is completely black.

All records are of specimens taken at light-traps in Sarawak.
Range: Borneo and Sumatra.

Odontolabis castelnaudi (70–90 mm)   PLATE 5A♂ C♀
A smart, elegant creature with yellow wing sheaths. The head, mandibles, prothorax and legs are black. The mentum is much wider and broader than the pronotum. Mandibles are narrow, branched into two tips with a very small rounded tooth on the second; underneath this tip lie a few miniature spherical teeth. At the base

another tooth projects inwards. The elytra usually turn dirty chestnut or brown when not well preserved and dried. Hence special care has to be taken.

The male closely resembles *O. femoralis*, but can be easily separated because the entire underside of the body and the tibiae and femora of the legs of *O. castelnaudi* are entirely polished black. The female has smooth elytra of bright yellow with the head greatly reduced in size and the mandibles even more so.
Range: P. Malaysia, Sumatra and Borneo.

Odontolabis dalmani (60–65 mm)   PLATE 5B ♂
The adult male beetle is slender-bodied and dirty-looking. The mandibles are hard but are not very long, about 12 mm in length; the tips are saw-like and flattened. The head is black and much smaller in area than the prothorax. The pronotum covering the eyes is pointed at the posterior edges. The elytra hava a shield of well-trimmed brown fur-like pubescence. The legs are quite long and black.

Rarely seen in collections and found in thick forested areas over 600 m above sea-level.
Range: P. Malaysia, Sumatra, Java and Borneo.

Odontolabis femoralis complex (45–85 mm)   PLATE 5D ♂ E ♂ F ♀
Males are variable in respect of size and of the shape and length of the mandibles. Most of the males resemble *O. castelnaudi* in shape and size, but the anterior of their head is flattened forming an oblong-shaped frontal. The underside of the body has dull orange-brown, squarish markings on the metasternum which are not found in *O. castelnaudi*. The head is rectangular. Both this part and the pronotum are black and densely covered with fine granulations. The elytra are smooth and yellow. Illustrations of two forms are shown. It is worth looking closely at the structure of the mandibles and then comparing their differences.

There is no record of variations in the female sex so far. Elytra of this sex are yellow with a V-shaped black portion, and very small mandibles.

Both male and female are apparently common in Peninsular Malaysia, but are rarely obtained in Borneo.
Range: Thailand to P. Malaysia, Borneo.

Odontolabis gazella (58–64 mm) PLATE 6A♂
This rare insect is one of the most handsome stag beetles, with deep shining yellowish-orange elytra. The head and pronotum are shiny brown. The shoulders and the margins of the prothorax are very finely granulated. This species resembles *O. brookeana* both in size and shape, but has the tips of the mandibles more pointed and the inner cutting edges more irregular and sharp. The entire jaws are polished black.

It occurs at moderate elevations on hills.
Range: P. Malaysia, Sumatra, Java and Borneo.

Odontolabis bellicosus (80–100 mm) PLATE 6C♂
A remarkably beautiful stag beetle. The mandibles have forked tips with another two long pointed projections from the long narrow and hardened mouth-parts. A bowl-shaped depression is clearly evident on the black head. The elytra are smooth and the insect is entirely black.

It dwells in secondary forest, in logs which are badly rotted with clusters of fungi. A very rare species and especially so in Peninsular Malaysia.
Range: Sumatra and Borneo, eastwards to Celebes and westwards to P. Malaysia.

Odontolabis latipennis (55–60 mm) PLATE 6B♂
In shape, habits and habitat, it is very similar to *O. gazella*, but the whole body of this species is washed black with elytra deep chestnut to black. Mandibles are short, broad, rather blunt, and saw-like; the femora of the first pair of legs thickened. The head is rectangular and is smaller than the prothorax which is somewhat trapeziform in shape. The elytra, head and prothorax are black.

A rare insect, found in deep primary forest.
Range: P. Malaysia.

Odontolabis sommeri (40–55 mm) PLATE 6D♂ E♂
A medium-sized beetle with reduced mandibles and head. The jaws are straight, and evenly serrated. The elytra are pale yellowish-brown, likewise the head; but in some specimens the elytra are much brighter yellow in colour. The pronotum and legs are darker. Not much is known of this species.

Illustrations show two typical forms of the male.
Range: Taiwan, southward to Philippines, Borneo, Java, Sumatra, P. Malaysia and the surrounding islands.

Odontolabis wallastoni (50–55 mm)   PLATE 6F♂ G♂ H♀
Another highly attractive insect with an entirely black head and pronotum. Elytra are yellowish-brown with a big V-shaped black mark running right through from the top to the bottom. Both the head and prothorax are rectangular, the head being broader with the dorsal part depressed. The area near the compound eyes is finely granulated. Both the femora and tibiae are narrow and black, and mandibles with irregular conical teeth.
Range: P. Malaysia.

Prosopocoilus cinnamoeus (60–65 mm)   PLATE 8A♂ C♂
A comparatively common species which can be found in burrows in soil, usually beneath rotted logs. It has long dark brown mandibles with five teeth at their extremity, and a forked and raised growth is seen at the base. It is slender-bodied with short brown legs. The head and pronotum are dull dark chocolate brown, the wing covers olive brown.
Range: P. Malaysia to Sumatra and Java.

Prosopocoilus elaphus (70–75 mm)   PLATE 8B♂
Another interesting large insect, also polished black. The long modified appendages of the mouth-parts include a pair of narrow, sickle-like decumbent mandibles. Inner edges from the tip to the middle are beset with small sharp teeth, the last of which is much bigger than the others. The male has a broad rectangular head. The female is smaller, measuring about 35 mm, with small triangular mouth-parts. It is commoner than the male and dwells under loose bark and in cracks of trees, mostly of the genera *Melanorrhoea* and *Eugenia*. It is found below 750 m above sea-level at all stages of its life.
Range: Thailand to P. Malaysia

Prosopocoilus feai (30–35 mm)   PLATE 8D♂
A rather uncommon small dark brown insect with straight blade-like mandibles. Only the inner edges near the tips of the mandibles are

dentate. It has fine granulations on the head and pronotum. The body is slender and prolonged. No female of this species has been collected by the author.

The beetle is frequently found in dead logs, living in nests of ants, probably of the family FORMICIDAE.

Range: P. Malaysia.

Prosopocoilus forceps (45–50 mm) PLATE 8E♂

In shape quite like *P. feai*, this species is shining reddish-dark brown in colour. Mandibles are deflexed and of considerable length, about 12 mm long, with saw-like teeth on the inner side of the apex. Since this beetle is usually taken at light-traps, nothing is known of its habits, habitat and life history.

Range: Borneo to P. Malaysia and Sumatra.

Prosopocoilus forcifer (45–55 mm) PLATE 8F♂

This distinctive lustrous brown insect has denticulate mandibles of almost the same length as its body, the base being broadened. It has short geniculate feelers. In flight, the hind wings beat against the hard elytra making a loud noise. It is occasionally attracted to carrion and light-traps, but is rarely seen in collections.

Range: P. Malaysia and Sumatra.

Prosopocoilus occipitalis (32–36 mm) PLATE 8G♂ H♂ I♀

Another lustrously coloured brown insect. Though small it is capable of reducing fallen dead tree trunks and branches to fragments and then to dust, using its tough sausage-shaped mandibles. These are thick, short and very strong, cylindrical in shape and forked at the apex; their base is widened, with a long conical projection.

This beetle is found in the interior of dead logs or in deep holes in the soil. The eggs are oblong and brownish-red and the larvae feed on foliage and are milky white with large mouth-parts. A common species, found in numbers in burrows under the soil during the months of May to early September.

Range: P. Malaysia eastwards to Celebes and Philippines.

Prosopocoilus zebra (30–35 mm) PLATE 8J♂ 9A♂ B♀

Quite a common species in Borneo where it is known as 'Zebra Stag Beetle.' It has two narrow black longitudinal bands on the elytra. On the pronotum another two narrower black lines are seen near the margins, and a broad vase-like black portion covers the central part. The head is small, granulated, and dark brown and the elytra are orange.

Mandibles short, straight, thickened and double-toothed at the posterior. Another form which is very rarely seen in collections, form *telodonta*, has straight, long mandibles measuring about 15 mm in length with bifurcated extremities. This form is illustrated in the plate too. The mandibles of the female are shorter and much reduced in size.

Rare in mainland Malaysia but recorded as common elsewhere in its range.

Range: Borneo, Java, Sumatra to P. Malaysia.

Rhaetulus didieri (60–65 mm) PLATE 9E ♂

One of the most handsome beetles with unusual mandibles; these are strangely built omega-like structures from the lateral view.

A true highland species, this has only been collected above 750 m in heavily forested areas.

Mandibles bifurcated at the tips, toothed at the edge and of remarkable length. The head is smaller than the prothorax which bears saw-like edges. Both the head and pronotum are black. The smooth sheath of the hardened elytra are chestnut at the posterior, and their apexes are black. Tibiae of all legs are chestnut, whereas the rest of the body is black.

The larva (Fig. 23) is creamy-white with a rather smooth fleshy body. There are some short setae on the upper surface of the body. It measures between 50 and 60 mm in length. It feeds on the rotting tree trunks of the genus *Shorea* and pupates after two and a half months deep in the core of rotting trunks.

A rare insect occasionally taken at light traps, this beetle also inhabits freshly felled or uprooted trees.

Range: P. Malaysia.

PASSALIDAE (SUGAR BEETLES OR BESSBUGS)

On the whole, sugar beetles are black-coloured flat beetles found dwelling in small groups in decaying wood. This family has only two known species in Malaysia, and differs from the LUCANIDAE in having the mentum of the labium deeply emarginate, and a deep median groove running through the pronotum (Fig. 24). Longitudinal striae are clearly to be seen on the surface of the elytra.

LUCANIDAE   PASSALIDAE

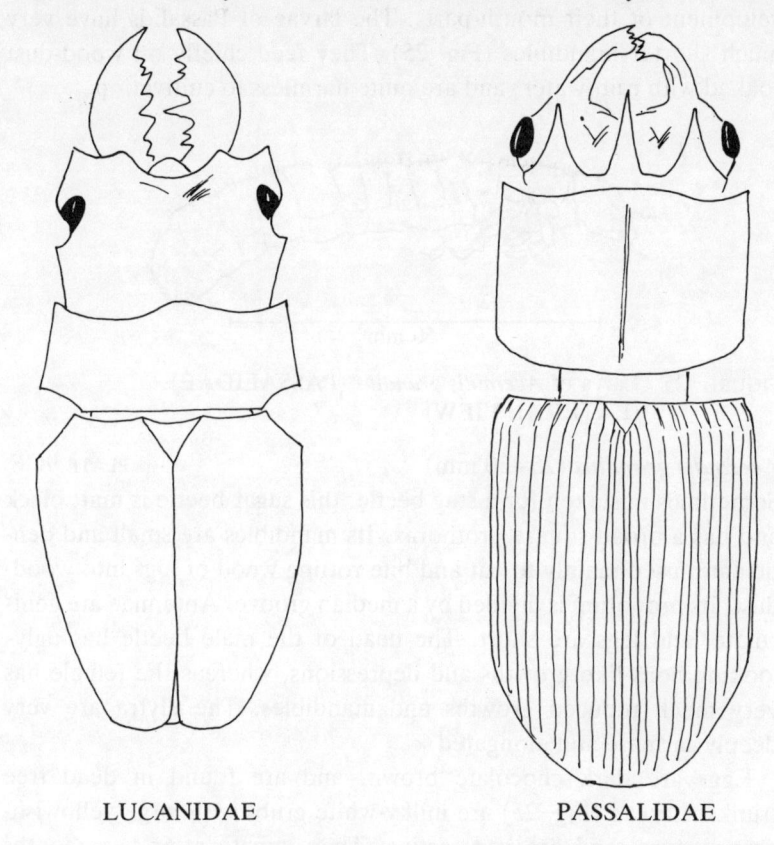

FIGURE 24   The external body features of a stag beetle (LUCANIDAE) and a sugar beetle (PASSALIDAE) (DORSAL VIEW)

These beetles lead a somewhat nocturnal life and hide themselves deep in the trunks of rotting trees. The adults of both sexes are cannibal and have been observed feeding on their offspring. They also eat decaying matter admixed with their digestive juices which are exuded from their mouth before eating. They live in small social communities in decaying fallen trees in the forest, and are easy to find and collect.

Larvae are slender and long. They are milky-white in colour with spiracular bristles along the sides of the fleshy body, and normally measure between 30 and 40 mm in length. They dwell in rotting tree trunks together with the adults. They are similar to the larvae of LUCANIDAE but are easily distinguishable by the growth and development of their mouth-parts. The larvae of Passalids have very much shorter mandibles (Fig. 25). They feed chiefly on wood-dust soaked with rain-water, and are quite harmless to cultivation.

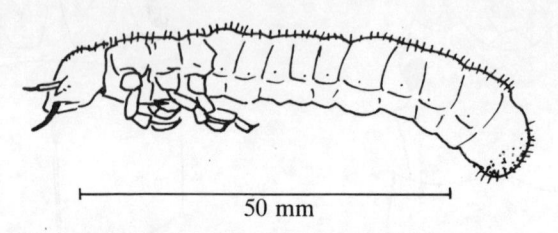

FIGURE 25   Larva of *Aceraulis grandius* (PASSALIDAE) (LATERAL VIEW)

Aceraulis grandius (25–30 mm) PLATE 9C ♂
Sometimes mistaken for a stag beetle, this sugar beetle is matt black and has a broad square prothorax. Its mandibles are small and denticulate, used mainly to cut and bite rotting wood of logs into wood-dust. Its pronotum is divided by a median groove. Antennae are geniculate, and legs are short. The head of the male beetle has ugly-looking horn-like growths and depressions, whereas the female has very much reduced growths and mandibles. The elytra are very deeply carinate and elongated.

Eggs are dark chocolate brown, and are found in dead tree trunks. Larvae (Fig. 25) are milky-white grubs with large yellowish-orange eyes, and are very active. They pupate after two months deep in the core of rotting trunks. Freshly emerged beetles are reddish in colour, and take a further few days to blacken. This is a gregarious insect and is locally common in dead logs in clearings; it is sometimes seen wandering in shady paths.
Range: Taiwan, Indo-China, Borneo and P. Malaysia.

Passalus tridens (50–60 mm) PLATE 9F ♂
This horned Passalid beetle is dark coloured and flat, and often seen in groups of about four in rubber and durian plantations in which much dead wood is found. The mentum of the male is deeply notched with a flat-headed short horn. The mandibles are long and boomerang-shaped with dentate tips. The jaws of the female

are smaller and the head bears shorter horns. The elytra of both sexes are longitudinally striated. The legs are comparatively short and black.

Confined to lowlands and foothills. Found in galleries in decaying logs, it lives with its young, which are very pugnacious and gregarious. Adults are cannibalistic and have been observed to feed on freshly dead caterpillars, and also on their own young. The larvae as well as the adults are harmless to those living trees which are important to forestry.
Range: Taiwan to South-east Asia.

SCARABAEIDAE (SCARAB BEETLES, DUNG BEETLES AND CHAFERS)

Scarabs include the biggest and bulkiest known beetles. Many are found dwelling in the debris of decaying trees, flowering plants, plant roots and carrion. The brilliantly coloured chafers fly in the day and feed on the nectar of flowering plants or on foliage. Collectors use light-traps to attract and trap many species of this family at night. Dung beetles are easily collected at droppings of animals and in traps with bait.

Species from the subfamily DYNASTINAE, such as *Chalcosoma atlas* and *Eupatorus gracilicornis* have marked sexual dimorphism with the male bearing fantastically developed horns on the head and prothorax whereas the female lacks these or has only very small growths corresponding to them. Normally, the antennae are lamellate with the last three to seven segments expanded laterally on one side into an elongate, or oval, movable connected disc.

Eggs hatch into whitish larvae, frequently seen curled into a comma-like position (Fig. 26), feeding mainly on plant roots, dung and other decomposing materials. There are three pairs of legs attached to the thoracic segments. The bodies are fleshy with blackened spiracular plates and bristles surrounding each spiracle are found on the abdominal segments. They pupate deep in the ground or under heaps of decaying matter or inside stems of canes and palms or on foliage.

Though the larvae of *Oryctes rhinoceros* and *Xylotrupes gideon* do not do much harm to plants, the adults remain among the worst

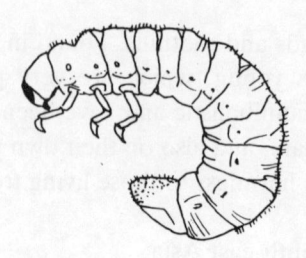

FIGURE 26 Larva of *Oryctes rhinoceros* (SCARABAEIDAE) (LATERAL VIEW)

pests in coconut and oil palm plantations, feeding on young developing palms. Some larvae of chafers, such as young of *Adoretus compressus* and *Apogonia destructor*, are injurious to garden plants, cocoa and vegetables. An example of a larva which causes considerable destruction to sugar-canes is that of *Lepidiota stigma*.

Adoretus compressus (10–12 mm)   PLATE 9H♂
Of the genus *Adoretus* this species is probably the commonest and is notorious for the damage it does to leaves of banana, coconut, coffee, kapok, pepper, rose, sugar cane, and many other garden plants.

The insect is elongated in shape and greyish-brown in colour owing to a short dense yellowish-white pubescence. Its grubs live on vegetable detritus and are brownish-white with black markings surrounding the spiracles. They measure about 14 mm long. They eat slowly and pupate after having undergone five moults. Adults are easily collected at affected plants in late afternoon to twilight.

A. compressus is common and often abundant in coffee plantations in Sumatra and Java, where it causes serious infestation to this cultivated crop.
Range: Throughout South-east Asia.

A closely related species is *A. sinicus* (11–12 mm), which is dull brown and lacks longitudinal stripes on its elytra. This rose beetle is diurnal in habit and is known for its infestation of coffee and bana-

nas. The larva dwells among the dead leaves of vegetables or bananas. They reach a length of 14 mm before they pupate.
Range: Java and Timor, throughout South-east Asia.

A third species, *A. umbrosus* (11–12 mm) of which the habitat is the same as the species described above, has elytra with four light stripes running from the dorsal part to the posterior (of the elytra). It can be captured at night when feeding on leaves and flowers of rose plants. In the daytime these insects conceal themselves in the soil near the base of their food plants.
Range: Throughout Sundaland including Timor Island.

All *Adoretus* species are herbivorous at all stages of their life.

Agestrata orichalcea (35–45 mm)   PLATE 9D ♂
This is a shiny green beetle with a squarish stout head. The body is metallic copper in colour and the head, prothorax, elytra and legs are metallic green. Its mouth-parts are small and hardly visible. It is a bulky insect with short legs and exceptionally short forelegs. The adult is common in flowering *Lantana* shrubs and foliage in meadows and woodlands.

Larvae have been observed in bamboo thickets, feeding on the underside of the leaves. They are gregarious and, when disturbed, curl up in a semi-circle, draw in their jointed thoracic legs and drop to the ground. They are milky-white and when fully grown usually measure between 48 and 52 mm in length.

There are a number of undescribed species of this genus in Malaysia; *A. orichalcea* is among the commonest.
Range: Philippines, westwards to P. Malaysia. Probably found in
       Borneo too.

Anomala viridus (17–22 mm)   PLATE 9I ♂
Another lowland species having glossy green wing covers, head and pronotum. The female lays her eggs below the surface of the soil. These are white and the larva is milky-white with a brownish-orange head on which minute mouth-parts are visible. The body is heavily covered with short mesial hairs or setae.
Range: P. Malaysia to Sumatra and Java.

A common lowland species, *A. anchoralis*, which affects *Dahlia* and cultivated crops such as cucumber and chilli, is light brown and has an anchor-like blackened portion on its wing sheaths. The elytra are longitudinally carinated.

Grubs are small with black markings and short setaceous pubescence running down the centre of the back. They have been observed in shoots of growing leaves of sugar cane and maize. In Borneo, they are seen in cocoa and tobacco plantations.
Range: Borneo, Java, Sumatra and P. Malaysia.

In Malaysia, a larger species, *A. dorsalis* (14–17 mm), which is yellowish-brown with a broad black stripe on the elytra, is commonly found feeding on the leaves of maize and tapioca plants.

A pest on cultivated and garden plants.
Range: P. Malaysia.

Related to *A. viridis* is *A. obsoleta* (10–12 mm), which is smaller and bronzy-brown. The shape is similar, with dark brown head and pronotum. The larva lives on vegetable foliage and is found in heaps of unwanted vegetables and spoilt fruits. The meson of the body of the whitish grub is usually densely covered with very short setae.
Range: P. Malaysia to Java.

In all the *Anomala* species, the head is smaller than the prothorax; at times, when the beetle bends its head downwards to feed on leaves, the head is barely visible. All the species are herbivorous.

Catharsius molossus (55–60 mm) PLATE 9J ♂
The English name is the 'Dung Beetle', and as its name suggests, the insect feeds solely on dung. It belongs to the subfamily formerly known as COPRINAE (now SCARABAEINAE).

The head bears a blade-like projection with a horn on it, and with the assistance of the powerful forelegs it can roll small spherical pieces of dung to burrows which it digs in the top soil. The dung is to feed the young.

The elytra are deep lustrous blue and markedly convex and carinate; the prothorax, head and legs are black. After death the blue colour of the elytra turns to black.
Range: Throughout Sundaland.

Heliocopris bucephalus (50–55 mm) PLATE 9G ♂
Another tropical dung beetle, frequently seen devouring the waste

of animals and rolling spherical pieces of excreta into galleries it has made in the surface of the ground, as food for its brood.

The frontal part of the broadened prothorax is raised, with horned edges. A slender conical horn is seen jutting out at the base of its blade-like, semi-circular but flattened head. The female is easily distinguished by its flattened and hornless head, and smaller size. The tibiae of the first pair of legs are strong and powerful, spurred and well-built. The tarsi of the forelegs are short. The femora of all the legs are thick and strong to assist the insect when it is rolling food back to its gallery. The body and legs are coloured reddish-brown with the head and prothorax much darker. The elytra are striated.

A very common insect, particularly in April and May.
Range: India to Indo-China and P. Malaysia.

Heliocopris dominus (55–60 mm)   PLATE 10A♂

This is a less common species, but like all dung beetles, is of importance to agriculture, because it enriches the top soil by bringing balls of dung into its burrows. These waste products become natural fertilizers and the burrowing loosens up the soil, making it more porous. A neat insect, with the apex of the notum highly raised, with a horn projecting forward, it bears a flattened trapezium-shaped mentum. The elytra are dull black and longitudinally striated with deep grooves. From the top view the margins of the elytra are U-shaped. Legs are powerful and covered with short brown pubescence. Like the adult, the larva feeds on dung brought in by its parents. It is sluggish and brownish-white. It lives deep in the network of galleries made by both the adults and larvae.

Quite a rare beetle in mainland Malaysia but found abundantly in central Thailand.
Range: India to Indo-China, Thailand and P. Malaysia.

Chalcosoma atlas complex
(70–130 mm)   PLATE 10B♂ C♂ D♀ 11A♂

Above 1200 m in the highlands of Malaysia lives the enormous black 'Atlas Beetle', also known locally as the 'Three-horned Beetle' due to the lengthened projections from the head and prothorax. This is probably the biggest and bulkiest beetle in Malaysia.

On the prothorax there arise three prominent growths, two at the raised edge of the apex of the pronotum, and another in the centre immediately behind the head, pointing straight forward. The fourth growth curves its way upwards from the mentum of the head with a pointed end, and at the mid-length a small conical tooth branches out in an upward direction. Some male specimens have the anterior projections greatly reduced in size. The elytra are smooth and well-polished. The legs are long and slender.

The females have no growths on the prothorax and head and are much smaller, measuring about 65 mm in length. They are dull brown in colour and the elytra are densely covered with light brown pubescence. They are commoner than the males and often found at the food of street lampposts in hill resorts. The species is frequently attracted to light-traps and is common in the months of July and August.

Range: India to Sundaland.

Chalcosoma caucasus complex (55–100 mm)   PLATE 12A♂ B♀
Another magnificent insect which is probably the second largest of all Malaysian beetles. It resembles *C. atlas* in body structure, habits and habitats but has a lustrous greenish body, and dwells in hilly areas between 300 and 1800 m above sea-level.

Shapes of the four horns found on the head and prothorax are similar to those of *C. atlas* except that the one which arises from the base of the mentum of the head is less recurved, with a hooked tip and a saw-like edge between the tip and the third quarter, and no other projection. Its huge larva has been observed to do some harm to the roots of dadap and coffee in Java.

Another very common form with short undeveloped horns, measuring about 70 to 75 mm, occurs in the lower parts of the hills.

There is a marked sexual dimorphism; the male is characterized by the presence of horns on the prothorax and head, and the female with no such process, is usually small in size and is commoner. She measures 50 to 60 mm in length.

Range: Indo-China across to Thailand and P. Malaysia; Sumatra to Java and Borneo.

Chalcosoma moellenkampi complex (75–100 mm)   PLATE 13A♂ B♀
This bulky Bornean species is closely allied to *C. caucasus* and is found in mountainous regions.

All the specimens the author has were collected at night from light-traps set on the slopes of Mount Kinabalu at the top of a cliff at about 1500 m above sea-level. Like most beetles, when in flight, the elytra open up sideways, allowing the fragile membranous hind wings to take the insect into flight, and balancing it in mid-air.

The elytra are a glossy greenish-black with the head and pronotum fully black; not greenish, as in *C. caucasus*. On the mentum and notum are the usual four projections. Like all other *Chalcosoma* species, some males have the projections greatly reduced in size. Legs are strong, stiff and long.

Range: Borneo.

Cheirotonus parryi (50–70 mm)   PLATE 14A♂ B♂ C♀

This is a beautiful and distinctive beetle. The oral-shaped body looks like a kind of small tropical fruit, a resemblance which may serve as natural camouflage. It has very long and slender forelegs which seem to slow down its movement. It belongs to the subfamily EUCHININAE.

It lives on fermenting juices of trees and is confined to hills of the main range of Peninsular Malaysia. The head is very small, bearing a pair of lamellate antennae. The prothorax is dome-shaped, with the suture heavily covered with yellow pubescence. It is purplish-green, rough and finely granulated.

The surface of the elytra is green, and small patches of an orange pattern are seen along the partially-hidden striae, running longitudinally through this surface. The underside of the body is honey-brown in colour. The legs are greenish-brown, long and hairy, except the forelegs, which have tibiae extremely prolonged and heavily-spined. The femora are long too but rather smooth with a tooth jutting out near the mid-length.

The female is similar to the male in colour, size and shape, with shorter forelegs which have broadened and spurred femora. There is no yellow pubescence on the marginal suture of the prothorax as found in the male. The last anal segment is left uncovered by the elytra.

It is quite common especially in hill-stations, where it is strongly attracted to lights.

Range: Eastern India to Burma, Thailand, Indo-China and P. Malaysia.

Eupatorus gracilicornis (60–65 mm)   PLATE 15A♂ B♀
Elytra bright yellowish-orange; head and pronotum, smooth and black. The prothorax has four prominent growths, short, sabre-like, with blunt tips. The head is small and a strongly curved horn, long and protrusive, rises from the base of the postmentum. The elytra are elongated. The body is brown in colour, with tufts of setae on the ventral side. The legs are brown with spurred tibiae.

In Malaysia this easily identifiable insect is known to occur on Maxwell Hill, Fraser's Hill and Mount (Gunung) Kubu on the mainland. It has not been recorded from any of the other local hill-stations.

The female of this species looks very much like the female of *C. atlas*, but is smaller and browner. The female appears to be commoner than the male.
Range: Assam to Indo-China, Thailand and P. Malaysia.

Euselatus sponsa (18–22 mm)   PLATE 15D♂
A small but common rose-chafer, this species is apparently subject to considerable variation. The body is reddish-brown, beautifully keeled with patterns of yellow amongst the striae.

It is an inhabitant of cultivated forest clearings and open woodlands. The insect is ubiquitous and between the months of May and June, it is found in great numbers on *Lantana* plants.
Range: Philippines and Borneo to P. Malaysia.

Exopholis hypoleuca (22–24 mm)   PLATE 15H♂
Another chafer with light brown elytra. A conspicuous row of white spots is noticeable all along the margins of the abdominal segments. The scarabaeiform grubs are white, and feed on the young developing roots of tea and seedlings of many species of plants. They pupate after a few months deep in the ground. Normally, the pupal stage is about a month, but in the dry season the pupae may spend three to four months in aestivation. Adults frequent foliage of coffee, maize and groundnut in twilight.
Range: Throughout Sundaland.

Fruhstorferia sexmaculata (25–30 mm)   PLATE 15E♂ I♀
A small bulky-looking light-green beetle with a pair of prominent narrow excrescences projecting sideways in the shape of a

horseshoe. These divaricate protrusions are reddish in colour, very narrow and oddly projected from the postmentum of the rather stout azure head. The legs are short and red. The female is of the same size and structure as the male with grass-green elytra (darker on the head and pronotum) and lacking the horseshoe-shaped growths. A highland species, it is quite rare, but appears occasionally between the months of April and July.
Range: Taiwan to Borneo and P. Malaysia.

In Borneo, a similar insect was taken which is probably a new species or subspecies. Its elytra are darker green, not lustrous and it has very short horseshoe-shaped growths greatly curved into an almost complete circle.

Lepidiota stigma (35–50 mm)   PLATE 15C♂
A medium-sized cockchafer found in the soil near roots of tapioca, groundnut and sugar cane, in which considerable damage has been observed. *L. stigma* is one of the most important root pests.

The insect has an oval body and is entirely brown in colour, densely covered with yellowish-white scales which may be worn off in older specimens. A common beetle, not attracted to light-traps. The life history is similar to *Oryctes rhinoceros* below.
Range: Java, Sumatra to P. Malaysia.

Apogonia destructor (8–10 mm)   PLATE 15F♂
This beetle may be brown, bluish or greenish-black in colour, and is listed as a pest of cultivated crops. Adults are often found in numbers in sugar cane and groundnut plantations, especially after an afternoon downpour.

The female oviposits about 60 eggs at a time into a burrow in the soil, usually during the rainy season. Larvae feed on humus and attack the roots of plants such as sugar cane, maize, cocoa, groundnut and soya beans. They are sluggish and gregarious.
Range: P. Malaysia, Sumatra and Java.

Holotrichia leucophthalma (24–27 mm)   PLATE 15J♂
This local race is chestnut in colour, commonly found in tapioca and sugar cane plantations. The male is sometimes found in numbers. The forelegs of this insect are strongly arched at the third tarsal seg-

ment, and their tibiae are broad, flattened and spined. All the legs are hairy and brownish-grey.

The larvae feed on roots of sugar cane, grasses, tapioca, *Hevea*, *Amarathus* and *Portulaca*. They are worm-like, and often curl up into a crescent shape. The bodies are fleshy with black spiracular bristles and plates surrounding each spiracle on the thoracic and abdominal segments. There is one brood annually. They are root pests at all stages.

Range: Java, north-west to Sumatra and northern P. Malaysia.

Oryctes rhinoceros (35–45 mm)   PLATE 15G♂ 16B♀
Of the subfamily DYNASTINAE, the Rhinoceros Beetle is known from the process on its head, which resembles a rhinoceros's horn. Found only in the hot lowlands, this dark brown or black insect is characterized by the long backwardly recurved horn on the head of the male; in the female it is nearly obsolete. Another visible difference between the sexes is that the last abdominal segment of the female is semi-circular and covered with bristles.

Eggs are laid in decaying trunks, decomposing matter, dumps of coconut husks or leaves, and dung-heaps. They hatch into greyish-white grubs with a reddish-brown head and enlarged abdomen (Fig. 26). Pupation is within a cocoon made of earth or fibrous xylem of palm trees, in the ground or in the heart of wounded trees such as coconut, or in sugar cane, or even under cowpats, humus and most often in decaying stumps.

The adults are destructive, boring into trees to feed on the sweet exuding sap, and strongly affect the growth of young coconut palms, oil palms, *Nipa* palms, *Areca* palms, sugar cane and sago.

Range: India, South-east Asia, Korea and southern part of Japan. Probably in Taiwan too.

Oryctes trituberculatus (55–60 mm) (PLATE 16E♂), a larger species, is found living with *O. rhinoceros*. It differs from the latter by the presence of three small teeth horizontally in line on the raised pronotum. (*O. rhinoceros* has only two small teeth with blunt tips on the pronotum.) The prothorax is more rugose. There is also an adornment on its head. The female is very much like the female of *O. rhinoceros* but is very much larger. Its habitat and life are also very similar.

Both species of *Oryctes* are of economic importance and are notorious for the serious damage they inflict on sugar cane, coconut and oil palms.
Range: Sumatra, P. Malaysia, Borneo, Java to Celebes.

Trichogomphus lunicollis (60–65 mm)   PLATE 16A♂
A montane species with a very distinctive bifurcated growth on the mesomentum of the prothorax. The forks of the growth arch and bend forward. On the head is another process, very thick at the base and pointed at the tip with a conical tooth near the mid-length. The prothorax is finely granulated and irregular. The elytra are smooth and polished shiny black. An entirely black insect, and frequently taken at light-traps.
Range: P. Malaysia, Sumatra and Java.

Xylotrupes gideon (55–60 mm)   PLATE 16C♂ D♂
Another black insect with a long growth on the pronotum. This growth is slender and protrudes forward with a forked end bending downward. A similar projection is present on the head, with a bifid tip and a small growth at the mid-base facing inwards. The entire insect is a shiny black or dark brown. The female is smaller, not exceeding 40 mm, and lacks the conspicuous projections of the male. The larvae are grizzled and found in the stumps of palm trees, or the surrounding ground. The adult insect is often seen on rubber trees feeding on latex on peeled bark and tapping wounds.
Range: India, southern China and Indo-China, South-east Asia, New Guinea and Bismarck Islands.

Rhomborrhina splendida (32–35 mm)   PLATE 29D♂
This insect inhabits the lowland forest and is often found in numbers. Both sexes resemble the montane species *Jumnos ruckeri* but lack any blue hues in the glossy grass-green chitin and the forelegs are much shorter.
Range: Taiwan to Borneo.

Also resembling the above species is *Plectrone nigrocoerulea* (22–27 mm), PLATE 29C♂, which is smaller with a more slender body and is deep blue in colour. A common insect which is found throughout the year in lowland forest.
Range: Philippines to Borneo and P. Malaysia.

A smaller Cetoniid, *Macronota abdominalis* (11–15 mm) figured in PLATE 29E♂, is also found in the same habitat as the forementioned species. This insect is dark brown with the greater part of its elytra reddened and spotted with yellow.
Range: Philippines across Borneo to P. Malaysia.

Polyphylla fullo (30–35 mm)   PLATE 29B♂
A montane species which is closely related to the European *Polyphylla* species. Often taken at light-traps on cold, moonless nights in Cameron Highlands above 1200 m altitude.
  Generally the insect is reddish-brown, white and yellow. The body is elongate, and elytra are smooth with patterns of red and white; antennae long and feather-like. The author has taken two specimens feeding on nectar of roses in Tanah Rata. This species is rare throughout mainland Malaysia.
Range: Europe to P. Malaysia.

Jumnos ruckeri pfanneri (45–55 mm)   PLATE 32D♂ E♀
J. ruckeri pfanneri belongs to the subfamily CETONIINAE. The entire insect is glossy green with forelegs slightly prolonged. The submentum is squarish, jutting forward from the highly convex pronotum. The elytra are smooth and carry a sheen. All the legs are rather long and slender. It is a particularly rare species but may be found in the early morning sipping oozing sap of a tree of the genus *Shorea* on Gunung Jasar (1690 m above sea-level) in Cameron Highlands.
  J. r. pfanneri is different from the nominate race, *J. r. ruckeri* (PLATE 32F♂ G♀), by being leaf-green in colour without any bluish hues or shades; and having longer forelegs. Both beetles are inhabitants of the montane forest and have only been taken in flight or resting on a tree sipping sap.
Range: P. Malaysia.

Diceros dives (30–35 mm)   PLATE 32H♂ I♀
This is one of the smaller Cetoniids and it differs from other species by having big squarish black markings on its elytra. Overall, the insect is metallic green. Found on wounded trees, bleeding cracks of living trees and bamboos.

There are two distinctive pin-like prolongations at the frontal edge of the head measuring between 4 and 6 mm in the male, much shorter in the female.

It is known to breed in the heart of bamboos. The males are gregarious insects and several are frequently seen together among thickets of bamboos.

Range: P. Malaysia and Sumatra.

BUPRESTIDAE (SPLENDOUR OR METALLIC WOOD-BORING BEETLES)

Iridescent splendour beetles are among the most handsome insects in the world. As their name suggests, the beauty of their metallic hard chitin has inspired artists and provides a constant inspiration for designers of embroidery and jewellery. The adults vary greatly in size and colour but are of much the same shape.

The first two (or even three) abdominal sterna are usually fused together with the suture between them either very weakly marked or totally absent. The head, prothorax and the abdominal segments are closely joined together so that the beetle looks like a compact elongated glossy bullet. The tips of the elytra covering the anal segment are separated.

These wood-borers fly in the day in tropical shade. They live among foliage, and are found sipping nectar from flowering plants. They are easily collected by sweeping a strongly made net across the vegetation in open woods and forests. Often they take flight when threatened, or play dead when disturbed.

The larvae of most species are creamy in colour, cylindrical in shape with a small head and a peculiar broad, flattened thorax (Fig. 27). They are legless and bore galleries into roots of young host-

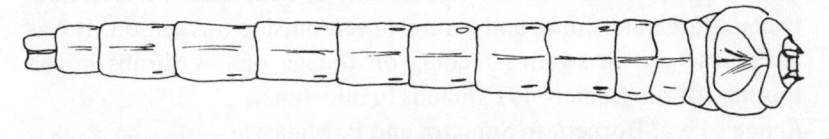

109 mm

FIGURE 27 Larva of *Megaloxantha bicolor* (BUPRESTIDAE) (DORSAL VIEW)

plants or under the bark of dying or living trunks and thick branches of trees. They pupate after five or six moults, depending on individual species. Most pupae remain for two to three months but some spend five to six months in aestivation especially during the dry season. In both the larval and adult stage some of these insects have the status of pests. The larvae of certain species bore the roots of *Albizzia* and *Citrus* trees. Adults have been occasionally noticed boring deep into trunks of *Nephelium* (rambutan), kapok and cocoa trees.

The appearance of Buprestids is seasonal, and they are frequently found in swarms between mid-February and mid-July.

Belionota prasina (21–23 mm)   PLATE 17L♂
Dwelling among foliage, this small Jewel Beetle has greenish-blue elytra; the prothorax is green with the suture ends of the notum near the margins of the scutellum fiery red. Antennae are short and thread-like on a widened head. The legs are short and narrow.

A very common beetle, frequently seen on the bark of kapok and casuarina trees.
Range: India to Indo-China, China, Taiwan, south to P. Malaysia, Sumatra, Java, Borneo and Maluku.

Callopistus castelnaudi (40–43 mm)   PLATE 17A♂ B♀
A glossy light green insect which, in yellow light, shows an azure colouring reflecting at the margin of the elytron. The head is hard and trapezium-shaped with large compound eyes and short glabrous antennae and the pronotum is broad. The whole body is rough and hard and coloured glossy green. The legs are short and plain green in colour.

It is a strong flier of great endurance, and likes flying under the hot afternoon sun. It occurs occasionally in Peninsular Malaysia between March and June, and is rarely seen outside this season. It was once observed in swarms feeding on foliage of low shrubs in the foothills of the Cameron Highlands in mid-June.
Range: Java, Borneo, to Sumatra and P. Malaysia.

Catoxantha opulenta (50–55 mm)   PLATE 17C♂ D♀
A large Buprestid with big swollen eyes. The antennae are serrate. Pronotum broad and finely granulated. Deeply sculptured sinuous

lines are visible on the surface of the elongated elytra. At the midlength of the wing covers are two yellowish-white narrow parallel bands laid horizontally between the median groove and the margin of each elytron. The whole insect, including its legs and undersurface, is lustrous green. The notum has reflected yellowish- and brownish-green colours. A median groove divides the pronotum into two equal halves. In some specimens, the two sternites of the underside of the abdomen are tinted glossy milk-yellow.

This striking insect is common when in season, and it is fond of the conifer *Agathis flavescens* in forest at about 700 m, above sea-level.
Range: India to Java via P. Malaysia.

Chrysochroa buqueti (43–46 mm)   PLATE 17E♂ F♀
This handsome insect has the elytra chalk-white with their tips and two square markings near the mid-length royal blue. Head small, glossy granular red. Pronotum metallic royal blue in the centre, shining red on the edge at each side. Legs short and bluish. The chalk-white colour of the elytra tends to turn yellowish when not well-dried in the sun before or during mounting. The body is purplish and heavily covered with pubescence.

Collected frequently on the foliage of low shrubs in lowland montane areas, it is not a true primary forest species. The larva is said to feed on *Mangifera indica* (mango trees).
Range: India to Burma and Thailand, P. Malaysia and Java.

Chrysochroa castelnaudii (37–40 mm)   PLATE 17G♂ H♀
Another bluish Buprestid which has head and pronotum brilliantly tinted prussian-blue. Elytra are shiny prussian-blue also but are separated into two parts by a broad band of plain white or dirty pale yellow. Fine blue antennae, short and glabrous. Huge eyes and short slender legs. Blue-bodied and fond of sipping oozing sap from wild durian trees.

This insect is commonest during the months of May and June. Its larvae have been observed feeding on the fruit of durian trees.
Range: P. Malaysia and Sumatra, east to Borneo and Palawan Island (Philippines).

Chrysochroa ephippigera (35–38 mm)   PLATE 17I♂ J♀
Among the most beautiful beetles in Malaysia with its iridescent

rainbow colours. Head short and wide with large glabrous eyes. Pronotum gaily azure with bright brownish hues. Elytra have a white broad band at the mid-length. The dorsal part of the elytra shows mixed iridescent colours which extend to the pronotum; the posterior is shiny greenish-azure. The ends of the elytra are truncate, forming a short straight line.

One brood a year. The legless larva eats the living tree trunks of kapok, boring a network system of galleries through the whole diameter of the trunk which it inhabits; foresters regard it with hostility, but jewellers often use the glossy elytra of the adult to manufacture ornaments. The larva measures 43 to 46 mm with a small head and a big, flattened, squarish thorax. It is cylindrical and creamy-white in colour. It pupates after three months in the larval stage.
Range: Indo-China to P. Malaysia.

Chrysochroa fulgidissima (44–46 mm) PLATE 17K ♂
As brilliantly green as the following species, *C. fulminans*. The body is green with an azure head. Antennae short, rather flexible, and thread-like. The pronotum is trapezium-shaped with two tinted spots of red near the posterior corners of the notum. The elytra are iridescent bluish-green.

In contrast to *C. fulminans*, this species is marked in such a way that a narrow reddish-brown line is clearly evident along (but not touching) the margin of the edge of each elytron. A rather rare species. Its grubs tunnel in the wood of mahogany trees, spoiling the timber.

It has a seasonal annual appearance which begins in late February and usually lasts for three months.
Range: India, southern China, Indo-China and northern P. Malaysia.

Chrysochroa fulminans (37–40 mm) PLATE 18A ♂ B ♀
A small but very common species, extremely beautifully coloured leaf-green, in such a way that the colour is constantly changing due to the different angle of the light-rays which fall upon the highly reflective surface of the elytra. These are valued for making articles of jewellery. The end of the elytra is split, and characteristically tinted red.

The larva is legless, almost flattened, with a widened thorax measuring about 70 mm and bores into the heart of kapok, cocoa, *Citrus, Albizzia*, and other leguminous trees. Pupation occurs after four months. The adult beetle feeds chiefly on the sap of these trees or sucks nectar from their flowers.
Range: P. Malaysia to other parts of the Sundaland.

Chrysochroa wallacei (45–48 mm)   PLATE 18C♂ D♀
Another marvellous insect, *C. wallacei* is dark green admixed with a lustrous dark blue, appearing at the margins of the elytra and prothorax. Legs fairly short, and elytra lightly striated.

Also seasonal in appearance, this insect loves to sit on the thick branches of cinnamon and other trees in the forest making a shrilling sound. The author once observed scores of the adult insects on the bark of a wild durian tree in the lowland forest of Perak.
Range: P. Malaysia, Sumatra and Borneo.

Chrysochroa weyersii (45–48 mm)   PLATE 18F♂ G♀
Similar to the above species but a darker green.

The larva is a wood-borer and a pest of forestry. This beetle appears in numbers from mid-March to mid-May on *Lantana, Aristolochia*, and *Cordia* bushes from lowland clearings up to forest at over 600 m.
Range: P. Malaysia, Sumatra and Borneo.

Agrilus acutus (7–8 mm) is a rather small beetle wiith the pronotum adorned with deeply striated markings. On the lower part of the elytra two bands of white hairs are clearly seen upon the bluish-green chitin of the insect. The larva is a yellowish-white grub, 12 mm long, and is injurious to jute plants and *Citrus* trees.
Range: Java, Sumatra and southern P. Malaysia.

Demochroa gratiosa (25–27 mm)   PLATE 18E♂
Another small beetle, washed with intense dark green. The head is small and the prothorax granular. Elytra heavily striated and broadened anterior to the distal end. At the mid-length of the wing sheaths there is a broad band of yellowish-white. The underside of the body is heavily tinted glossy red, particularly in the last three sternites.

A common insect, occasionally captured on the foliage and flowering twigs of *Lantana* shrubs.
Range: Indo-China and P. Malaysia.

Iridotaenia sumptuosa (35–37 mm)   PLATE 18H ♂
Appears commonly in the open forest, stridulating with a high shrilling sound, during its season, between February and April. At times, a great number of this species can be captured at one particular spot.

An entirely glossy dark leaf-green clumsy-looking insect, with the margins of the elytra, behind the mid-length, toothed like a saw.
Range: P. Malaysia, Sumatra and Borneo.

Iridotaenia chrisostome (10–15 mm)   PLATE 18I ♂
A handsome insect with a small green head, deeply notched in the centre. Antennae serrate and brown. The pronotum is green with two glossy red markings, one at each corner of the lower part. The elytra are dark green, and there are two narrow yellowish-bronze lines running longitudinally along the submarginal lengths of the wing sheaths. The legs are green and of moderate length.

I. chrisostome has a legless, somewhat flattened, elongated larva with enlarged thoracic segments. The larvae are borers of a number of trees including kapok, cocoa, *Citrus* and *Nephelium* (rambutan).
Range: P. Malaysia and Java; probably in Sumatra too.

Megaloxantha daleni (26–27 mm)   PLATE 18J ♂
This species is very closely related to *M. bicolor* from Java. The entire body is a glossy dark bluish-green. Antennae serrate. The head is small. The elytra have striae and two chalky-white patches are present anterior to their apical end. The end of the elytra covering the tip of the abdomen is notched.
Range: P. Malaysia and Java.

Megaloxantha hemixantha (47–49 mm)   PLATE 18K ♂ L ♀
A Malaysian species, heavily marked green with a dirty yellow patch on the surface of each elytron. These patches are a boomerang shape, at one third back from the tip of the elytra, and are outlined in black. Elytra slightly carinate. Commonly seen during the early months of the year.
Range: P. Malaysia.

Megaloxantha nigricornis (56–58 mm) PLATE 18M♂ N♀
A species closely related to *M. bicolor* is *M. nigricornis*, which is smaller and darker in colour. Its wing sheaths are very glossy greyish dark green with larger white elytra-patches. Two bulbs of yellow are visible at the corner of the basal margin of the notum. The underside of the body is pale yellow, sometimes turning dirty light brown. Females are larger with the glossy green colouring less intense, and prefer flying higher in the forest, often 9 to 12 m up in the flowering trees.

The yellowish larvae live in great numbers on creepers of the genus *Aristolochia*, and make numerous burrows into the core of their food plants.
Range: P. Malaysia, Sumatra and Borneo.

Megaloxantha purpurascens (41–43 mm) PLATE 19A♂
The smallest of the group, *M. purpurascens* is a very common insect which is light green in colour. A strong reflection of purplish-brown is visible on the elytra. The pronotum is at times, and at certain angles, purple or deep indigo in colour.

It is slender-bodied and found on the foliage of *Lantana* and *Hibiscus* plants. The females have a broader body and frequent showy flowers.
Range: P. Malaysia and Borneo.

Chrysobothris militaris (8–15 mm) PLATE 18O♂
A small but attractively marked and coloured beetle with polished dark blue elytra engrossed with six small oval spots of metallic green. The pronotum is shining green bearing glossy reddened submarginal edges. Rarely found in collections. It is a fast flier and a dweller in mangrove forest.
Range: P. Malaysia.

An allied species, *C. chrysonotata* (10–12 mm), is bronzy-yellow with three golden spots on each elytron and is not uncommon in southern Peninsular Malaysia. It is small but of great economic importance because it is a notorious pest of valuable timber.
Range: Java northwards to Sumatra and southern P. Malaysia.

ELATERIDAE (CLICK BEETLES OR SKIPJACKS)

The click beetles are famous for their acrobatic ability to jump when turned on their backs, producing a clicking sound. They may jump several times until they land the right way up. They are slender-bodied with woody-coloured hard elytra acting as a natural camouflage. When disturbed they drop to the ground and sham dead for some moments.

The prothorax is loosely joined to the body so that they have no difficulty in righting themselves with a somersault when on their backs. The labrum in the mouth-parts is separated from the clypeus. The tibial spurs of the legs are small and weak. Antennae usually serrate; sometimes pectinate and filiform.

The larvae are very hard-bodied, slender, milky-brown and are found in the soil near roots of trees (Fig. 28). They are known popularly as 'wireworms', and may be injurious in tree nurseries and reafforestation zones.

Many of the commoner Malaysian species are still unidentified and unclassified.

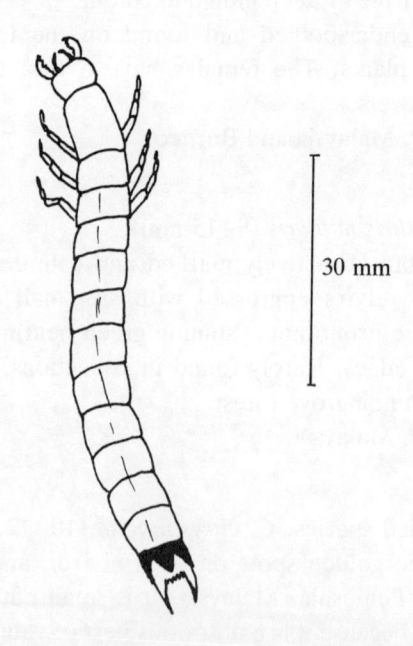

FIGURE 28 Larva of *Calais lacteus* (ELATERIDAE) (DORSAL VIEW)

Calais lacteus (23–25 mm) PLATE 19D ♂
The 'White Click Beetle' has its head and prothorax in the shape of a bell and is greyish-white in colour. The head is particularly small and can be hidden underneath the large broad suture of the prothorax. The elytra are spade-like and elongated, greyish-white with two small squarish black dots and a few smaller ones in front of the split end of the wing sheaths. They are heavily covered with pubescence. The antennae are filiform and short. The legs are also short, with undeveloped tibiae. Found throughout the year, but commoner in April and May.
The wireworm larva (Fig. 28) is slender, milky-brown and hard-bodied. It feeds voraciously on roots of leguminous trees which are of importance to forestry.
Range: Throughout South-east Asia.

A dirty-looking brownish click beetle, *Melanotus rubidus* (30–32 mm), is a common species whose larva lives among the roots of coffee plants. It is greyish-white with black marks along the side of its body surrounding the spiracles. The head is enlarged.
Range: Java to Sumatra and P. Malaysia.

Campsosternus leachei (34–36 mm) PLATE 19H ♂
An iridescent green insect. The prothorax and elytra are smooth and strongly tinted with red due to structural coloration. The head is very small, with serrate, hairy antennae and minute mouth-parts. The eyes are partially hidden by the overhanging suture of the pronotum. The body is slender and glossy.
The larvae are distinguished from those of other species by their slender, hard and shiny bodies. They are commonly called 'glossy' or 'metallic' wireworms and are found either in the earth or in compost.
This insect is commonly found on foliage and may be mistaken for a splendour beetle.
Range: P. Malaysia.

Oxyropterus audoniwi (60–70 mm) PLATE 19B ♂
A strangely shaped insect, dirty light chocolate brown in colour. The head is small with visible mouth-parts and labium and the

antennae are pectinate and light brown. The elytra are slender with the tips of each elytron separated.

A truly Malayan species, found hiding in joints of large branches in trees, usually above 6 m from the ground. It probably feeds on the sap of *Bignoniaceae* and *Leguminosae* species.
Range: P. Malaysia.

A similar species but of a different genus is *Sinuaria aenescense* from Borneo. It is easily separated from the above species by having darker brown pronotum and elytra, and an unusual prothorax which is divided by a raised median area. In habits and habitat it is very similar to *O. audoniwi*.
Range: Northern Borneo.

Hemiops nigripes (12–15 mm)   PLATE 19L♂
Distinguished by bright yellow elytra, darkened on the pronotum and head, this small click beetle can be taken along jungle paths and seepages during the daytime feeding on *Lantana* plants and is found commonly at all elevations. It is a weak flier but makes short flights when danger is near.
Range: Thailand to P. Malaysia and Sumatra.

LAMPYRIDAE (FIREFLIES)

The head is more or less concealed by the pronotum and usually is not visible. The trochanters are short and the front coxae small and globose. The mid-coxae are contiguous, a point that distinguishes them from the LYCIDAE, in which the mid-coxae are separate. Lampyrids are nocturnal insects with an elongated, soft body, and the males are sometimes beautifully coloured.

These beetles are well known for the presence of a luminescent organ on the abdomen. The females are usually wingless and look very much like larvae. Both the larvae and the adults are luminous and omnivorous, the females feeding on foliage during the day and on insects after twilight. The luminous organs are yellowish-green, whether glowing or not. On cool, damp nights, the males can be seen flying like fiery sparks through low bushes and shrubs, while the females flash their lights in the grass. Their courtship involves an exchange of flashing signals at dusk or after dark.

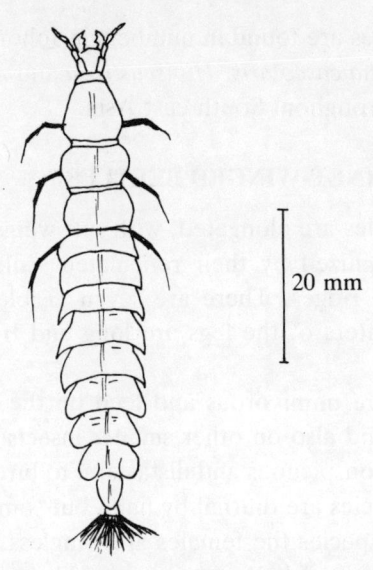

FIGURE 29   Larva of *Pteroptyx* sp (LAMPYRIDAE) (DORSAL VIEW)

The larvae of Lampyrids are predators, with biting, fang-like mouth-parts to suck out the blood of small snails (Fig. 29). They lurk in thick patches of grass, and under low vegetation.

***Pteroptyx* sp (15–20 mm)** PLATE 19M♂

The males have small heads, usually covered by the broadened prothorax. Both the prothorax and elytra are brownish-orange with the tips of the wing covers tinted dark blue. They are often found in numbers, emitting flashes of light in synchrony, and frequently remain stationary at vantage points, displaying their lighted plates of greenish-yellow. These organs are found on the underside of some of the abdominal segments.

The females are worm-like and also have light organs.

The body of the larva (Fig. 29) is greyish-red and bears dark grey spots at the sides of the body. Its mouth-parts include a pair of long, sharp perforated maxillae, used for sucking the blood of small snails, slugs and other small creatures. The larvae are easily recognized by the luminous organs borne on the hind segments of the abdomen, which emit a bright light at night, and also by fan-like filamentous appendages at the anal end of the abdomen. They are nocturnal in habit and hide themselves in the daytime.

Both sexes are found in numbers in Johore, usually on plants such as *Sonneratia caseolaris, Hibiscus rosa* and *Ardistia elliptica*.
Range: Throughout South-east Asia.

LYCIDAE (NET-WINGED BEETLES)

These beetles are elongated, with soft wings and bodies, and can be easily recognized by their reticulated sculptured elytra, bearing a network of ridges. There are seven visible abdominal sterna, and the trochanters of the legs are long and transversely joined to the femora.

Adults are omnivorous and feed on the juices of decaying plant materials and also on other smaller insects. They are often brightly coloured, conspicuous and distasteful to birds.

Most species are diurnal by habit but some females are nocturnal. In several species the females are wingless. The females of the two species described below have worm-like bodies, along the margins of which are a string of luminous organs which flash on and off, signalling in a predetermined code. The light produced is a weak, cold light, rather like that from a fluorescent tube, and it is apparently caused by a chemical reaction.

The larvae are predaceous and are found on foliage and tree trunks in open woods.

Chalchromus sp (13–16 mm)   PLATE 19N ♂

The male has glossy blue elytra and the pronotum is deep orange to black. The elytra are short and never cover the last two abdominal segments of the insect. The body is elongated. The antennae are serrate and black. The mouth-parts bear long, strong maxillary palpi used to suck the body fluid of its prey.

The female resembles the female of *Duliticola* sp but is smaller and not as beautifully decorated with glowing plates as is the latter. Its body is much narrower.

The male can be collected at flowering plants in the afternoon and the female is found at night around lights, especially at hill-stations above 762 m.

Range: Borneo to P. Malaysia.

Duliticola sp (25–30 mm)   PLATE 7D ♀

The male insect is quite similar to the above species but is much bigger and more reddish-brown in colour. It secretes an acrid substance and smell which is believed to be extremely repugnant to birds.

The female (45–50 mm) is wingless and retains a form similar to that of the larva. For this reason, and from a fancied resemblance to the extinct trilobites, these wingless females have come to be called 'trilobite larvae'. It is occasionally found in highlands (above 750 m) near roadsides, displaying its distinctive sets of glowing small red bulbs upon its brown coloured body. The colour of the body tends to turn dull black some time after the insect is killed. The glowing bulbs will turn light brown in contrast to the black body.
Range: Borneo and P. Malaysia.

EROTYLIDAE (PLEASING FUNGUS BEETLES)

These are more or less oval, medium-sized beetles. They are found on fungi and wounds on trees, feeding on the sap.

EROTYLIDAE have the tarsi distinctly five-segmented, with the fourth tarsal segment greatly reduced in size, and bearing simple claws. The forecoxal cavities open behind and lack a trochantin (a small sclerite in the thoracic wall immediately anterior to the base of the coxa). The antennal clubs usually have three or four segments. Erotylids are usually black, with reddish-orange markings on the elytra, but some small highland species have metallic blue or green elytra.

Encaustes sp (28–32 mm)   PLATE 19I ♂
This insect is black with the prothorax bearing two orange or light orange patterns. The elytra are lightly striated and black in colour. The head is comparatively small and somewhat flattened with capitate antennae.

It is fairly common and is found living in decaying logs and tree stumps among fruiting bodies of fungi.
Range: Borneo and P. Malaysia.

Encaustes verticalis (28–32 mm)   PLATE 19J ♂
Quite a striking insect with black and orange patches and patterns on the pronotum and elytra. The legs are black with a tint of brownish-orange at the femur and tibia. The adult beetle is oval, somewhat bullet-like. The antennae are capitate and black in colour.

The habitat of this species is similar to that described for the previous species. They also have been observed on the fronds of *Calamus* palms.
Range: Borneo and P. Malaysia.

COCCINELLIDAE (LADYBIRDS)

Ladybirds are probably the most popular of all beetles. Most have brightly coloured hemispherical, convex elytra, but some species resemble a piece of excrement, a sort of camouflage to put off their enemies. All of this family are small insectivorous insects found dwelling in gardens and open woodlands.

The larvae of COCCINELLIDAE are our allies. In Java, larvae of certain species have been introduced to destroy aphids and scale-insects. Such natural biological control of crop-pests is of great value and importance to agriculturalists, because it does not destroy other forms of life. The larvae are soft-bodied and variously coloured and spotted. Their mouth-parts have sickle-like mandibles and the legs are comparatively long. Usually the body of these Coccinellid grubs is protected by long distinctive integumental processes (Fig. 30).

The pupae are also conspicuously coloured and are enclosed in the skin of the last larval instar, which is not shed at pupation. They are commonly found under the leaves of *Lantana* and *Convolvulaceae* species.

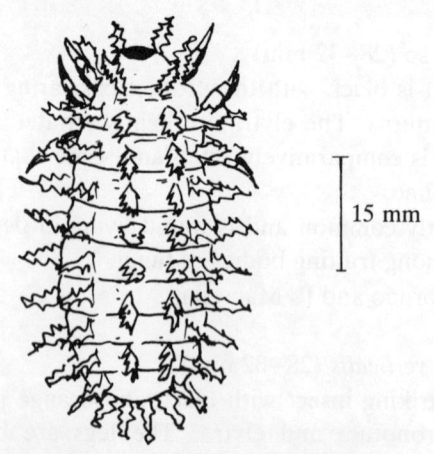

FIGURE 30 Larva of *Epilachna indica* (COCCINELLIDAE) (DORSAL VIEW)

Adults are common throughout the year and act as predators by feeding on ova, nymphs and adults of many plant-pests.

Anisolema sp (12–15 mm)　　　　　　　　　　　　PLATE 19E ♂
The species of this Bornean genus have rounded bodies, exceptionally small heads, and short simple clavate antennae.

The prothorax and the elytra are totally black and are coated with a thin layer of fine white pubescence. The margins of these two parts are slightly tinted yellowish-white. The legs are generally short, small and black.
Range: Borneo and Mindanao Island (Philippines).

Coccinella arcuata (6–8 mm)　　　　　　　　　　PLATE 19F ♂
One of the commonest ladybirds, inhabiting the lowland woodlands of Peninsular Malaysia, particularly in the south, and also found in rice fields, feeding on rice leaf-hoppers and their young. They also eat aphids and many types of plant lice. The insect is oval with a very small head and clavate antennae. It is bright orange-red with a large spot on the pronotum, and four transverse black bands on the elytra.

The spindle-shaped eggs are laid on plants in clusters of ten to twenty. The newly hatched larvae are brownish-black with a yellow cross-band at the distal end. They prey on aphids and mealy-bugs. Pupation occurs on the leaves of plants. The whole life cycle is about 15–20 days.
Range: Java to P. Malaysia.

An even commoner species, *C. transversalis* (5–6 mm), has a black body with some yellow markings on its elytra. The notum is black with a yellow anterior edge. It is very often found on the foliage of *Mimosa* and *Lantana* in clearings, searching for scale-insects.
Range: Throughout South-east Asia and Australia.

Epilachna indica (10–12 mm)　　　　　　　　　　PLATE 19G ♂
One insect which certainly will fall into your net while beating is *E. indica*, a yellow-headed ladybird with twelve small black round spots on the surface of its red elytra. The prothorax is yellow and so are its legs.

The eggs are pale yellow, spindle-shaped and easily seen on leaves in bundles of one to two dozens. The larvae (Fig. 30) are yellow and armed with numerous branched soft spines. Fully grown larvae turn grey overall before they pupate. The life cycle is about a month.
Range: South-east Asia to Australia.

Another easily captured ladybird is *E. vigintioctopunctata* (20–23 mm), which is a meadow and garden dweller. It is distinguished by the twenty-eight round dots found on its elytra. The body is red and resembles the above species.

The life history is also similar, and the ova, larvae and pupae are hardly distinguishable from those of *E. indica*. The only visible difference in the larvae is that those of this species are often more yellowish in colour and armed with numerous branched yellowish spines. They are commonly found feeding on aphids on the foliage of tomato, beans, chillies, Cucurbitaceous plants, *Hevea* and *Hibiscus*.
Range: South-east Asia to Australia.

TRICTENOTOMIDAE (FALSE LONGHORN BEETLES)

These ugly-looking insects are known from the forests of the South-east Asian region and only two species are recorded from mainland Malaysia.

They have enormous, hard, biting mouth-parts and quite long antennae (at least half the length of the body) with the last three antennal segments differentiated in size and shape, usually bigger and bifurcated. The elytra are hard and heavily dusted with a greenish-yellow powder-like pubescence which can be removed by slight friction.

Their habits and habitat are somewhat similar to those of the Cerambycids, and they are confined to deep woods above 750 m above sea-level. The life histories of these large insects are still unknown.

Autocrates aeneus (75–80 mm)   PLATE 20A ♀
This highland species has straight prolonged mandibles. The head is small and it has a pair of brownish compound eyes, and quite long

filiform antennae. The last three antennal segments are bituberculate, that is, split into two small plates at each antennal segment. The mandibles are saw-like at the inner edges and used mainly to cut wood into pieces. Those of the male have the extremities projected upwards to 5 to 10 mm, whereas those of the female are straight measuring between 7 and 11 mm.

The suture of the broad pronotum is thorny. The elytra are slender and elongate. The insect is entirely greenish-black with a very thick yellow wool on the prothorax and elytra which tends to drop off at the least friction. The legs are greyish-black. Adults are easily located in primary forest on the bark of *Vaccinium glabrescens* plants. At times, they are taken at light-traps.
Range: Himalaya to P. Malaysia.

Trictenotoma davidi (55–60 mm) PLATE 20D ♀
Another false longhorn beetle found in mainland Malaysia is *T. davidi*, which is known to occur in the lowland montane forest.

Mandibles straight, and shorter than in the above species. Quite long filiform antennae. Smaller in size and more yellowish. The head is of considerable size with a moderately large prothorax. Elytra slender and elongated. Legs short. Tips of the elytra split. The entire insect is black and heavily covered with a yellowish green pubescence. A common insect, often seen resting on the bark of *Eugenia* trees.
Range: Southern China, Taiwan and P. Malaysia.

CERAMBYCIDAE (LONGHORN, LONGICORN, OR TIMBER BEETLES)

This is most probably the second largest family in the Order COLEOPTERA with several thousand species occurring all over the world. It includes countless beetles with elegantly shaped and beautifully coloured bodies bearing the most distinctive antennae, often longer than the body. These flexible filiform antennae are found projecting from the frontal prominences of the head of the males, and are very much shorter in the females. The mouth-parts include a pair of short, powerful, sharp mandibles used for biting and cutting.

Most of the adults are slender insects, the eyes often emarginate. There are five or six visible sterna. All tarsi are apparently four-segmented. Experiments show that a number of the known species make shrill grating sounds by moving the prothorax and the neck of the scutum up and down against the mesothorax, probably to deter predators. One fine example is the species, *Batocera albofasciata*, which, when held in the hand, will stridulate with shrilling noises continuously until it is set free.

Many of the larvae of these insects are injurious to forest and fruit trees. Eggs are laid in the cracks of bark of living trees. The larvae are long, fleshy, tapering whitish grubs with horny heads (Fig. 31) which bore through the timber. When full-grown they pupate in chambers in the wood. Some species are known to take several years to reach maturity.

Very considerable damage is caused annually to valuable timber trees, fruit trees and some cultivated crops by longhorn beetles. The larvae of *Batocera albofasciata* and *Xystrocera festiva* attack the trunks of kapok and *Parkia* trees. Another common pest, *Rhytitodera simulans* (which is not shown in the plates) has larvae which live in the trunks of mango and durian trees. Local cultivators use an insecticide containing carbolineum to control this destructive insect.

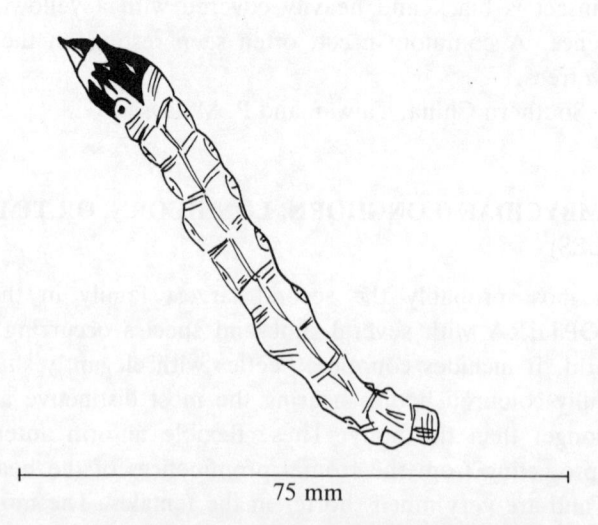

FIGURE 31   Larva of *Batocera albofasciata* (CERAMBYCIDAE) (LATERAL VIEW)

Anhammus deleni (38–42 mm) PLATE 20B♂ C♀
A longhorn beetle with long antennae, those of the male being about 11 mm. The antennae of the female are much shorter, about half the length of those of the male. The pronotum is rough with some growths. The marginal edges of the suture are sharpened into thorn-like processes. Elytra dark brown and black, sprinkled with small bright yellow spots. Legs long and slender. The whole body, including the legs and antennae, is yellowish-brown.
Range: P. Malaysia to Sumatra, Java and Borneo.

Anoplophora longehirsuta (50–55 mm) PLATE 20G♀
Fine light blue with five broad black transverse stripes across its elytra. The third band is the widest of the five, and is at the central part of the elytra on the median line. This band is joined with the next two bands at the posterior with two narrow longitudinal black lines, one on each elytron. A very narrow horizontal line is found on the head. The pronotum has a black patch in the centre and the outer margin is blackened.

The male differs from the female in having long antennae measuring 100 mm, while those of the female are about 65 mm. Another distinctive character of the female is that only the last two transverse bands of the elytra are joined with the longitudinal lines.
Range: P. Malaysia.

Anoplophora medembachi (40–45 mm) PLATE 20E♀ F♂
A beautiful greenish-blue insect which confines itself to thick secondary forest.

The head and pronotum are outlined in black. The elytra have four broad black transverse lines, and the shoulders are coarsely granulated. The tips of each antennal segment are blackened. The antennae of the male are about 80 mm long and those of the female about 50 mm. The abdomen of the female is not covered by the tips of the elytra, and is more rounded.
Range: P. Malaysia to Sumatra and Java.

Another light blue beetle with elongated elytra is *A. zonatrix* (40–50 mm), which is shown in PLATE 21A♀. The centre of the notum is blackened. The elytra have six narrow rows of black lines. Legs short and bluish-grey. The base of every segmental joint of the

antennae is blackened. The male has antennae about 110 mm, whereas in the female they are slightly less than 70 mm. The posterior margins of the elytra of the female are broader and rounder than those of the male which are narrow and small.
Range: P. Malaysia.

Aethalodes verrucosus (20–25 mm) PLATE 21B ♂
This insect is distributed throughout Malaysia in lowland forest. Both sexes are rather rare.

The insect is dirty-grey. Legs, particularly the hind ones, comparatively short. The joints of the head and scutum, and the elytra are greyish-black. Part of the centre of the prothorax and the whole surface of the wing sheaths are coarsely granulated. Towards the posterior end of the elytra, the granules become smaller and finer, and the whole surface of the elytra bears brownish-red patches. The body is elongated. Antennae long in the males, being about 30 mm. The females have shorter antennae, measuring about 20 mm, and they are slender and brownish-grey.
Range: P. Malaysia to Borneo.

Aristobia approximator (28–32 mm) PLATE 21C ♂
Though not found abundantly, this species is sometimes captured visiting flowers and on the bark of cinnamon and mahogany trees. It is a very distinctive and conspicuous beetle, with bright orange patches of various shapes and sizes all over the black wing covers. The head is bright orange with two oval black dots just behind the orange antennae, which are filiform and rather short, with a cluster of black wool-like hairs on the third segment of each. The first and second antennal segments are a glossy black. The notum is bulky, ridged and thorned. It is orange with four visible black lines, two at each margin, right across to the body underneath the elytra, and another two narrow ones on the surface. Legs long and black.
Range: Burma to Indo-China and P. Malaysia.

Batocera albofasciata (40–50 mm) PLATE 21D ♂
This is probably the commonest species of a large and important genus, and is found on the margins of clearings from cocoa plantations, and from the lowland undergrowth to thick secondary forest.

The insect is mouse-grey with four pairs of sulphur-yellow dots (all of different sizes) on the wing sheaths. These dots have a tendency to turn white after death. The pronotum is marked with two blood-red spots which also fade after death. Antennae filiform, brown with fine bristles from the second to the last segment.

The female lays 200 or more eggs at a time under the bark of kapok and dadap trees. The larva (Fig. 31) is milky-white and legless. The head has brown stripes and the mouth-parts are brown. When fully grown it is about 80 mm. It pupates after three months in the larval stage.

Range: Sumatra, Java and P. Malaysia.

Another common representative of the genus is *B. hector* (50–60 mm), shown in PLATE 27B♂, which is light brown in colour and densely covered with golden pubescence, especially the surface of the elytra. The fully grown larva is about 100 mm in length and is a notorious pest of dadap, *Albizzia*, nutmeg, and *Ficus*. This insect is known in English as the 'Dadap Borer'.

Range: Java, Sumatra and P. Malaysia.

In Borneo there is a closely related species, *B. parryi* (50–60 mm) (PLATE 27A♀), which resembles the above except that it has four pairs of white spots on the elytra. A very common insect.

Range: Borneo.

Batocera davidis (65–70 mm) PLATE 21E♂
Though not abundant on the plains in Sabah, this beetle is common in forested areas below 750 m.

The male is a light-brown insect with antennae more than 120 mm long, with short conical spurs throughout their length. There are two vermilion spots on the notum. The wing sheaths are heavily pubescent, the dorsal area roughly granulated and seven pairs of light red spots are seen on the surface. The red spots have a tendency to turn white or dirty yellowish-white after death. Legs short and greyish-brown. Adults often stridulate with a shrilling sound.

The larvae are whitish, elongate-cylindrical, and legless. They are found boring in freshly cut logs in logging sites.

Range: South China to Taiwan and Borneo.

Combe brianus (30–35 mm) PLATE 21F♂ G♀
A familiar little longhorn beetle, occasionally seen settling and walking on the bark of dadap and *Koompassia excelsa*.

This insect is distinguishable by its dark shiny blue and white patterns and stripes. The antennae are rather short, about 40 mm, greyish-white with dark grey segmental joints. Legs short and body elongated. The elytra do not cover the last abdominal segment of the insect. The anal segment is covered with short, well-trimmed tufts of hairs.
Range: Throughout South-east Asia.

Cyriopalus wallacei (35–40 mm) PLATE 21H♂ I♀
A medium-sized beetle with pectinate brown antennae. The body, head, notum, elytra, and legs, are yellowish-brown. It is often seen and captured in flight in the afternoon. The males have been observed settling on the leaves and stems of wild banana plants in the forest.
Range: Sumatra and P. Malaysia.

Diastocera wallichi (40–45 mm) PLATE 22A♂
This striking insect has a brownish-green body. Its antennae are filiform, with tufts of brownish-black hairs on the third, fourth and fifth segments. The others are densely covered with short hairs.

The head is small and dark leaf-green, the prothorax is bulky, and is light green admixed with some yellowish-green pigments. The elytra are the same colour as the prothorax, with three pairs of black lines outlined with thick green, on each elytron. The legs are of considerable length, femora reddish-brown, tibiae and tarsi dark green.

Easily and frequently collected on flowering plants.
Range: Himalaya to P. Malaysia.

Dorysthenes planicollis (45–50 mm) PLATE 22B♂
A common beetle but only in the forests of Borneo and Sumatra. The entire insect is dark chocolate, almost black.

A pair of large mandibles is seen at the mentum of the head. The edges of the pronotum bear three small triangular projections. Legs long. Antennae short, thick, and serrated.
Range: Borneo and Sumatra.

Epepeotes luscus (25–30 mm)   PLATE 22C♂
This longhorn beetle is as common as *B. albofasciata*. It is dirty greyish-brown in colour, with two small round spots on the shoulders of its elytra.

It has been observed that the female lays more than a thousand eggs at a time in cracks in the bark of trees. The eggs hatch into creamy-white larvae which grow to 45 mm in length. The head of the larva has horns which assist it to bore into tree trunks and branches. Pupation takes place after three months. Food plants include mango, cocoa, *Ficus* species and jack-fruit.
Range: P. Malaysia to Java and the Philippines.

Epepeotes lateralis (28–33 mm)   PLATE 22I♂ J♀
Confined to grassland, hedges, and the undergrowth of the tropical forest.

The feather-like pectinate antennae are short and about the same length as the body in the male; they are shorter in the female. This beetle is elongated and brownish-black with light-brown thickly pubescent elytra and deeper brown notum and pronotum. Legs rather long and brownish-black.
Range: Sumatra, P. Malaysia and Borneo.

Macrotoma fisheri (80–100 mm)   PLATE 26J♂
A highland species, confined to forest above 750 m, this is a drab-coloured insect, brown throughout. Mouth-parts visible with slightly prolonged mandibles having saw-like inner edges used for biting and cutting. The head is quite large with thickened but short antennae (about 65 mm), slightly shorter than the full body length. Pronotum coarsely granulated, with the outer margins denticulated. Wing sheaths light brown and parallel, lightly striated, and separated at the tip. The head and pronotum are darker, as are the legs, which are somewhat flattened, and spurred.
Range: Burma, Indo-China, southern China, P. Malaysia, Java
         and Sumatra.

Euryphagus lundi (20–25 mm)   PLATE 22D♂
A small, bright blood-red insect with black legs and short, black, filiform antennae. Head broad with red mandibles. Pronotum oval and finely granulate. Scutellum dark grey. Wing covers striated, with the posterior tip blackened.

Occasionally taken at roadsides near flowering *Lantana* plants.
Range: India to Java, Borneo.

Glenea (Macroglenea) elegans (30–35 mm)   PLATE 22E♂
A small, elongated beetle which is commonly found in coffee and cocoa plantations. The head is small, with greyish-white antennae, about 25 mm.

The head and the square prothorax are transversely coloured with black and white stripes. Elytra black with a tint of blue near the scutellum and shoulders of the dorsal part. A few distinctive white markings are found on the surface of the elytra. The lower margin of the elytra is arched.
Range: Indo-China, P. Malaysia, Sumatra, Java, Borneo and Nias Island (off Sumatra).

Eurybatus lesnei (44–48 mm)   PLATE 22F♂
Medium-sized, red coloured with six black spots, this insect is confined to highland forest. The head is broad and red, with the base of the filiform, short antennae blackened. The notum is circular and has a velvety black oval spot in the mid-length. Elytra narrow with a curved tip covering the last abdominal segment. The whole of the wing sheaths are grey with three pairs of yellow dots, and the scutellum and legs are black.

The larva is pale yellow and measures about 35 mm when fully grown. This species inhabits montane forest and adults are frequently seen attracted to roses at the hill stations.
Range: Java to P. Malaysia.

Leprodera elongata (35–43 mm)   PLATE 22G♂ H♀
This beetle is greyish-brown and chocolate. The antennae measure 120 mm and are filiform, very slender and fragile, especially after being dried. Elytra granulate, coarser in the dorsal parts. A broad belt of chocolate brown runs horizontally across the elytra at the mid-point. A pair of chocolate patches are visible at the margins but do not reach the median parting of the elytra. The legs are brown, the forelegs exceptionally long.

This species is occasionally found near debris in logging sites.
Range: P. Malaysia, Sumatra, Java and Borneo.

Neocerambyx gigas (75–85 mm) PLATE 25A♂ B♀
An enormous beetle. The male has very long antennae measuring 150 mm, those of the female only 70 mm. Sexual dimorphism is thus clearly marked. The entire beetle is densely covered with a neat, even layer of white, brown and black pubescence. The antennae are filiform and lighter brown in colour than the body, but turn black after death. Body elongated and hairy.

Not a very common insect. Found hiding in thorny shrubs, such as giant *Mimosa* and *Lantana*, and thick bushes.
Range: P. Malaysia to Borneo.

A very close relative of *N. gigas* but smaller in size is *N. grandis* (60–70 mm), illustrated in PLATE 24A♂ B♀. Its antennae are generally shorter and the first five antennal segments are not spherical in shape at the joints as they are in *N. gigas*. Similar habitat to *N. gigas* though the author believes this species is much rarer.
Range: P. Malaysia.

Omocyrius jansoni (20–25 mm) PLATE 25D♀
Not uncommon in lowland forest. The head is oval and the prothorax elongated. The unusual antennae have bulbous terga on the third and fourth segments. The pronotum is lengthened and brown, as are the elytra, which bear a number of small yellow dots.

The forelimbs have the tibiae lengthened and lighter brown than the rest of the legs.
Range: P. Malaysia.

Pachyteria dimidiata (25–30 mm) PLATE 25D♀
The insect is dark blue. Biting mouth-parts are seen at the mentum of the small head. Antennae thickened, with the first five segments dark blue, and the others light yellow.

The general colour of the insect is deep lustrous blue with a broad yellow band across the elytra. It is not uncommon in secondary forest.
Range: India to Indo-China and P. Malaysia.

Pachyteria equestris (28–32 mm) PLATE 26A♂
A handsome longhorn beetle with a small head and biting mouth-parts. Antennae thick and filiform, with the first to fifth segments

yellow while the others are dark blue. The circular pronotum is red. The top half of the elytra is red, the bottom half bluish-green. The tip of the elytra never covers the last abdominal segment. The forelegs have greenish-blue femora and tibiae, and yellow tarsi. Mid-legs and hind legs blue, the hind legs being somewhat longer.
Range: P. Malaysia.

Pachyteria virescens (35–40 mm)   PLATE 26B ♂
Rather a rare insect with a deep iridescent green body. The head is ash-coloured and the mouth-parts are clearly visible, as in other species of this genus. The antennae are thickened, with the first five segments grey and the following six segments bright yellow. The notum is purplish-red; and the wing covers metallic green. All legs are also green, the forelegs being slightly darker. The hind legs, as usual, are longer.
Range: P. Malaysia.

Pachyteria imitans (32–35 mm)   PLATE 26C ♂
Superficially this species resembles *P. equestria*, and it can be easily separated by its elongated body, its blackened antennae at the last four segments, and a lateral pale yellow line below the mid-length of each elytron. The males frequent flowering plants and cultivated crops. A common insect.
Range: P. Malaysia.

A further species of the genus is *P. lambi* (22–24 mm), PLATE 26D ♂. It differs from the above species by having the upper half of its elytra brightly yellow-washed and the last six antennal plates bright yellow, the remaining plates being dark blue. It is slightly smaller in size. The legs, as in the above species, are dark blue, and the prothorax is brownish-red. A common species that dwells in secondary forest at all elevations.
Range: P. Malaysia.

Euryorthrum carinatum (18–20 mm)   PLATE 26E ♂
A smaller Cerambycid which bears some resemblance to the *Pachyteria* species. The entire insect is dull blue with a yellow transverse line at the mid-length of the elytra. Its antennae are somewhat pectinate instead of filiform, with brownish-orange plates.

An inhabitant of the lowland forest. Both the larvae and the adults are true foliage feeders.
Range: P. Malaysia.

Paraleprodera diophthalma (30–32 mm) PLATE 26F ♂
A dweller in open woodlands and mangrove swamps. It is distinguishable from allied species by its greyish-yellow body and its slightly lengthened forelimbs. Antennae filiform, grey and only about 45 mm long. Head and notum pale yellow, with broad marginal grey lines. The elytra have a pair of small horseshoe-shaped chocolate brown patches near the shoulders; and a bigger pair of chocolate brown triangular patches covering the central part of the sides.
Range: Taiwan to P. Malaysia.

Zonopterus consanguineus (43–48 mm) PLATE 27D ♂
This insect is slightly bigger than species of the *Pachyteria* genus. Although it superficially resembles *Pachyteria* species, it is distinguished by its slightly lengthened hind legs, greatly flattened tibiae and femora, and more prominent mouth-parts.

The beetle is black with two broad yellow bands across the elytra. The last six segments of the antenna are tinted yellow. All tarsal claws are yellow too. Not a very common beetle.
Range: P. Malaysia.

Epicedia maculatrix (25–30 mm) PLATE 27C ♂
A wood-brown beetle with two large triangular black spots near the margins of the elytra and two more small black dots in the upper half. A wood-borer, it frequents kapok trees and is found in great numbers.
Range: P. Malaysia.

Parepicedia fimbriata (35–40 mm) PLATE 26H ♂
An ugly insect, completely dark brown, with two patches of black, outlined with light yellow, on each elytron. Antennae less than 55 mm in length. The female has shorter antennae. The head, pronotum and dorsal parts of the elytra are heavily granulated. The forelegs have elongated tibiae and hairy tarsal claws.

Commonly captured in undergrowth in deeply forested areas.
Range: P. Malaysia, Sumatra and Borneo.

Pseudomyagrus waterhousei (25–30 mm) PLATE 26G♂ I♀
The body is pale blue with wing covers adorned with fifteen small squarish black spots. Legs and antennae blue. The antennal joints are blackened. The female bears shorter antennae, has broader and more convex elytra, and the entire insect is darker sky-blue.

This is a rare insect, found in thick primary forest in Peninsular Malaysia. Females are less rare than males.
Range: P. Malaysia, Sumatra and Nias Island.

Rhaphipodus hopei (90–100 mm) PLATE 23A♂
A giant Cerambycid, among the biggest in Malaysia, and not uncommon in hilly areas. It is frequently seen on the bark of dead trees, confined to forest above 750 m.

The mandibles are straight with rough cutting edges. The head is large; the antennae short and brown. The prothorax is rectangular; wing sheaths elongated and lightly striated. The insect is completely brown, darker on the head, including the mandibles, prothorax and legs. The legs are covered with sharp bristles.
Range: Burma, Indo-China, south to P. Malaysia and Sumatra, Borneo.

Trirachys orientalis (45–50 mm) PLATE 28A♂ B♀
Dull and small, this is a very common species, found mostly in lowland forest on the bark of rotting trees.

The antennae are filiform and long. The pronotum is oval and roughly structured. The elytra are slender with yellowish-brown and black pubescence. All legs are yellowish-brown and narrow.
Range: Southern China to Taiwan and P. Malaysia.

Xylorhiza adusta (35–40 mm) PLATE 28C♂ D♀
Quite a striking beetle, this species looks like a piece of wood and is well camouflaged among rotting tree trunks. It is a very common beetle and easily captured, especially when it is feeding on the oozing sap of tree wounds.
Range: India, China, Taiwan and Indo-China to P. Malaysia and Sumatra.

Xystrocera festiva (35–40 mm) PLATE 28E♂ F♀
General colour reddish-bronze with a greenish longitudinal stripe on

the outer margin of each wing cover. This insect is known for the damage it causes to the bark of *Parkia* trees, from which its larvae can strip the entire bark.
Range: Java to P. Malaysia.

An equally common species of this genus is *X. globosa* (35–40 mm), shown in PLATE 28P♂, which resembles the species above except that the greenish stripes do not run along the outer margins of the elytra but are in between the median line and the margins.
Range: Java to P. Malaysia.

Celosterna sulphurea (50–60 mm)   PLATE 27E♂
An entirely sulphur-coloured longhorn beetle with antennae light brown. The shoulders of the elytra are finely granulated. The elytra are elongated and the sulphur colouring on them tends to turn burnt-brown when placed to dry in the sun. A very rare insect.
Range: P. Malaysia.

Resembling *C. sulphurea* is *Joesse sanguinolenta* (45–55 mm), as illustrated in PLATE 27F♂. It is smaller and dull brownish-red. The antennae like those of *C. sulphurea* are short and narrow. Not an uncommon insect, it is often seen settling on trunks and thick branches of *Parkia* and kapok trees in lowland forest.
Range: South-east Asia.

Xylotrechus affinis (8–9 mm)   PLATE 29G♂
The head and prothorax are black above and densely covered with grey pubescence. There is a bare round spot on each side of the disc of the prothorax. The elytra are elongate and bear four bands of ashy-grey pubescence, as illustrated in the plate. The underside of the body is also covered with ashy-grey pubescence, with the episterna of both the meso- and metathorax being more densely covered with whitish pubescence. The legs are black and slender. The antennae are short and filiform with the proximal six antennal joints black, veiled with grey pubescence and the remaining joints pale fulvous. The frons of the head is parallel-sided and is not constricted between the eyes. It is furnished with three feeble carinae, one at the middle line, the others midway between the middle and the margins of the head.

This is a common insect and can easily be taken at hill-tops or hill-stations above 1050 m.
Range: P. Malaysia.

Xylotrechus consocius (9–10 mm) appears to be most nearly allied to the above species, which greatly resembles it in colour, but differs in having the frons of the head constricted between the eyes and furnished with four carinae. The anterior bands on the elytra are much smaller in size. It is also common.
Range: P. Malaysia and Southern Thailand.

Arcyphorus conformis (9–10 mm)   PLATE 29F♂
The head and prothorax above are black and faintly covered with grey pubescence. There is a large oval spot on the disc of the prothorax and another small, rounded spot on each side of the prothorax. It is entirely covered with shallow punctures. The elytra are dark-brown with bands of grey pubescence arranged in a similar way as those on *X. affinis*. The femora of the mid-legs are carinate on each side and near the ventral area are broader. The first joints of the tarsus of the hind legs are slightly longer than the remaining joints together.
  A montane species which can be easily taken in flight in the early morning at hill-stations.
Range: P. Malaysia.

Mimistena biplagiata (6–7·5 mm)   PLATE 29H♂
The general colour of this longhorn beetle is glossy black, with the elytra tinged with metallic-green and marked with a yellowish-white elongate spot between the middle and the base of each elytron. The head is sparsely covered with ashy-grey pubescence. The antennae are a little longer than the length of the body, with the eighth, ninth and the basal half on the tenth antennal joints fulvous. The prothorax is strongly punctured and is furnished with an oblique tubercle at the edge of the disc. It has a narrow transverse band of silver grey pubescence near the base and apex. The underside of the body is glossy-black, bearing transverse bands of silver white pubescence at the sides of the abdomen, and an oblique band on the metasternum. The prosternum and mesosternum are less densely covered with greyish-white pubescence. The legs are brownish-black and the clubs of the femora are reddish-brown.

This species frequents secondary forest above 750 m though at times it can be taken in lowland forest.
Range: P. Malaysia.

Macrochenus melanospilus (22–31 mm)   PLATE 291 ♂ J ♀
The head and prothorax are black above and faintly covered with grey pubescence. These two parts are marked with three longitudinal white bands. The scutellum is ashy-white. The elytra are clothed with ashy-white pubescence which is interrupted by numerous black spots of various sizes and shapes, and these spots have a tendency to coalesce in places. Sexual dimorphism is marked by the length of the prothorax, that of the male being twice as long as that of the female.

M. melanospilus is a rare insect and can be captured at bleeding wounds of kapok trees, usually above 6 m from the ground. The author has taken some specimens in cocoa plantations at the foot of Mount Kinabalu in Sabah.
Range: P. Malaysia and Borneo.

CHRYSOMELIDAE (LEAF BEETLES AND TORTOISE BEETLES)

This family includes a very large number of sun-loving insects found principally on flowers and foliage. Tortoise beetles (subfamily CASSIDINAE) are commonly captured at *Lantana* shrubs near limestone caves, hills and open woods. They are generally small, oval or round in shape, with highly arched backs of flamboyant colours.

Typically, leaf beetles have a superb metallic sheen on the elytra with a very small head which can sink under the prothorax. The legs are rather short. At the tip of the antenna is a two to three-segmented club. They exhibit great diversity in colour and shape. The tarsi of most species are apparently three or four-segmented. When disturbed, they habitually sham dead by drawing in their limbs and falling to the ground.

Larvae (Fig. 32) from this family resemble those of the Coccinellids. They have horny growths on their fleshy bodies, and pointed, soft spines, are voraciously active and many species are found on the leaves of Cucurbitaceous plants. Agriculturalists regard them as serious pests because they voraciously eat cultivated

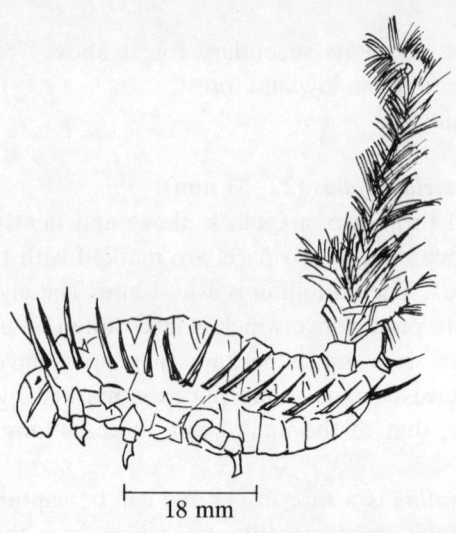

FIGURE 32   Larva of *Aspidomorpho miliaris* (CHRYSOMELIDAE, subfamily CASSIDINAE) (LATERAL VIEW)

crops such as potato, as well as garden plants. The adult members are foliage-feeders which can defoliate and even kill a plant.

The larvae of tortoise beetles, subfamily CASSIDINAE, are elongate-oval, somewhat flattened, and covered with bristles. A striking forked process is seen projecting at the posterior of the body. The cast skins and the excrement are attached to this. They are very active in the morning on the foliage of *Lantana, Mimosa*, wild canes, and palm trees. The pupae are naked and are often protected by the remains of the last larval skin which hardens and forms an integument.

Aspidomorpho inquinata (10–12mm)   PLATE 28G ♂
A small metallic yellow insect with golden, broad, hemispherical elytra, giving a striking effect. The scutum is wide and thin, and has a translucent sheen covering the whole head. Antennae clavate, and legs short. The body of this insect is flattened. It is always prepared to take flight when danger threatens.

Locally, it is called the 'Miniature Flying Saucer Beetle', and its English name is the 'Tortoise Beetle'. It is placed in the subfamily CASSIDINAE.
Range: Java to P. Malaysia.

Aspidomorpho miliaris (10–15 mm) PLATE 28H♂
A beautifully marked pale yellow beetle with black pencillings and linings. The yellowish-brown suture of the pronotum almost covers the whole head. The elytra are spade-like, thin and fragile, with black spots located at the four outer angles beneath a winding longitudinal black band, on each elytron. The yellow colour tends to turn brown after death.

Eggs are laid in batches of between 30 and 60. The larvae (Fig. 32) are gregarious and armed with rows of soft spines along each side of the light yellow body; head and legs brown. They use their excreta as camouflage. The total developmental period is about three weeks. The adults live on sweet potatoes, beans, and species of *Convolvulaceae*.
Range: Throughout Sundaland.

Laccoptera tredecimpunctata (7–9 mm) PLATE 28I♂
A bright orange-brown tortoise beetle with two black spots on its translucent scutum. The surface of the elytra is marked with eleven black dots. There is usually a spot beneath the scutellum.

The larvae are similar to those of *A. miliaris* and also use their excreta to act as a protective cover. They are mostly found on the tops of leaves of *Ipomoea* species.
Range: Java, Sumatra and P. Malaysia.

Prioptera decempunctata (11–14 mm) PLATE 28J♂
Confined to lowland and open woodlands, this insect is pear-shaped and light yellowish-brown in colour. There are two small round black dots on its pronotum. The elytra are highly convex; two large red spots are seen near the middle on each elytron, and another smaller and slightly faded dot is present at the bottom edge. A fairly common beetle, easily collected when it is feeding on the sap of wounded flowering twigs in the morning and at noon.
Range: P. Malaysia to Java.

Aulacophora coffeae (7–8 mm) PLATE 28K♂
An elongated but small insect, very often found in woodlands and gardens. Usually very active in the early morning and late afternoon, flying or walking or feeding hungrily on the foliage of Cucurbitaceous plants, sometimes in great numbers. It is light yellow with the

middle and hind pairs of legs entirely black. A strong postmedian transverse depression is present on the prothorax.

The female oviposits beneath the surface of the soil. Larvae reach maturity after three or four weeks.

Range: P. Malaysia, Sumatra and Java.

A. flavomarginata (7–8 mm) has elytra a shiny blue-black, as shown in PLATE 28L♂. The head and prothorax are yellow.
Range: P. Malaysia to Java.

Other known common Chrysomelids are *A. niasiensis* (6–7 mm) and *A. atripennis* (10–11 mm). The former is yellowish-brown with tibiae of the mid and hind legs, and the abdomen, blackened; whereas in the latter, the body is larger and yellowish-red. Elytra and tibiae are black. All *Aulacophora* species are pests of cultivated crops and vegetables.
Range: P. Malaysia, Sumatra and Java.

Hispa armigera (4–5 mm)   PLATE 28M♂
This much smaller Chrysomelid inhabits rice-fields and sugar cane plantations. It is bluish-black with prominent spines all over the body. The antennae are clavate and glabrous. It is a notorious agricultural pest.
Range: Java to P. Malaysia and Borneo.

Nisotra gemella (3–4 mm)   PLATE 28N♂
Commonly known as the 'Flea Beetle', mainly because it hops like a flea. The body is round, with head, notum and legs red; the elytra are metallic-blue.

This species is placed under the subfamily ALTICINAE which is formerly known as HALTICINAE. Adults are seen feeding on the flowers of kapok, *Hibiscus*, and cocoa.

The eggs are found in the soil in big batches. The young larvae are pale brown, turning greyish in their later stages. They probably feed on the root-hairs of kapok and cocoa tree. After three weeks, they pupate.
Range: Java to P. Malaysia.

Sagra buqueti (28–30 mm)   PLATE 28Q♂ R♀
This leaf beetle is iridescent with steely blue-green elytra bearing a

broad dark purplish-red band right along their median groove. The head is small with thick clavate antennae, and small biting mouth-parts. The pronotum also is small, but the wing sheaths are high, spade-like and somewhat convex. The legs are green with thickened femora, those of the hind legs being exceptionally large. These hind limbs form the most distinctive feature of this common insect.
Range: Java, Sumatra and P. Malaysia.

S. borneensis (10–13 mm) shown on PLATE 28O♂, is another commonly found Sagrinid which is completely shining naval-blue in colour, and is much smaller in size than *S. buqueti*. It inhabits secondary woodlands.
Range: P. Malaysia to Borneo.

A rarer Chrysomelid which is often mistaken for a member of the *Sagra* genus is *Alurnus* sp (PLATE 29A♂), which is mostly yellow in colour and of the same size as *S. buqueti* (25–30 mm). The insect is soft-bodied and seldom found in collections.
Range: P. Malaysia.

CURCULIONIDAE (WEEVILS OR SNOUT BEETLES)

Weevils form the largest superfamily in the INSECTA and many of them are serious pests, feeding solely on seeds and grains. Over 40 000 species have already been described, studied and named, but many more are still waiting to be discovered and classified, especially in the tropics.

Some weevils are noted for their value as pollinators of oil palms and other cultivated crops. An experiment carried out by the local Agricultural Department found that the weevil, *Elaeidobius kamerunicus*, originally from West Africa, greatly assists in the pollination of oil palms.

The chitinous bodies of weevils are exceptionally hard, but their legs tend to drop or break off quite easily on capture and after death. A very distinctive prolonged beak or snout called the *rostrum* is seen jutting out from the head with small but visible mouth-parts at the tip of the long proboscis (Fig. 3).

The clavate antennae are elbowed at the end of the first joint and tend to fold neatly backwards when at rest.

The females have longer snouts and drill deep holes in seeds and fruits to oviposit. The larvae are legless (Fig. 33), and tunnel into the stems, shoots and tissues of young developing plants. Many of them are injurious to cultivation.

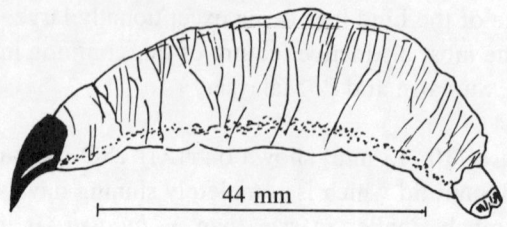

FIGURE 33   Larva of *Rhynchophorus ferrugineus* (CURCULIONIDAE) (LATERAL VIEW)

Alcides cinchonae (8–11 mm)   PLATE 31A ♂
A small light leaf-green weevil, found plentifully on kapok trees and the young leaf shoots of Cinchona.

The forelegs have elongated tibiae, toothed at the base. The larvae have been recorded as doing heavy damage to the young twigs of cultivated plants.

Adults usually turn light brown or black after being captured and after death.
Range: Java, Sumatra and P. Malaysia.

Another common *Alcides* species is *A. leeweeni* (9–10 mm). This insect is almost completely black. The posterior of the elytra is greenish. The tibiae of the forelimbs are provided with a tooth-like spine. They live with other *Alcides* species. The females are as common as the males. They are sometimes found in numbers on a single tree.
Range: P. Malaysia to Java.

Cryptorhynchus gravis (5–6 mm)   PLATE 31B ♂
This beetle is greenish-grey in colour. It is often seen on the bark of kapok and cocoa trees. The larva lives and pupates in mango fruits, its total life cycle normally being completed in 25 to 35 days.
Range: India to Java and P. Malaysia.

A Malaysian species, *C. mangiferae* (7–9 mm), is commoner. It is slightly bigger but almost the same colour and has similar habits. It

is found in numbers on mango trees, particularly during the fruiting seasons.
Range: P. Malaysia and Sundaland.

Cyrtotrachelus buqueti (50–55 mm)   PLATE 30A♂
Confined to forested areas, this species is among the most handsome of the snout beetles, with an orange and black body. The bright orange colour tends to turn burnt brown after death.

The head bears a long arrow-like snout which is completely black. The prothorax is large with three bright longitudinal stripes on it, one of which lies in the median groove while the remaining two are at the margins of the notum. The elytra are black with bright orange patches. The tip of the abdomen is naked, pointed and hairy. All legs are black in colour, the forelimbs being exceptionally long (55–65 mm).
Range: P. Malaysia.

A rarer insect in the genus, closely related to the above species in habits and habitat, is *C. dux*. It is black and reddish-brown. Its forelegs, over 80 mm long, distinguish it from all the other members of this genus.
Range: Assam to P. Malaysia.

Lophobaris serratipes (4–5 mm)   PLATE 31C♂
An entirely black weevil which is found in great numbers in pepper trees, boring into the flowers and fruits. The body is densely covered with hair-bearing tubercles, and the snout is short and slender, often bending backwards when at rest or on capture, and after death.

During its larval stage, it feeds on clusters of peppercorns, which gives it its common name, the 'Pepper Weevil'.
Range: Java, Sumatra, P. Malaysia and Borneo.

Macrochirus praetor (75–80 mm)   PLATE 30B♀
An enormous weevil, with a small head and long, narrow proboscis. The huge pronotum is brown and square. The elytra are orange brown and striated, leaving the last abdominal segment of the insect uncovered. The legs are long, slender and black. The male can be

distinguished from the female as it has enlarged mouth-parts at the extremity of the rostrum.

Not uncommon in secondary forest where it is found on sap exuding from trees.
Range: P. Malaysia to Java.

Protocerius colossus (45–50 mm) PLATE 30C♀
The entire insect is very dark purple to black, somewhat similar to the above in shape but much smaller and darker. A broad purplish line is seen on the notum, and it is tinted purple at the base of the snout. Its uncovered abdomen is less pointed. The elytra are heavily and deeply striated. Overall the legs are shorter and covered with short setae.

It is found throughout the year, occasionally seen visiting flowers and young developing shoots of the plants and palms.
Range: P. Malaysia.

Rhynchophorus ferrugineus (25–55 mm) PLATE 30E♂ F♀
Locally called the 'Red Palm Weevil', this species is very common and very variable in size and colour. It is red brown with four black spots on the pronotum. It frequents wild palms in open forest and oil palm plantations.

The white larva (Fig. 33) feeds on the sap of young palm trees, and is often seen drilling holes into the stems with its sharp and pointed mouth-parts. A pest of oil palms.
Range: Sundaland to Australia.

Another common species which is likely to fall into the hands of collectors is the 'Red Stripe Weevil', *R. schachi*, shown on PLATE 30D♂. It is darker with a narrow red median line on the pronotum.
Range: Southern Thailand and P. Malaysia.

Rhynchophorus palmarum (40–50 mm) PLATE 32A♂ B♀
A reddish-brown weevil with deeply striated elytra, and short beak and legs. The tibiae of the legs are covered with short setae. The species is quite common and sometimes found in numbers in oil palm estates and cocoa plantations.
Range: Sumatra and P. Malaysia.

Sitophilus (Calandra) granaria (3-4 mm) PLATE 31D ♂
A small black weevil of great economic importance. It is a serious pest of stored grain and flour. The minute larvae are whitish-yellow with black heads. They bore into and feed on stored products, as do their parents. They pupate after one or two weeks. The whole life cycle is less than a month, and there are many broods each year.
Range: World-wide.

Sitophilus (Calandra) oryzae (3-4 mm) PLATE 31E ♂
A tropical race very similar to *S. granaria*. It feeds mainly on stored rice grains and can easily be found in your rice tin at home. The minute larvae are whitish in colour and pupate after 10 days in a white silky cocoon.
Range: India to Sundaland, Australia, and north to Thailand, Indo-China, China, Taiwan, Korea, Japan, northern part of Africa and southern Europe.

A common species found in young shoots of sugar cane and paddy fields is the black weevil, *Hypomeces squamosus* (13-15 mm). Its larva feeds voraciously on sugar cane and severely restricts its growth if it is not checked and controlled.
Range: P. Malaysia.

Sphenophorus (Cosmopolites) sordidus (12-15 mm) PLATE 31F ♂
A more important pest of agriculture in Malaysia is the 'Banana Weevil'. The adult beetle is black with strongly grooved, greyish elytra. It dwells among banana plants, usually near the base of the stems. The larva causes heavy damage on the banana stem by tunnelling deeply into it. Pupation also takes place in the stem. The whole life cycle is four to five weeks.
Range: P. Malaysia.

Brachycerus congestus (18-22 mm) PLATE 32C ♂
This species has to date only been recorded from Africa. The author has taken two identical insects from Pulau Langkawi on two different visits, both in January. This beetle is oval, dark brown to black, with a highly arched body, and is distinguishable from other species by the surface of its elytra which is densely covered with numerous small, raised ball-like structures.

A very rare weevil, found in open forest in the lowlands. The exact status of its occurrence is not known yet nor are its habits, habitat and life history.

Range: Africa to P. Malaysia. Possibly found in India, Burma and Thailand too.

BEETLES AND MAN

Beetles, like all other forms of life, are part of the complicated ecosystem including man. They can become pests when man alters the ecosystem, generally without any thought for the consequences, to grow food, to establish industrial estates, and to open up land for settlement.

Most beetles are harmless to man: some are positively beneficial as pollinators, but certain species are serious pests of agricultural crops.

The public in general are much more aware of the ill effects of injurious beetles than those of the beneficial ones, though on the whole, the latter are greater in number than the former. Both groups play important roles in the natural ecosystem and agriculture.

INJURIOUS BEETLES

Cultivated crops, shrubs, bushes, plants, and trees in a natural state as well as preserved food products, stored grains and man's possessions, are subjected to attack by a wide range of insect pests. Some attack animals too and a few beetles are agents in the transmission of certain human and animal diseases. Flea beetles transmit a virus disease called Spindle Tuber to potato plants; this disease greatly affects the productivity of the plants. Some beetles are ecologically among the most formidable of our insect enemies. A few are injurious and cause damage and harm to plants at all stages of their development, particularly during the larval stage.

Most harmful COLEOPTERA are feeders on foliage, causing injuries which may vary from a reduction in the yield of the crop to the complete destruction of the plant. It is estimated that beetles destroy at least 15% of the total food that farmers and agriculturalists are trying to produce annually.

Larvae of BUPRESTIDAE, CHRYSOMELIDAE, and CURCULIONIDAE are feeders on plant tissues, foliage, and borers in stems, flowers, fruits, and stored food grains. Such feeding skeletonizes the plant tissues and may later defoliate them completely.

Species that burrow deep in the fruits, stalks, wood of living trees, and the internal tissues of the plant include CERAMBYCIDAE, BUPRESTIDAE, and CURCULIONIDAE. These feed on the sap from the stems and trunks of trees. Such borrowing, tunnelling and boring into the plant tissues may eventually cause stunted growth, delayed maturity and poor fruit development. Worst of all are the females of the CURCULIONIDAE, which not only attack the external tissues of plants but also feed on the internal ones, tunnelling numerous deep holes with their long snouts and injecting a substance which badly affects plant growth. Galls may be produced by the plant in response to eggs which have been laid by the females in plant tissues.

Another serious type of plant damage is caused by the larvae of ELATERIDAE and SCARABAEIDAE which feed underground on roots. Leaves of the plants may turn yellow, and margins and tips may develop a scorched or burnt appearance. The quality of the harvested products is often adversely affected as the plants become weak and prone to attack by other insects and fungi.

Beetles also do harm to stored products, fabrics, clothing and other kinds of fibre upholstery. Stored products such as rice grains and flour are attacked by *Sitophilus granaria* (CURCULIONIDAE). Fabrics and clothing are attacked by dermestid beetles. Bean and nut weevils tunnel in and may destroy or contaminate stored beans and nuts. Both the larvae and adults of the museum beetle, *Tribolium castaneum* (TENEBRIONIDAE), attack dried and preserved insects in collections.

BENEFICIAL BEETLES

Man benefits from insects in many ways; and of all the beneficial beetles, the COCCINELLIDAE, Ladybirds, are the most familiar, preying mainly on aphids, scale insects and their broods. These insectivorous beetles have few enemies themselves and protect themselves from them by exuding an oily, acrid and bad smelling fluid. Species of ant beetles (CLERIDAE) and hister beetles (HISTERI-

DAE), too, during their larval stage devour small borers, bark-borers, and shot-hole borers and also eggs of bees, wasps and locusts.

Some sixty years ago some species of the HISTERIDAE were introduced into Fiji Island from Java to prey upon banana root borers and their broods; this biological control was quite successful.

Both the larvae and adults of ground and tiger beetles are predators of great economic importance, preying upon many pest species and helping to keep them under control. These *aphytophagous* insects have also done much to keep down the high reproductive capacity of many scale insects, aphids and ants. Larvae of DYTISCIDAE, too, prey upon mosquito larvae, the mosquito being a formidable enemy of man in the tropics.

Flower-nectar feeders such as fan beetles, RHIPIPHORIDAE, and brister beetles, MORDELLIDAE, help to ensure cross-pollination of plants which biologically results in the reproduction of higher plants and better food production. Such pollination is effected by pollen sticking to the bodies of beetles, and then being rubbed off when the beetles are feeding on another flower.

Symbiosis between plants and insects is basic to the reproduction of many higher grades and kinds of plant species which nature has provided man. Cross-pollination by insects, particularly weevils, is one of the most important services beetles have done for man by increasing the yield and production of food we grow. One fine example is the introduction of a West African weevil, *Elaeidobius kamerunicus*, to oil palm plantations in Malaysia to assist pollination between the palms which has resulted in an increase in yields.

In Africa, New Guinea, Europe and Malaysia, people use some species of beetle in the treatment of diseases. Certain drugs, such as cantharidin which is made from the dried bodies of blister beetles, MELOIDAE, (probably *Lytta* sp), are made and used medicinally as an aphrodisiac.

The tropical species of SILPHIDAE and SCARABAEINAE, which feed on decomposing animals, carrion and dung, often convey these into the soil, as food for their young, which helps to fertilize the soil and improve its structure. Woodboring beetles such as CERAMBYCIDAE, BUPRESTIDAE and CURCULIONIDAE play important roles in hastening the conversion of fallen trees and logs into soil. Insect scavengers from the families LUCANIDAE and PASSALIDAE feed on decomposing plants and logs, and assist in converting such waste materials into simpler substances which are then returned to the soil. Their activities, including excretion, the dead bodies of beetle grubs, and the decaying materials brought into the soil can considerably enrich its fauna. Added to this, many grubs of SCARABAEIDAE burrow into the ground, creating numerous galleries which help to increase soil porosity, structure and profile.

Beetles can also help to destroy undesirable plants. An experiment was carried out by the United States Agricultural Department between 1944 and 1948. This involved the introduction of species of European Chrysomelid and Buprestid beetles into California to control the growth of the noxious Klamath weed, which is poisonous to livestock. The result was very satisfactory and the concept is highly recommended by research stations.

The grubs of DYTISCIDAE are utilized as food by many fresh water fishes, and those of SCARABAEIDAE and PASSALIDAE are used as baits for catching game birds, and for fishing. Malays dig up SCARABAEIDAE larvae to feed chickens and other livestock. In other parts of the world, grubs of some SCARABAEIDAE are utilized as human food too. In Africa, many tribes search for and eat the larvae of CETONIINAE.

Larvae and adult beetles are used in experimental work. These studies include the study of beetles in general; their life history; habits; habitat; anatomy and physiology; their reaction to environmental factors and other biological phenomena.

In Agricultural Departments, various beetles are used experimentally in testing the toxicity of new insecticides. All in all, beetles are of great economic importance.

Beetles have aesthetic as well as commercial value. Years ago, jewellers, artists, and businessmen noticed the texture of the iridescent elytra of many BUPRESTIDAE species, and the natural metallic colours which adorn these insects have been utilized by jewellers and designers for designing bracelets, necklaces, glass trays, pictures and bookmarks. Many of these beetles are mounted in glass frames and sold to the public. Many others are exported overseas to entomological dealers. Some are taken by private collectors who place them in glass frames as decorations for their homes. Others are donated to museums or zoological departments for research.

Thus, the good work done by these insects must be balanced against the harm, but only very few persons actually appreciate this. Perhaps the good is often less evident than the bad. In spite of this, man is constantly inventing more powerful insecticides to control beetles and other insects; and thus makes himself not just a collector or a student of entomology but also a destroyer and an enemy of the whole insect kingdom. The same could be said of a commercial collector, or a person who purchases a set specimen in a case.

INTEGRATED PEST CONTROL

In crop production, the control of pests, particularly beetles, is often essential to obtain high yields. Since most crops suffer, to some extent, from attacks of insect pests, a brief discussion of control measures is given below.

Biological and chemical control measures are often considered to be incompatible because insecticides are usually imposed upon the existing ecosystem in chemical control. On the other hand, biological control may also be inadequate by itself and it is better to regard all control measures as complementary.

BIOLOGICAL CONTROL

Biological control is defined as the destruction or suppression of pests by the introduction, encouragement or artificial increase of their natural enemies. It is essential for a successful *introduced* parasite or predator to have greater fecundity than its host and to be adaptable to the new environment and to be able to disperse. An effective parasite will attack only one host species or at most two or three, so as not to endanger the presence of other harmless insect species.

Strictly speaking, many pests are held at numbers so low that they are not economically important and in such situations, biological control may hold good over a considerable period of time until the pests overcome this natural control barrier, and cause further economic damage. Then chemical control measures may be necessary to keep the economic destruction to a minimum.

Care must be taken in the implementation of any pest control measures, particularly involving the use of chemicals, to ensure that the ecosystem is not destroyed. At all times the increase of natural enemies of the pest in terms of predators and parasites should be encouraged to assist in controlling the pest. It is also desirable to grow pest resistant crops where this is possible.

The role of nature in biological control
Nature has its own way of controlling the multiplication of insect pests; birds, spiders and other creatures are natural enemies of many insects, hunting and preying upon them at all stages of their development. Such ecological factors are called the natural balance. During the sixties, an ecological approach was developed to avoid upsetting the natural balance and causing drastic changes to the habitat or environment which normally forms their home. One such approach involved introducing certain beetles, viz. COCCINELLIDAE, to prey on pest species such as aphids and flea beetles on plants. Another involved the importation of natural enemies to regulate insect pests. These measures aimed to develop natural rather than chemical controls, keeping the multiplication of beetle pests to a minimum. Since the majority of ants and spiders are to some extent predaceous, they have been used to prey on larvae of COLEOPTERA (beetles) as well as LEPIDOPTERA (butterflies and moths).

CULTURAL CONTROL
Common cultural controls in destroying insects include mechanical means such as the constant destruction of breeding sites of pests by burning them or burying them deep into the ground. Deep and thorough ploughing has long been considered beneficial in insect control, for this often results in burying the insects. Recent tests on growing deep covers over breeding sites of *Oryctes rhinoceros* and *Xylotrupes gideon* have also been found to be very successful.

Diversification in farming and crop rotation are sanitary measures which in some ways help to eliminate insect pests and their breeding sites, but are not necessarily very effective measures in the short term.

Use of pathogenic organisms
The idea of pest control by pathogenic organisms was first investigated by Metchnikow in 1880 when he applied the Green Muscardine Fungus, *Metarrhizium (Isaria) anisopliae*, against *Anisoplia* (a

cockchafer) and *Cleonus* (a weevil), which do much damage to cultivated crops in Russia. Later, Petch in his general work in a series of papers in the *Transactions of the British Mycological Society* records a number of trials of artificial dissemination of fungi to control pests. Attempts to produce such epidemics have met with limited success but this method is still very promising.

In recent years, the study of bacteria pathogenic to insects has developed greatly, and the control of a number of insect pests, mainly LEPIDOPTERA, has been successfully achieved by ordinary spraying methods using a preparation of bacterial spores, such as *Bacillus thuringiensis*. Other pathogens like viruses and protozoa, have also been considered for biological control, but they are more difficult to exploit artificially. This is another promising line for deeper investigation in connection with the effects they have on the insect pests.

Mechanical methods
Mechanical means serve to ward off injurious animals or to kill them directly without making use of poison. Although handpicking of insect pests is hardly practical on agricultural crops, it is useful with garden crops. Light-traps, baits and collecting with nets may help to reduce their population. Banding of fruit trees is quite useful to prevent attacks of larvae.

CHEMICAL CONTROL

Man's efforts to control harmful insects with insecticides have encountered two intractable difficulties. The first is that the pesticides developed up to now have been so broad in their effect that they have been toxic not only to the pest at which they were aimed but also to other insects. To make matters worse some are passed along the food chain and present a hazard to other organisms including man. The second difficulty is that insects have shown a remarkable ability to develop resistance to insecticides.

'In poisoning the pests that each year destroy crops worth billions of dollars, are we also unwittingly poisoning ourselves?' The editor of the National Geographic Society of the U.S.A. raised this question in the issue, 'The Pesticide Dilemma' (February, 1980).

Insecticides

Insecticides may be likened in many ways to antibiotics. They are used in controlling the infestation of certain insect pests in cultivation. However in the application of these toxic products many other harmless and beneficial insects may be killed. Additionally such dangerous chemicals can prove fatal to birds, mammals and even man. Their full genetic effects in the long term are currently under study. Thus, the safest insecticides are those with a narrow spectrum effect, killing only the species of pest at which they are directed, without affecting man and his environment.

Scientists have noticed that the more they throw pesticides and insecticides at their enemies the more are they surviving: already what were once extremely successful pesticides are losing their effectiveness because of the evolution of resistant strains of pests. The development of these strains is called loss of biological efficiency. It is a natural response to the introduction of these products into the animal's environment and it is extremely well-documented.

The ill-considered use of insecticides, while raising crop yields, has already brought whole populations of mammals, birds and fishes to the brink of extermination. Rachel Carson in her *Silent Spring* (1962) produced a powerful indictment that portrays the results of human carelessness and irresponsibility in the mass use of persistent chemicals against insects, weeds and animal pests, which upset the balance of nature and the ecosystem. Arrayed in *Silent Spring*, all the facts have stimulated a reappraisal of the adequacy of information on pesticide and insecticide residues and their persistence in our environment. Additionally, it has produced public anxiety that both pesticides and insecticides might prove unmanageable poisons.

International legislation on the implementation and use of pesticides and insecticides was thus tightened because of irremediable environmental damage through the ignorant misuse of such deadly chemicals. In most countries, precautionary measures are required by the users. In Malaysia, the local government has published numerous guides on the methods of applying and spraying of selected brands of insecticides to farmers and cultivators, and has set programmes to educate young farmers in agricultural management. Special guidance has also been given by the staff of Agricultural Stations to assist farmers in the handling of toxic chemicals which includes the wearing of prescribed protective clothing specified for particular operations; keeping such poisons away from children; and avoiding breathing in the spray or fumes of the insecticides when spraying or mixing.

INTEGRATED CONTROL

In recent years, integrated control has become popular among entomologists and agriculturalists. This control may be defined as the management of the totality of relations, existing or introduced, between the crop and the pests, to achieve the best productive result. This approach also includes the study of pests in relation to the climate, to the plant, and to the other living creatures in the environment, which influence the economic control measures incorporated within the ecosystem.

Although integrated control is based on the best ecological studies and experiments, the techniques for its application in full are still under development. In addition, a further study based on the efficiency of agro-management, the changing climatic conditions, the effect of applying toxic chemicals and the relation between crop production and the existing ecosystem should be carried out too.

Methods of integrating biological and chemical controls are now under consideration. It is hoped that they will eventually achieve the ultimate victory against the *so-called* insect pests.

GLOSSARY

Abdomen   The last part of the three divisions of the body of an insect (Fig. 3)
Acrid   Bitterly pungent, irritating, corrosive
Aedeagus   The male intromittent organ, the penis
Aestivation   Dormancy during a warm or dry season
Anal end   The last abdominal segment (Fig. 3)
Anatomy   The science dealing with the form and structure of living organisms
Antenna (*pl* antennae)   Segmented and jointed sensory organ found in pairs on the head above the mouth-parts (Fig. 3)
Antennal club   The enlarged distal segment of a clubbed antenna (Fig. 6)
Antennal groove   A groove in the head capsule which joins the basal segments of the antennae (Fig. 6)
Anterior   In front, before
Anther   The pollen-forming part of the stamen
Antibiotic   A chemical compound produced by and obtained from certain living cells especially lower plant cells, such as bacteria and moulds, or an equivalent synthetic compound, which is antagonistic to some other form of life, especially pathogenic or noxious organisms.
Aphytophagous   Feeding on vegetable debris, animal materials and/or larvae of other insects.
Apical   At the end, the outermost part
Apterous   Wingless
Aquatic   Living in water
Arboreal   Living in, connected with trees
Arcuate   Bent like a bow
Arolium (*pl* arolia)   A structure of segments at the apex of the last tarsal segment between the claws (Fig. 7)
Asperate   With rough or harsh surface

Band A broad transverse marking
Bifid Forked
Bifurcate Divided into two, forked
Bituberculate With two tubercles or swellings

Camouflage Disguise or deception; the act or means of disguising things to deceive an enemy
Cannibalistic Having the habit of eating its own kind or young
Capitate With an apical knob-like enlargement; capitate antennae (Fig. 5).
Carina (*pl* carinae) A keel-like part or ridge
Carinate Ridged or keeled
Caudal Pertaining to the tail or the posterior end of the abdomen
Cercus (*pl* cerci) One of a pair of appendages at the end of the abdomen
Chestnut Bright reddish-brown colour
Chitin A nitrogenous polysaccharide occurring in the cuticle of arthropods
Class A subdivision of a phylum
Clavate Club-shaped; clavate antennae (Fig. 5)
Cleft Forked or split
Clubbed With the distal part enlarged
Clypeus A sclerite, between the frons and the labium on the lower part of the face
Coalesce To grow together or into one body; to unite so as to form one mass
Cockchafer Large beetle of the family SCARABAEIDAE that flies with a loud whirring sound and is destructive to vegetation
Cocoon A silken covering enclosing the pupa
Commensal Applied to animals or plants which live as tenants of others and share their food
Complementary Complementing each other (of two or more things)
Complete metamorphosis The full development of an insect which includes all the stages: egg (ovum), larva, pupa and adult
Compost Prepared mixture of rotten organic matter or manure for use in horticulture
Compound eye An eye composed of many smaller hexagonal facets called ommatidia that are very closely joined together (Fig. 3)

Contiguous   In close proximity without actually touching
Coxa (*pl* coxae)   The basal segment of the leg (Fig. 7)
Cross pollination   The transference of pollen from one plant to another of the same species by wind or insects
Cuticle   The non-cellular outer part of the body wall of an insect

Data   Facts (in this context including things known from the habits and habitat of an insect)
Decumbent   (Of a plant) Reclining on the ground but with ascending apex or extremity
Deflexed   Bent downward
Defoliate   To destroy the leaves of a plant or tree or an area of forest
Dentate   Toothed
Denticulate   With minute tooth-like projections
Dipterocarp   A member of the genus DIPTEROCARPUS, comprising East Indian trees characterized by two wings on the summit of the fruit, formed by enlargement of two of the calyx lobes
Dissemination   The act of scattering, sowing in various places
Distal   Towards the end of an appendage
Diurnal   Active during the daytime
Divaricate   Extending outwards and then curving inward or towards each other distally
Diversification   The act of making something different or various
Dorsal   Top or uppermost
Dorsomesal   Along the mid-dorsal line

Ecdysis (*pl* ecdyses)   The process of shedding or moulting the exoskeleton
Ecology   The scientific study of the interrelations of living organisms and their environment
Ecosystem   The fundamental unit in ecology, comprising the living organisms and the non-living elements interacting in a certain defined area
Elytron (*pl* elytra)   A thickened forewing
Emarginate   Notched
Emergence   Coming out of an adult from the last nymphal skin or the pupal case
Encasement   A case-like covering
Entomologist   A person who studies entomology

Entomology   A branch of natural history which deals with the study of insects

Epidemic   Simultaneously affecting large numbers in a community, used mainly of disease

Epimeron (*pl* epimera)   The posterior of two sclerites typically composing the pleuron (the lateral expansion of a tergite) in insects

Episternum (*pl* episterna)   The anterior portion of a pleuron

Excrescence   An outgrowth

Exoskeleton   A supporting structure on the outside of the body

Exuviae   The cast skins of an arthropod

Facet   The external surface of an individual compound eye unit

Family   A subdivision of a superfamily. Latin family names end in *-idae*

Fecundity   The ability to produce offspring frequently and in large numbers

Femur (*pl* femora)   The leg segment between the trochanter and the tibia (Fig. 7)

Filamentous   Very fine, thread-like

Filiform   Hair-like or thread-like; filiform antennae (Fig. 5)

Flabellate   With fan-like processes; flabellate antennae (Fig. 5)

Frons   An impaired sclerite on the front of the head

Gall   An abnormal growth caused by the attack of a pest or disease organism

Gena (*pl* genae)   The part of the head on each side below and behind the compound eye; the cheek (Fig. 6)

Geniculate   Elbowed; geniculate antennae (Fig. 5)

Genitalia   The sexual or reproductive organs; external sexual organs

Genus (*pl* genera)   A group of closely related species; the first name in a binomial or trinomial Latinized scientific name

Glabrous   Smooth, hairless

Granular   Composed of or bearing granules or grains

Granule   A small grain or particle

Gregarious   Living in groups

Grub   A scarabaeiform larva, without abdominal prolegs, only three pairs of thoracic true legs, usually sluggish

Gula A sclerite on the ventral side of the head between the sub-mentum and post-sternum (Fig. 6)
Gular suture Longitudinal suture of one side of the gula (Fig. 6)

Head The anterior body region which bears the antennae, compound eyes and mouth-parts (Fig. 3)
Herbivorous Feeding on plants
Hibernation The period in which a larva passes the whole of the 'winter' months in a state similar to sleep

Insecticide An agent that kills insects
Insectivorous Feeding on insects
Instar The stage of an insect between successive moults, the first instar being the stage between hatching and the first moult
Integument The outer covering of the body (of a larva)

Keeled Ridged

Labial palpus (*pl* labial palpi) One of a pair of small feeler-like structures arising from the labium (Fig. 6)
Labium The lower lip in the mouth-parts (Fig. 3)
Labrum The upper lip in the mouth-parts (Fig. 4)
Lamellate With plate-like segments; lamellate antennae (Fig. 5)
Larva (*pl* larvae) Caterpillar or grub
Lateral On or pertaining to the side
Ligula The terminal lobes of the labium (Fig. 6)
Longitudinal Lengthwise of the body
Luminescent Producing light

Mandible One of the anterior pair of mouth-part structures, a jaw (Fig. 6)
Mandibulate With jaws fitted for chewing and cutting
Margined With a sharp or keel-like lateral edge
Maxilla (*pl* maxillae) Paired mouth-part structure immediately posterior to the mandibles
Maxillary palpus (*pl* maxillary palpi) A small feeler-like structure arising from the maxilla (Fig. 6)
Median In the middle, on the mid-line of the body

Membranous Like a membrane, thin film of tissue, on the hind wings of a beetle, usually transparent
Mentum The distal part of the labium (Fig. 3)
Mesial Middle, median
Mesomentum The middle portion of the mentum
Meson The intermediate portion between two sutures
Mesothorax The second segment of the thorax (Fig. 1)
Metabolism The process by which food is built up into living matter or by which living matter is broken down into simpler substances
Metamorphosis (*pl* metamorphoses) Change in form during development
Metathorax The third segment of the thorax (Fig. 1)
Metasternum (*pl* metasterna) The ventral sclerite of the metathorax
Millimetre 0.001 metre or 0.03937 inch
Mollusc (*pl* molluscs) One of a class of animals with soft bodies (and often hard shells)
Moniliform Bead-like, with rounded segments; moniliform antennae (Fig. 5)
Morphology Branch of biology dealing with the form and structure of animals and plants
Moult A process of shedding the exoskeleton; the ecdysis

Nocturnal Active at night
Notum (*pl* nota) The dorsal surface of a body segment

Ocellus (*pl* ocelli) A simple eye of an insect or other arthropod
Ommatidium (*pl* ommatidia) A single visual unit of a compound eye
Oral Pertaining to the mouth
Ostium bursae An opening in the anal end of the female which receives the aedeagus of the male on fertilization
Oviposit To lay or deposit eggs

Palpus (*pl* palpi) A segmented process borne by the maxillae or labium
Parasite An animal living on or in another and getting its food from it

Pathogen Any disease-producing agent or micro-organism
Pathogenic Pertaining to or causing a disease
Pectinate With projections like the teeth of a comb; pectinate antennae (Fig. 5)
Perforate Pierced with a hole or holes
Pheromone Any of a class of hormonal substances secreted by an individual and stimulating a physiological or behavioural response from an individual of the same species
Phylum (*pl* phyla) One of the major divisions of the animal kingdom
Physiology The science dealing with the function of various parts and organs of living organisms
Phytophagous Feeding on plants
Pilose Covered with soft hairs
Pollen grain Fine powder produced by flowers which fertilizes other flowers when carried to them by the wind, insects, etc.
Pollination The process in which pollen grains are transferred to the stigma of the pistil of a flower
Pollinator An agent that causes pollination
Post-median After the median
Post-mentum After the mentum
Predaceous Feeding as a predator
Predator An animal that preys and feeds on other animals
Proboscis The extended beak-like mouth-parts
Proleg One of the fleshy abdominal legs of certain insect larvae but not larvae of COLEOPTERA
Pronotum (*pl* pronota) The dorsal sclerite of the prothorax
Prothorax The first segment of the thorax (Fig. 1)
Protozoa Animals of the simplest type formed of a single cell (and usually microscopic)
Proximal The topmost or the uppermost part
Pubescence Short fine hairs
Pubescent Downy, covered with short fine hairs
Pupa (*pl* pupae) The stage between the larva and the adult in insects with complete metamorphosis; a dormant stage
Pupate Transform to a pupa
Pygidium The last dorsal segment of the abdomen (Fig. 3)

Reafforestation The re-planting of forests

Recurved Curved upward or backward
Reticulate Like a network
Rostrum Beak or snout (Fig. 6)

Scape The basal segment of the antennae (Fig. 6)
Scarabaeiform In the form of a scarab
Scavenger An animal that lives on decaying flesh and materials or animal wastes
Scent gland A gland producing an odorous substance or scent
Scientific name An internationally recognized Latinized name of a species or subspecies which consists of the generic, specific and sometimes the subspecific names. When printed, these are italicized
Sclerite A hardened body wall plate bounded by sutures
Scutellum A more or less triangular sclerite of a thoracic notum (Fig. 3)
Scutum The middle division of a thoracic notum (Fig. 3)
Segment A subdivision of the body or an appendage (Fig. 1)
Semiaquatic Living in wet places or partially in water
Serrate With saw-like edge; serrate antennae (Fig. 5)
Setaceous Bristle-like
Seta (*pl* setae) A bristle
Sinuous Having many curves, bends or turns
Species A group of animals or plants, subordinate in classification to a genus which is able to breed with each other but not with other groups
Spermatophore Reproductive cell in the fertilizing fluid of a male
Spindle-shaped Elongate and cylindrical, thickened in the middle and tapering at the ends
Spiracular bristle A bristle very close to a spiracle
Spiracular plate A plate-like sclerite next to or surrounding the spiracle
Spiracle A minute external opening at the side of each thoracic and abdominal segment, used for respiration
Spur A movable spine on the leg located at the apex of the segment
Sternite A sclerite on the ventral side of the body
Stigma (*pl* stigmata) The uppermost tip of the pistil (female structure of the flower) with sticky surface for receiving pollen-grains
Stria (*pl* striae) A groove or depressed line

Striate   With grooves or depressed lines
Stridulate   To make a noise by rubbing two structures or surfaces together
Stripe   A longitudinal colour marking
Subclass   A major subdivision of a class
Subfamily   A major subdivision of a family; Latinized subfamily names end in *-inea*
Subgenus (*pl* subgenera)   A major subdivision of a genus
Submentum   The basal part of the labium (Fig. 6)
Suborder   A major subdivision of an order
Subphylum (*pl* subphyla)   A major subdivision of a phylum
Superfamily   A group of closely related families. Latinized superfamily names end in *-oidea*
Superficial   Of or pertaining to the surface, external or outward body
Suture   An external (visible) grooveline in the body wall
Symbiosis   The living together of two dissimilar organisms, especially when this association is mutually beneficial
Synchrony   Coincidence in time; simultaneousness

Tarsal claw   A claw at the apex of the tarsus (Fig. 7)
Tarsal spur   A large spine located at the distal end of the tibia
Tarsus (*pl* tarsi)   The segmented part of the leg beyond the tibia
Taxonomist   A person who classifies and describes animals and plants into categories of varying rank, based on similarities and differences
Tergite   The dorsal surface of an abdominal segment
Tergum   The dorsal surface of any segment
Testaceous   Having a test or shell-like covering; of a brick-red, brownish-red, or brownish-yellow colour
Thorax   The body region between the head and abdomen
Tibia (*pl* tibae)   The segment of the leg between the femur and the tarsus (Fig. 7)
Tibial spur   A large spine located at the distal end of the tibia
Trilobite   Any marine arthropod of the extinct group *Trilobita*, from the Palaeozoic era, having a flattened, oval body varying in length
Toxic   Poisonous, pertaining to poisoning
Toxicity   The ability of a chemical to produce injury once it reaches a susceptible site in or on the body

Transverse suture   A suture across the mesonotum (Fig. 7)
Trochanter   The segment of the leg between the coxa and the femur (Fig. 7)
Trochantin   A small sclerite in the thoracic wall immediately anterior to the base of the coxa
Tubercle   A small knob-like or rounded protuberance

Vector   A carrier, an animal (often an arthropod) that transfers an infective agent from one host to another
Vein   A thickened line in the wing
Ventral   Lower or underneath the underside of the body
Vertex (*pl* vertexes)   The highest point, or the crown, or the top of the head

Weevil   A beetle with a snout or beak which is of economical importance
Wireworm   An elateriform larva with a slender, elongate and heavily sclerotized body, usually hairless and without prolegs

An Explanatory Note on Some Terms Used in the Text
Assam   A part of Tibet in China, north-east India, northern Bangladesh and northern Burma.
Borneo   East Malaysia and Kalimantan of Indonesia.
Himalaya   Northern India, northern Bangladesh, Nepal and part of Tibet in China, including Sikkim.
Indo-China   Vietnam, Cambodia, Laos and Thailand.
P. Malaysia   Peninsular Malaysia which zoogeographically includes Singapore Island.
South-east Asia   Vietnam, Cambodia, Laos, Thailand, Malaysia, Singapore, Indonesia and the Philippines.
Sundaland   This zoogeographical subregion indicates an ancient continent, consisting of Peninsular Malaysia, Singapore, Sumatra, Borneo, Java, Palawan, Balabac Island and their satellite islands, which existed less than a million years ago, most of which have now sunk into the sea, forming the shallow Sunda Shelf and the remaining islands and Peninsular Malaysia.
Note that all the above are zoogeographical names of places and are used for convenience only, with no political significance.

BIBLIOGRAPHY

ARROW, G.J. (1910), *The fauna of British India, including Ceylon and Burma. Coleoptera: Lamellicornia (Cetoniinae and Dynastinae)*, Taylor and Francis, London.
ARROW, G.J. (1917), *The fauna of British India, including Ceylon and Burma. Coleoptera: Lamellicornia*, **II**, *(Rutelinae, Desmonycinae and Euchirinae)*, Taylor and Francis, London.
ASLAM, N.A. (1961), An assessment of some internal characters in the higher classification of the Curculionidae *s.l.*, *Transaction of the Royal Entomological Society of London*, **113**, 417–489.
BANKS, C.S. (1906), The principal insects attacking the Coconut palm, *Philippine Journal of Science*, **I**, 143–167; 211–218.
BARLOW, H.S. (1975), Decline of the good earth, *The Planter*, Kuala Lumpur.
BARLOW, H.S. and CHEW, P.S. (1970), The Rhinoceros Beetle, *Oryctes rhinoceros*, in young oil palms replanted after rubber on some estates in Western Malaysia, Paper presented at the Malaysian Crop Protection Conference (unpublished), Kuala Lumpur.
BELL, R.T. (1967), Coxal cavities and the classification of the Adephaga (Coleoptera), *Annual of the Entomological Society of America*, **60**, 101–107.
BENESH, B. (1960), W. Junk's *'Coleopterorum Catalogus Supplementa' Pars 8: Lucanidae*, The Hague.
BENTHALL, J. (1972), *Ecology, the shaping enquiry*, Longman, London.
BLANEY, W.M. (1976), *How insects live*, Elsevier International Projects, Oxford.
BORAIKO, A.A. (1980), The Pesticide Dilemma, *National Geographic*, **152**(2), 144–183, Washington.
BORROR, D.J. and DELONG, D.M. (1964), *An introduction to the study of insects*, rev. edn., Holt, Rinehart and Winston, New York.

BRITTON, E.B. (1970), Coleoptera (Beetles), In: *The insects of Australia*, MACKERRAS, I.M. (ed.), Chapter 30, Melbourne.

CARPENTER, G.H. and MACDOWELL, M.C. (1912), The mouthparts of some beetle larvae, etc., *Quarterly Journal of Micro Science*, **57**, 373–396.

CARSON, R. (1964), *Silent Spring*, H. Hamilton, London.

CHAPMAN, R.F. (1969), *The insects (structure and function)*, English Universities Press, London.

CHUA, T.H. (1978), Population assessment, distribution and movement in *Cicindela sumatrensis* Hbst. (COLEOPTERA: CICINDELIDAE), *Malayan Nature Journal*, **31**(4), 195–201, Kuala Lumpur.

CLAVAREAU, H. (1913), W. Junk's *'Coleopterorum Catalogus' Pars 51: Chrysomelidae: Sagrinae, Donaciinae, Orsodacninae, Criocerinae*, The Hague.

CORBETT, G.H. (1921), The Rhinoceros Beetle. *Agricultural Bulletin of the Federated Malay States*, **IX**, Kuala Lumpur.

CORBETT, G.H. and PONNIAH (1924), The Red Stripe Weevil of Coconuts, *Bulletin No. 36 of the Department of Agriculture of the Straits Settlements and the Federated Malay States*, Kuala Lumpur.

CORNER, E.J.H. (1952), *Wayside Trees of Malaysia*, Vols. 1 and 2, 2nd edn., Government Printing Office, Singapore.

CROWSON, R.A. (1946), A revision of the genera of the Chrysomelid group Sagrinae (Coleoptera), *Transaction of the Royal Entomological Society of London*, **97**, 75–115.

CROWSON, R.A. (1967), *The natural classification of the families of Coleoptera*, 2nd edn., E.W. Classey, Hampton.

DAMMERMAN, K.W. (1929), *The agricultural zoology of the Malay Archipelago*, J.H. De Bussy, Amsterdam.

DAVIDSON, R.H. (1956), *Insect pests of farm, garden and orchard*, 6th edn., John Wiley and Sons, New York.

DIDIER, R. and SEGUY, E. (1952–1953), *Catalogue Illustre des Lucanides du Globe*, 2 vols. (*Atlas et Texte*), Paris.

EVANS, M.E.G. (1972), The jump of the click beetle (Coleoptera: Elateridae) — a preliminary study, *Journal of Zoology*, **167**, 319–336.

EVANS, M.E.G. (1973), The jump of the click beetle (Coleoptera: Elateridae) — energetics and mechanics, *Journal of Zoology*, **169**, 181–194.

FARD, P., et al. (1963), *Ecology*, Life Nature Library, New York.
FORD, R.L.E. (1973), *Studying insects, a practical guide*, Frederick Warne, London.
FOWLER, W.W. (1912), *Coleoptera. General introduction and Cicindelidae and Paussidae. Fauna of British India including Ceylon and Burma*, Taylor and Francis, London.
GAHAN, C.J. (1906), On a collection of Longicorn Coleoptera from Selangor and Perak, *Journal of the Federated Malay States Museums*, **1**(3), 109–123, Kuala Lumpur.
GAHAN, C.J. (1908), On the larva of *Trictenotoma childreni* Gray, *Melitomma insulare* Fairmaire and *Dascillus cervinus* Linn., *Transaction of the Entomological Society of London*, **1908**, 275–282.
GATER, B. (1925), Insects of African Oil Palms, *Malayan Agricultural Journal*, **XIII**, Kuala Lumpur.
GERBER, G.H., CHURCH, N.S. and REMPEL, J.G. (1971), The anatomy and physiology of the reproductive systems of *Lytta nutalli* Say (Col. Meloidae), **I**, The internal genitalia, *Canadian Journal of Zoology*, **49**, 523–533.
GRAHAM, F., Jr. (1970), *Since Silent Spring*, Fawcett Publications, U.S.A.
GRAVELEY, F.H. (1916), Some lignicolous beetle larvae from India and Borneo, *Records of the Indian Museums*, **12**, 137–175.
GRESSITT, J.L. (1966), Epizoic symbiosis: the Papuan weevil genus *Gymnopholus* (Leptopiinae) symbiotic with cryptogamic plants, oribatid mites, rotifers and nematodes, *Pacific Insects*, **8**, 221–280.
GRESSITT, J.L. and KIMOTO, S. (1963), The Chrysomelidae (Coleopt.) of China and Korea, Part II, *Pacific Insects Monograph*, **1A**, 1–299; (1961), **1B**, 301–1026; Supplement **5**, 921–932.
GRESSITT, J.L., et al. (1970), *Cerambycid beetles of Laos*, Paris.
HAGEN, K.S. (1962), Biology and ecology of predacious Coccinellidae, *Annual Review of Entomology*, **7**, 289–326.
HALFFTER, G. and MATTHEWS, E.G. (1966), The natural history of dung beetles of the subfamily Scarabaeinae (Coleoptera, Scarabaeidae), *Folia entomology of Mexico*, **12–14**, 1–312.
HENDERSON, M.R. (1959), *Malayan wild flowers, Monocotyledons and Dicotyledons*, Malayan Nature Society, Kuala Lumpur.
HINCKS, W.D. and DIBB, J.R. (1958), W. Junk's '*Coleopterorum Catalogus Supplementa*' Pars 142: *Passalidae*, The Hague.
HINTON, H.E. (1945), *A Monograph of the Beetles associated with*

Stored Products, Vol. I, British Museum (Natural History), London.

HODEK, I. (1973), *Biology of Coccinellidae, with keys for identification of larvae by co-authors G.I. Savoiskaya and B. Klausnitzer*, Prague, Czechoslovak Acadami Science, The Hague, Dr W. Junk N.V.

HOLLOWAY, B.A. (1960), Taxonomy and phylogeny in the Lucanidae (Insecta): Coleoptera), *Records of the Dominion Museum*, Wellington, **3**, 321–365.

HOLLOWAY, J.D. and BARLOW, H.S. (1979), The role of taxonomy, reference works and collections of insects in tropical ecology, (unpublished), Kuala Lumpur.

IMMS, A.D. (1957), *General textbook of entomology*, 9th edn., Methuen, London.

INAHARA, N. (1979), On representative species of Lucanidae from the World, *Memories of the Hiei Natural Science Museum* (**2**), Tokyo.

KAPUR, A.P. (1950), The biology and external morphology of the larvae of Epilachninae (Coleoptera, Coccinellidae), *Bulletin of Entomological Research*, **41**, 161–208.

KERREMANS, C. (1906–1914), *Monographie des Buprestides*, J. Janssens, Brussels. 7 vols.

LINSLEY, E.G., EISNER, T. and KLOTS, A.B. (1961), Mimetic assemblages of sibling species of Lycid beetles, *Evolution*, **15**, 15–29.

MACHATSCHKE, J.W. (1974), W. Junk's '*Coleopterorum Catalogus Supplementa': Scarabaeoidea, Melolonthidae, Rutelinae*, The Hague.

MARSHALL, G.A.K. (1916), *The fauna of British India. Coleoptera, Rhynchophora, Curculionidae*, Taylor and Francis, London.

MAULIK, S. (1978), *The fauna of British India, including Ceylon and Burma: Chrysomelidae* (*Hispinae and Cassidinae*), Taylor and Francis, London.

MCCLURE, H.E. (1978), Some arthropods of the dipterocarp forest canopy in Malaya, *Malayan Nature Journal*, **32**(1), 31–51, Kuala Lumpur.

MILLER and KEANA (1972), *Encyclopedia and Dictionary of medicine and nursing*, W.B. Sauders, Toronto.

MJOBERG, E. (1925), The mystery of the so-called 'Trilobite larva' or 'Perty's larvae' definitely solved, *Psyche*, Cambridge, **32**, 119–157.

MORIMOTO, K. (1962), Comparative morphology, phylogeny and systematics of the superfamily Curculionoidea of Japan, **I**, *Journal of the Faculty of Kyushu University, Fukuoka*, **II**, 331–373.

NICOR, H. (1943), *Biological control of insects*, Pelican Books, London.

OLDROYD, H. (1958), *Collecting, preserving and studying insects*, Macmillan, New York.

POLUNIN, I. (1968), Studies on firefly synchrony, *Malayan Nature Journal*, **21**(Supplement) May, xxvi–xxvii, Kuala Lumpur.

SCHENKLING, G. and JUNK, W. (1910–1940), *Coleopterorum Catalogus*, **1–70**, W. Junk Verlag, Berlin.

SHARP, D. (1882), On aquatic carnivorous Coleoptera or Dytiscidae, *Transaction of the Royal Dublin Society*, (2), **2**, 179–1003.

SHELFORD, R. (1907), The larva of *Collyris emarginatus* Dej., *Transaction of the Entomological Society of London*, **1907**, 83–90.

SHELFORD, V.E. (1909), Life-histories and larval habits of the Tiger beetles (Cicindelidae), *Journal of the Linnean Society of Zoology*, **30**, 157–184.

Shikoku Entomological Society (1979), A new subspecies of *Jumnos ruckeri* Saunders from the Malay Peninsula (Coleoptera: Scarabaeidae–Cetoniinae), *Transactions of the Shikoku Entomological Society*, Vol. 149(3/4), Japan.

STANEK, V.J. (1972), *The pictorial encyclopedia of insects*, reprint, Hamlyn Publishing Group, London.

STERN, V.M., *et al.* (1959), The integrated control concept, *Hilgardia* **29**(2), England.

TUNG, V.W.Y. (1981), A check-list cum census of species and subspecies of Lucanids (stag beetles), Order COLEOPTERA, of Malaysia, in press.

TWEEDIE, M.W.F. and HARRISON, J.L. (1970), *Malayan Animal Life*, Longman, Kuala Lumpur.

USHER, G. (1966), *A Dictionary of Botany*, Constable, London.

WALLS, I.G. (1979), *A–Z of garden pests and problems*, Collins, London.

WESTWOOD, J.O. (1839), *Introduction to the Modern Classification of Insects*, Vol. I, Longman, Brown, Orme, Green and Longmans, London.

WOOD, B.J. (1968), Pests of oil palms in Malaysia, *The Planter*, Kuala Lumpur.

WOOD, B.J. (1973), Integrated Control: Critical assessment of case histories in developing countries, *The Planter*, Kuala Lumpur.

WOTTON, A. (1978), *Insects are animals too*, David and Charles, Devon.

YASUDA, Y. and OKAJIMA, S. (1980), *Beetles of the World*, Gakken, Tokyo.

YUSOPE (1920), Insect pests of paddy, *Agricultural Bulletin of the Federated Malay States*, **VIII**, Kuala Lumpur.

FOOD PLANT INDEX

Agathis flarescens (Conifer) 71
Albizzia spp (Leguminosae) 70, 73, 89
Amarathus spp 66
Ardistia elliptica 80
Areca catechu (Areca palm) 66
Aristolochia 73, 75

Bamboo (*Bambusa* spp) 68, 69
Banana (*Musa sapientium*) 58, 59, 90, 107
Beans (*Phaseolus* spp) 84, 101, 110
Bignoniaceae spp 78

Calamus palm 82
Casuarina spp 70
Chillies (*Capsicum annum*) 59, 84
Cinchona spp (Cinchona) 104
Cinnamon 73, 88
Citrus spp (Lemon, lime, orange, pomelo) 70, 73, 74
Cocoa (*Theobroma cacao*) 36, 42, 48, 58, 60, 65, 70, 73, 74, 91, 92, 102, 104, 106
Coconut palm (*Cocus nucifera*) 9, 42, 57, 58, 66, 67
Coffee (*Coffea* spp) 42, 48, 58, 62, 64, 77, 92
Convolvulaceae 82, 99, 101
Cordia bushes 73
Cucumber (*Cucumis sativus*) 59
Cucurbitaceae (Cucumber, gourd, water-melon) 84, 101

Dadap (*Erythrina* spp) 62, 89, 90
Dahlia spp (Garden plant) 59

Durian (*Durio zibethinus*) 47, 71, 73, 86

Eugenia spp 52, 85

Ficus spp (Fig trees, India rubber) 89, 91
Fungi 19, 51, 81

Grain (*Gramineae*) 19, 103, 107, 109, 110
Grasses (*Gramineae*) 66, 78, 79
Groundnut (*Arachis hypogaea*) 64, 65

Hevea brasiliensis (Para rubber) 9, 36, 66, 67, 84
Hibiscus spp (Shoe flower, Roselle) 75, 84, 102
Hibiscus rosa (Hibiscus flower) 80

Ipomoea spp (Sweet potato) 101

Jack fruit (*Artocarpus integrifolia*) 91
Johannesteijsmannia altifrons (Undergrowth palm) 9
Jute 73

Kapok, or silk cotton (*Ceiba pentandra*) 36, 46, 47, 58, 70, 72, 73, 74, 86, 89, 95, 97, 99, 102, 104
Klamath weed 112
Koompassia excelsa 90

Lantana 59, 64, 73, 74, 75, 78, 82, 83, 92, 93, 99, 100

Leguminosae (Pulses; Green, mature plants) 73, 77, 78
Loranthus 36

Mahogany (*Swietenia* spp) 46, 72, 88
Maize (*Zea mays*) 60, 64, 65
Mango (*Mangifera indica*) 71, 86, 91, 104, 105
Melanorrhoea 52
Mimosa spp (Leguminosae) 83, 93, 100

Nephelium lappaceum (Rambutan) 70, 74
Nipa fructicans (Water palm) 24, 66
Nutmeg (*Myristica fragrans*) 89

Oil palm (*Elaeis guinensis*) 9, 42, 57, 66, 67, 103, 106, 111

Paddy, or rice (*Oryza sativa*) 107, 110
Palms (*Palmeae*) 57, 58, 66, 67, 100, 106

Parkia speciosa (Leguminosae) 86, 97
Pepper (*Piper nigrum*) 58, 105
Portulacae 66
Potatoes 100, 109

Red meranti (*Shorea* spp) 47
Rose (*Rosa* spp) 58, 68, 92

Sago palm (*Metroxylon sagus*) 66
Shorea spp 46, 54, 68
Shorea curtisii 47
Sonneratis caseolaris 80
Soya bean (*Glycine hispida*) 65
Sugar-cane (*Saccharum officinarum*) 58, 60, 65, 66, 67, 107

Tapioca (*Manihot utilissima*) 60, 65, 66
Tobacco (*Nicotina* spp) 60
Tomato (*Lycopersicum esculentum*) 84

Vaccinium glabrescens 85
Vegetables 58, 59, 60, 102

GENERAL INDEX

Note: Page references in bold indicate main descriptions.

abdominalis, Macronota xvii, **68**
Aceraulis grandius xiii, **56**
acuminatus, Aegus xii, **43**
acutus, Agrilus **73**
ADEPHAGA 4, **17**, 18
Adoretus compressus xiv, **58**
Adoretus sinicus **58**
Adoretus umbrosus **59**
adusta, Xylorhiza xvii, **96**
Aegus acuminatus xii, **43**
Aegus capitatus xii, **43**
Aegus falcifer xii, **43**
aenescense, Sinuaria **78**
aeneus, Autocrates xvi, **84**
aerata, Odontolabis xiii, **49**
Aethalodes verrucosus xvi, **88**
affinis, Xylotrechus xviii, **97**, 98
Agestrata orichalcea xiii, **59**
Agrilus acutus **73**
albersi, Cyclommatus xii, **45**
albofasciata, Batocera xvi, 86, **88**
Alcides cinchonae xviii, **104**
Alcides leeweeni **104**
Allotopus fruhstorferi xii, **44**
Allotopus moseri xii, **44**
Allotopus rosenbergi xii, **44**
ALTICINAE **102**
Alurnus sp xvii, **103**
anchoralis, Anomala **59**
Anhammus deleni xvi, **87**
Anisolema sp xv, **83**
Anisoplia sp 115
anisopliae, Metarrhizium 115
Anomala anchoralis **59**
Anomala dorsalis **60**

Anomala obsoleta **60**
Anomala viridis xiv, **59**, 60
Anoplophora longehirsuta xvi, **87**
Anoplophora medembachi xvi, **87**
Anoplophora zonatrix xiv, **87**
antaeus, Dorcus xii, **46**
Apogonia destructor xiv, 58, **65**
approximator, Aristobia xvi, **88**
arcuata, Coccinella xv, **83**
Arcyphorus conformis xvii, **98**
Aristobia approximator xvi, **88**
armigera, Hispa xvii, **102**
ARTHROPODA 3
Aspidomorpho inquinata xvii, **100**
Aspidomorpho miliaris xvii, 100, **101**
atlas, Chalcosoma xiv, 9, 11, 57, **61**, 62
atripennis, Aulacophora **102**
audoniwi, Oxyropterus xv, **77**, 78
Aulacophora atripennis **102**
Aulacophora coffeae xvii, **101**
Aulacophora flavomarginata xvii, **102**
Aulacophora niasiensis **102**
aurulenta, Cicindela xii, **35**
Autocrates aeneus xvi, **84**

Bacillus thuringiensis 116
basalis, Therates x, **36**
Batocera albofasciata xvi, 86, **88**
Batocera davidis xvi, **89**
Batocera hector xvii, **89**
Batocera parryi xvii, **89**
Belionota prasina xv, **70**

bellicosus, Odontolabis xiii, **51**
bicolor, Megaloxantha 69, 74, 75
biplagiata, Mimistena xviii, **98**
bonelli, Collyris, xii, 34, **35**
borneensis, Sagra xvii, **103**
Brachycerus congestus xviii, **107**
brianus, Combe xvi, **90**
brookeana, Odontolabis xiii, **49**
bucephalus, Dorcus **48**
bucephalus, Heliocopris xiv, **60**
BUPRESTIDAE 4, 8, 11, 17, 23, 33, **69**, 110, 111, 112
BUPRESTOIDEA 4
buqueti, Chrysochroa xv, **71**
buqueti, Cyrtotrachelus xviii, **105**
buqueti, Sagra xvii, 16, **102**, 103

Calais lacteus xv, 76, **77**
Calandra granaria **107**
Calandra oryzae **107**
Callopistus castelnaudi xiv, **70**
Campsosternus leachei xv, **77**
canaliculatus, Cyclommatus xii, **45**
CANTHAROIDEA 4
capitatus, Aegus xii, **43**
CARABIDAE 4, **36**, 37
CARABOIDEA 4
carinatum, Euryorthrum xvii, **94**
Casnoidea interstitialis xii, **37**
CASSIDINAE 7, 99, 100
castaneum, Tribolum 110
castelnaudi, Callopistus xiv, **70**
castelnaudi, Mormolyce xii, **38**
castelnaudi, Odontolabis xiii, 11, **49**, 50
castelnaudii, Chrysochroa xv, **71**
Catharsius molossus xiv, **60**
Catoxantha opulenta xiv, xv, **70**
caucasus, Chalcosoma xiv, **62**
Celosterna sulphurea xvii, **97**
CERAMBYCIDAE 4, 11, 16, 26, 33, **85**, 86, 110, 111
CETONIINAE 112
Chalchromus sp xv, **80**
Chalcosoma atlas xiv, 9, 11, 57, **61**, 62

Chalcosoma caucasus xiv, **62**
Chalcosoma moellenkampi xiv, **62**
Cheirotonus parryi xiv, **63**
chrisostome, Iridotaenia xv, **74**
CHRYSOMELIDAE 4, **99**, 100, 110
CHRYSOMELOIDEA 4
Chrysobothris chrysonotata **75**
Chrysobothris militaris xv, **75**
Chrysochroa buqueti xv, **71**
Chrysochroa castelnaudi xv, **71**
Chrysochroa ephippigera xv, **71**
Chrysochroa fulgidissima xv, **72**
Chrysochroa fulminans xv, 11, **72**
Chrysochroa wallacei xv, 3, **73**
Chrysochroa weyersii xv, **73**
chrysonotata, Chrysobothris **75**
Cibister roeselli xv, 11, **40**
Cicindela aurulenta xii, **35**
Cicindela sexpunctata 35
Cicindela sumatrensis xii, 3, **35**
Cicindela versicolor xii, **35**
CICINDELIDAE 4, 14, 16, **34**, 36, 37, 38
cinchonae, Alcides **104**
cinnamoeus, Prosopocoilus xiii, **52**
Cladognathus giraffa xii, **44**
Cleonus sp 116
CLERIDAE 1, 110
Coccinella arcuata xv, **83**
Coccinella transversalis 83
COCCINELLIDAE 4, 7, 16, 23, **82**, 110, 115
coffeae, Aulacophora xvii, **101**
COLEOPTERA 1, **3**, 4, 5, 14, 15, 16, 32, 85, 109, 115
Collyris bonelli xii, 34, **35**
Collyris tuberculata 36
colossus, Protocerius xviii, **106**
Combe brianus xvi, **90**
compressus, Adoretus xiv, **58**
conformis, Arcyphorus xvii, **98**
congestus, Brachycerus xviii, **107**
consanguineus, Zonopterus xvii, **95**
consocius, Xylotrechus **98**
COPRINAE 60

Cosmopolites sordidus **107**
crassipes, Selenocosmia 26
Cryptorhynchus gravis xviii, **104**
Cryptorhynchus mangiferae **104**
CUCUJOIDEA 4
CURCULIONIDAE 4, 10, 11, 16, 17, **103**, 104, 110, 111
CURCULIONOIDEA 4
curvidens, Dorcus xii, **46**
Cyclommatus albersi xii, **45**
Cyclommatus canaliculatus xii, **45**
Cyclommatus giraffa **44**
Cyclommatus lunifer xii, **45**, 46
Cyclommatus montanellus **46**
Cyclommatus terandus xii, **46**
Cyriopalus wallacei xvi, **90**
Cyrtotrachelus buqueti xviii, **105**
Cyrtotrachelus dux **105**

deleni, Anhammus xvi, **87**
daleni, Megaloxantha xv, **74**
dalmani, Odontolabis xiii, **50**
davidi, Trictenotoma xvi, **85**
davidis, Batocera xvi, **89**
decempunctata, Prioptera xvii, **101**
Demochroa gratiosa xv, **73**
destructor, Apogonia xiv, 58, **65**
deyrollei, Hexarthrius xii, **48**
Diamesus osculans xv, 40, **41**
Diastocera wallichi xvi, **90**
Diceros dives xviii, **68**
didieri, Rhaetulus xiv, **54**
dimidiata, Pachyteria xvi, **93**
diophthalma, Paraleprodera xvii, **95**
dives, Diceros xviii, **68**
dominus, Heliocopris xiv, **61**
Dorcus antaeus xii, **46**
Dorcus bucephalus **48**
Dorcus curvidens xii, **46**
Dorcus gypaetus xii, **47**
Dorcus parryi **47**
Dorcus reichei xii, **47**
Dorcus thoracicus **47**
Dorcus titanus xii, 42, **47**
dorsalis, Anomala **60**
Dorysthenes planicollis xvi, **90**

Duliticola sp xiii, **80**
dux, Cyrtotrachelus **105**
DYNASTINAE 8, 9, 57
DYTISCIDAE 4, 11, 16, **39**, 40, 111, 112

Elaeidobius kamerunicus 103, 111
elaphus, Prosopocoilus xiii, **52**
ELATERIDAE 4, 17, 23, **76**, 110
ELATEROIDEA 4
elegans, Glenea xiv, 3
elongata, Leprodera xvi, **92**
Encaustes sp xv, **81**
Encaustes verticalis xv, **81**
Epepeotes lateralis xvi, **91**
Epepeotes luscus xvi, **91**
ephippigera, Chrysochroa xv, **71**
Epicedia maculatrix xvii, **95**
Epilachna indica xv, 82, **83**, 84
Epilachna vigintioctopunctata 84
equestria, Pachyteria xvi, **93**, 94
EROTYLIDAE 4, **81**
EUCHININAE 63
Eupatorus gracilicornis xiv, 57, **64**
Eurybatus lesnei xvi, **92**
Euryphagus lundi xvi, **91**
Euryorthrum carinatum xvii, **94**
Euselatus sponsa xiv, **64**
Exopholis hypoleuca xiv, **64**

falcifer, Aegus xii, **43**
feai, Prosopocoilus xiii, **52**
femoralis, Odontolabis xiii, **50**
ferrugineus, Rhynchophorus xviii, 104, **106**
festiva, Xystrocera xvii, 86, **96**
fimbriata, Parepicedia xvii, **95**
fisheri, Macrotoma xvii, **91**
flavomarginata, Aulacophora xvii, **102**
forceps, Prosopocoilus xiii, **53**
forcifer, Prosopocoilus xiii, **53**
FORMICIDAE 53
fruhstorferi, Allotopus xii, **44**
Fruhstorferia sexmaculata xiv, **64**
fulgidissima, Chrysochroa xv, **72**

fulminans, Chrysochroa xv, 11, **72**
fullo, Polyphylla xvii, **68**
fulvipes, Palamnaeus 26

gazella, Odontolabis xiii, **51**
gemella, Nisotra xvii, **102**
gideon, Xylotrupes xiv, 9, 58, **67**, 115
gigas, Neocerambyx xvi, **93**
giraffa, Cladognathus xii, **44**
Glenea elegans xvi, 3, **92**
globosa, Xystrocera xvii, **97**
gracilicornis, Eupatorus xiv, 57, **64**
granaria, Sitophilus xviii, **107**, 110
grandis, Neocerambyx xvi, **93**
grandius, Aceraulis xiii, **56**
gratiosa, Demochroa xv, **73**
gravis, Cryptorhynchus xviii, **104**
gypaetus, Dorcus xii, **47**

HALTICINAE 102
hector, Batocera xvii, **89**
Heliocopris bucephalus xiv, **60**
Heliocopris dominus xiv, **61**
Hemiops nigripes xv, **78**
hemixantha, Megaloxantha xv, **74**
Hexarthrius deyrollei xii, xiii, **48**
Hexarthrius mandibularis xiii, **49**
Hispa armigera xvii, **102**
HISTERIDAE 1, 110, 111
Holotrichia leucophthalma xiv, **65**
hopei, Rhaphipodus xvi, 11, **96**
HYDROHILIDAE 1, 39
hypoleuca, Exopholis xiv, **64**
Hypomeces squamosus **107**

imitans, Pachyteria xvi, **94**
indica, Epilachna xv, 82, **83**, 84
innotata, Scirpophaga 35
inquinata, Aspidomorpho xvii, **100**
INSECTA 3, 9, 103
interstitialis, Casnoidea xii, **37**
interstitialis, Ophionea 38
Iridotaenia chrisostome xv, **74**
Iridotaenia sumptuosa xv, **74**
Isaria anisopliae 115

jansoni, Omocyrius xvi, **93**
Joesse sanguinolenta xvii, **97**
Jumnos pfanneri xviii, **68**
Jumnos ruckeri xviii, 67, **68**

kamerunicus, Elaeidobius 103, 111

Laccoptera tredecimpunctata xvii, **101**
lacteus, Calais xv, 76, **77**
lambi, Pachyteria xvii, **94**
LAMPYRIDAE 4, **78**, 79
lateralis, Epepeotes xvi, **91**
latipennis, Odontolabis xiii, 42, **51**
leachei, Campsosternus xv, **77**
leeweeni, Alcides **104**
Lepidiota stigma xiv, 58, **65**
LEPIDOPTERA 8, 115, 116
Leprodera elongata xvi
Leptocorisa varicornis 35, **92**
lesnei, Eurybatus xvi, **92**
leucophthalma, Holotrichia xiv, **65**
longehirsuta, Anoplophora xvi, **87**
Lophobaris serratipes xvii, **105**
LUCANIDAE viii, 4, 11, 26, 33, 41, 55, 56, 112
lundi, Euryphagus xvi, **91**
lunicollis, Trichogomphus xiv, **67**
lunifer, Cyclommatus xii, **45**, 46
luscus, Epepeotes xvi, **91**
LYCIDAE 4, **78**, **80**
Lytta sp 111

Macrochenus melanospilus xviii, **99**
Macrochirus praetor xviii, 11, **105**
Macroglenea elegans 92
Macronota abdominalis xvii, **68**
Macrotoma fisheri xvii, **91**
maculatrix, Epicedia xvii, **95**
mandibularis, Hexarthrius xiii, **49**
mangiferae, Cryptorhynchus **104**
medembachi, Anoplophora xvi, **87**
Megaloxantha bicolor 69, 74, 75
Megaloxantha daleni xv, **74**
Megaloxantha hemixantha xv, **74**
Megaloxantha nigricornis xv, **75**

Megaloxantha purpurascens xv, **75**
melanospilus, Macrochenus xviii, **99**
Melanotus rubidus **77**
MELOIDAE 1, 16
Metarrhizium anisopliae 115
miliaris, Aspidomorpho xvii, 100, **101**
militaris, Chrysobothris xv, **75**
Mimistena biplagiata xviii, **98**
moellenkampi, Chalcosoma xiv, **62**
molossus, Catharsius xiv, **60**
montanellus, Cyclommatus 46
MORDELLIDAE 1, 111
Mormolyce castelnaudi xii, **38**
Mormolyce phyllodes xii, **38**
moseri, Allotopus xii, **44**

Neocerambyx gigas xvi, **93**
Neocerambyx grandis xvi, **93**
niasiensis, Aulacophora **102**
nigricornis, Megaloxantha xv, **75**
nigripes, Hemiops xv, **78**
nigrocoerulea, Plectrone xvii, **67**
Nisotra gemella xvii, **102**

obsoleta, Anomala 60
occipitalis, Prosopocoilus xiii, **53**
Odontolabis aerata xiii, 49
Odontolabis bellicosus xiii, **51**
Odontolabis brookeana xiii, **49**, 51
Odontolabis castelnaudi xiii, 11, **49**, 50
Odontolabis dalmani xiii, **50**
Odontolabis femoralis xiii, **50**
Odontolabis gazella xiii, **51**
Odontolabis latipennis xiii, 42, **51**
Odontolabis sommeri xiii, **51**
Odontolabis wallastoni xiii, **52**
Omocyrius jansoni xvi, **93**
Ophionea interstitialis 38
opulenta, Catoxantha xiv, xv, **70**
orichalcea, Agestrata xiii, **59**
orientalis, Trirachys xvii, **96**
Oryctes rhinoceros xiv, 9, 57, 65, **66**, 115
Oryctes trituberculatus xiv, **66**

oryzae, Sitophilus xviii, **107**
osculans, Diamesus xv, 40, **41**
Oxyropterus audoniwi xv, **77**, 78

Pachyteria dimidiata xvi, **93**
Pachyteria equestria xvi, **93**, 94
Pachyteria imitans xvi, **94**
Pachyteria lambi xvii, **94**
Pachyteria virescens xvi, **94**
Palamnaeus fulvipes 26
palmarum, Rhynchophorus xviii, **106**
Paraleprodera diophthalma xvii, **95**
Parepicedia fimbriata xvii, **95**
parryi, Batocera xvii , **89**
parryi, Cheirotonus xiv, **63**
parryi, Dorcus 47

PASSALIDAE viii, 4, 26, **55**, 56, 112
Passalus tridens xiv, **56**
pfanneri, Jumnos xviii, **68**
phyllodes, Mormolyce xii, **38**
planicollis, Dorysthenes xvi, **90**
Plectrone nigrocoerulea xvii, **67**
POLYPHAGA 4, **17**, 18
Polyphylla fullo xvii, **68**
praetor, Macrochirus xviii, 11, **105**
prasina, Belionota xv, **70**
Prioptera decempunctata xvii, **101**
Prosopocoilus cinnamoeus xiii, **52**
Prosopocoilus elaphus xiii, **52**
Prosopocoilus feai xiii, **52**
Prosopocoilus forceps xiii, **53**
Prosopocoilus forcifer xiii, **53**
Prosopocoilus occipitalis xiii, **53**
Prosopocoilus zebra xiii, **53**
Protocerius colossus xviii, **106**
Pseudomyagrus waterhousei xvii, **96**
Pteroptyx sp xv, **79**
purpurascens, Megaloxantha xv, **75**

reichei, Dorcus xii, **47**
Rhaetulus didieri xiv, **54**
Rhaphipodus hopei xvi, 11, **96**
rhinoceros, Oryctes xiv, 9, 57, 65, **66**, 115

RHIPIPHORIDAE 1, 111
Rhomborrhina splendida xvii, **67**
Rhynchophorus ferrugineus xviii, 104, **106**
Rhynchophorus palmarum xviii, **106**
Rhynchophorus schachi xviii, **106**
Rhytitodera simulans 86
roeselli, Cibister xv, 11, **40**
rosenbergi, Allotopus xii, **44**
rubidus, Melanotus 77
ruckeri, Jumnos xviii, 67, **68**

Sagra borneensis xvii, **103**
Sagra buqueti xvii, 16, **102**, 103
sanguinolenta, Joesse xvii, **97**
SCARABAEIDAE viii, 4, 11, 16, 19, 33, **57**, 110, 112
SCARABAEINAE viii, 60, 111
SCARABAEOIDEA 4
schachi, Rhynchophorus xviii, **106**
Scirpophaga innotata 35
Selenocosmia crassipes 26
serratipes, Lophobaris xviii, **105**
Serrognathus titanus 47
sexmaculata, Fruhstorferia xiv, **64**
sexpunctata, Cicindela 35
SILPHIDAE viii, 4, 17, 19, **40**, 111
simulans, Rhytitodera 86
sinicus, Adoretus 58
Sinuaria aenescense 78
Sitophilus granaria xviii, **107**, 110
Sitophilus oryzae xviii, **107**
sommeri, Odontolabis xiii, **51**
sordidus, Sphenophorus xviii, **107**
Sphenophorus sordidus xviii, **107**
splendida, Rhomborrhina xvii, **67**
sponsa, Euselatus xiv, **64**
squamosus, Hypomeces **107**
STAPHYLINIDAE 1, 17
STAPHYLINOIDEA 4
stigma, Lepidiota xiv, 58, **65**
sulphurea, Celosterna xvii, **97**
sumatrensis, Cicindela xii, 3, **35**
sumptuosa, Iridotaenia xv, **74**

TENEBRIONIDAE 1, 110

terandus, Cyclommatus xii, **46**
Therates basalis xii, **36**
thoracicus, Dorcus **48**
thuringiensis, Bacillus 116
THYREOPTERINAE 38
titanus, Dorcus xii, 42, **47**
transversalis, Coccinella **83**
tredecimpunctata, Laccoptera xvii, 101
Tribolium castaneum 110
Trichogomphus lunicollis xiv, **67**
Trictenotoma davidi xvi, **85**
TRICTENOTOMIDAE 4, 84
tridens, Passalus xiv, **56**
Trirachys orientalis xvii, **96**
trituberculatus, Oryctes xiv
tuberculata, Collyris **36**

umbrosus, Adoretus 59

varicornis, Leptocorisa 35
verrucosus, Aethalodes xvi, **88**
versicolor, Cicindela xii, **35**
verticalis, Encaustes xv, **81**
vigintioctopunctata, Epilachna 84
virescens, Pachyteria xvi, **94**
viridis, Anomala xiv, **59**, 60

wallacei, Chrysochroa xv, 3, **73**
wallacei, Cyriopalus xvi, **90**
wallastoni, Odontolabis xiii, **52**
wallichi, Diastocera xvi, **90**
waterhousei, Pseudomyagrus xvii, **96**
weyersii, Chrysochroa xv, **73**

Xylorhiza adusta xvii, **96**
Xylotrechus affinis xviii, **97**, 98
Xylotrechus consocius **98**
Xylotrupes gideon xiv, 9, 58, **67**, 115
Xystrocera festiva xvii, 86, **96**
Xystrocera globosa xvii, **97**

zebra, Prosopocoilus xiii, **53**
zonatrix, Anoplophora xvi, **87**
Zonopterus consanguineus xvii, **95**

A

B

C

D

E

F

H

G

I

|0   4 cm

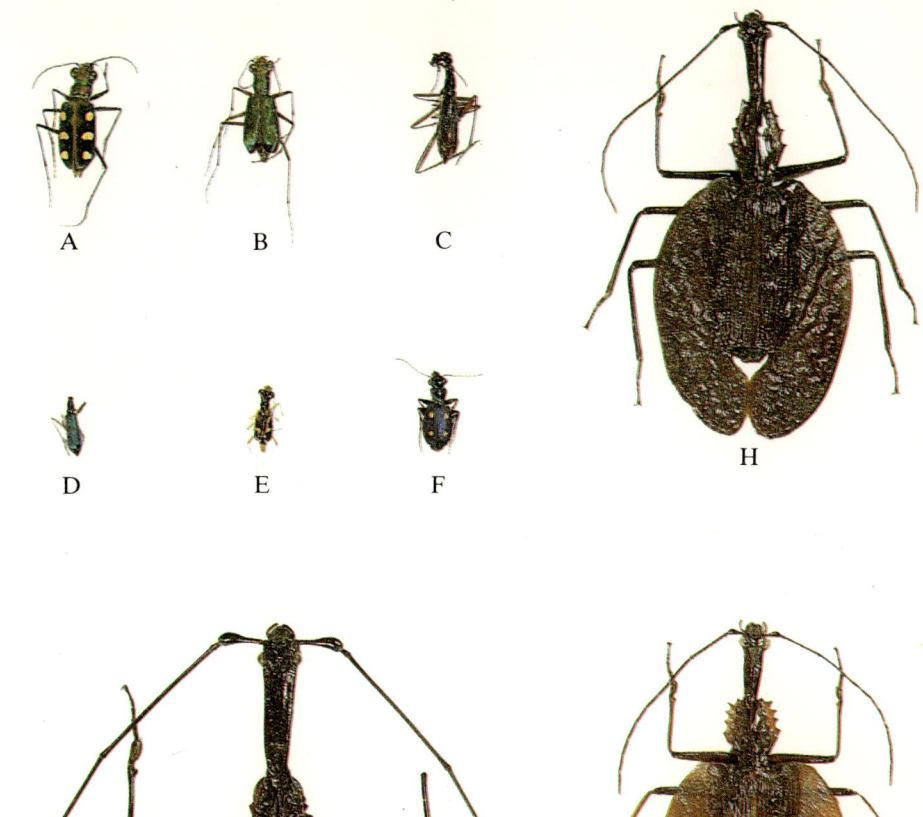

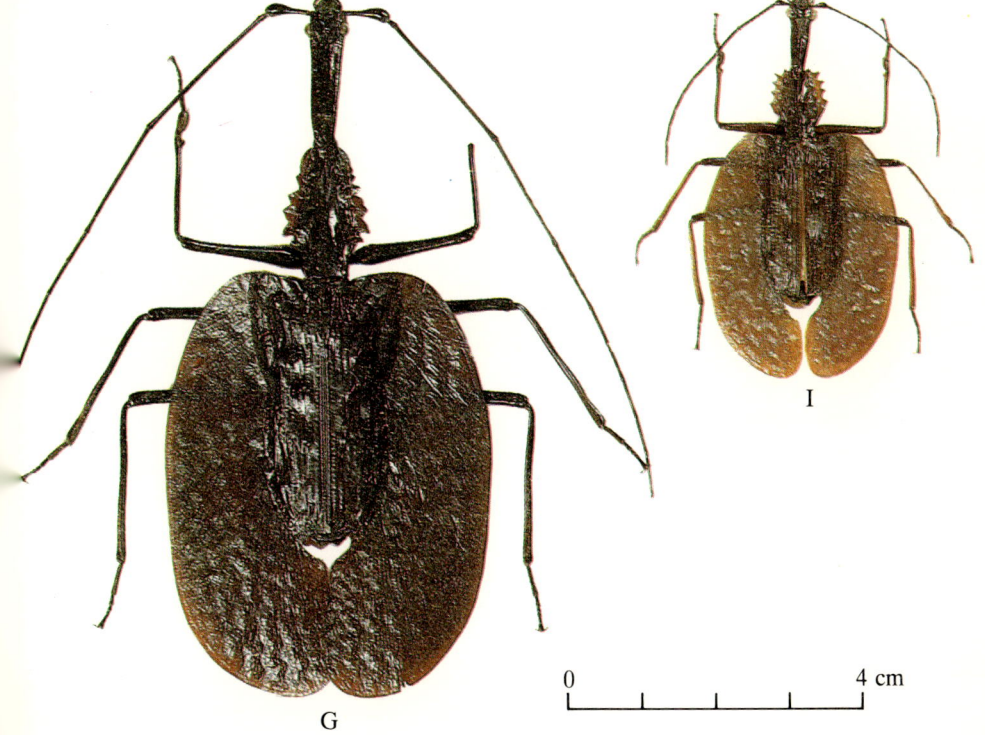

PLATE 1

A

B

C

D

G

E

F

H

0　　　　　　　　　4 cm

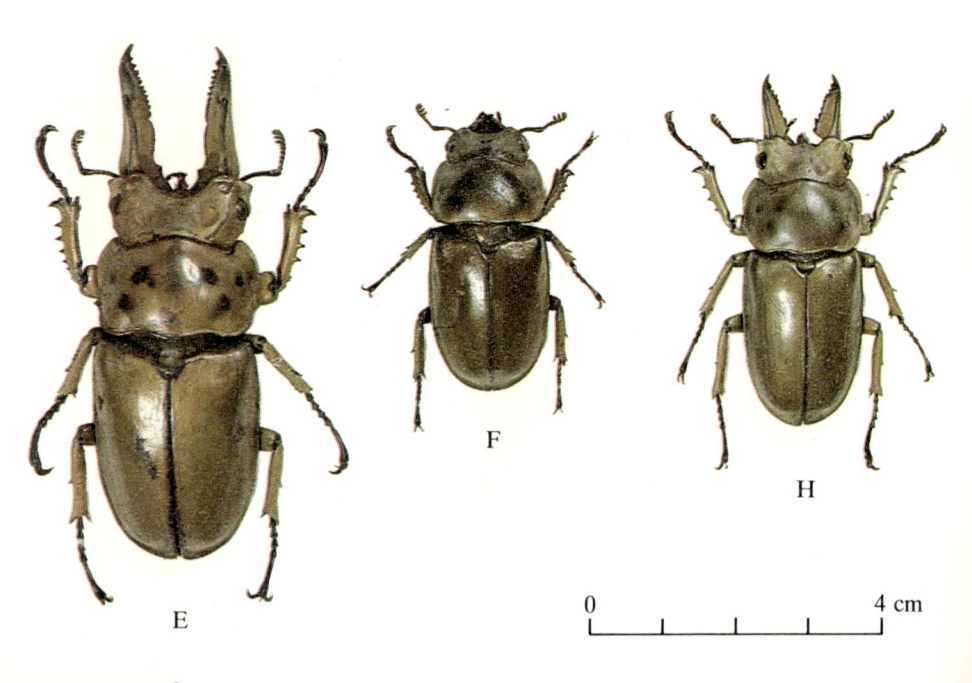

PLATE 2

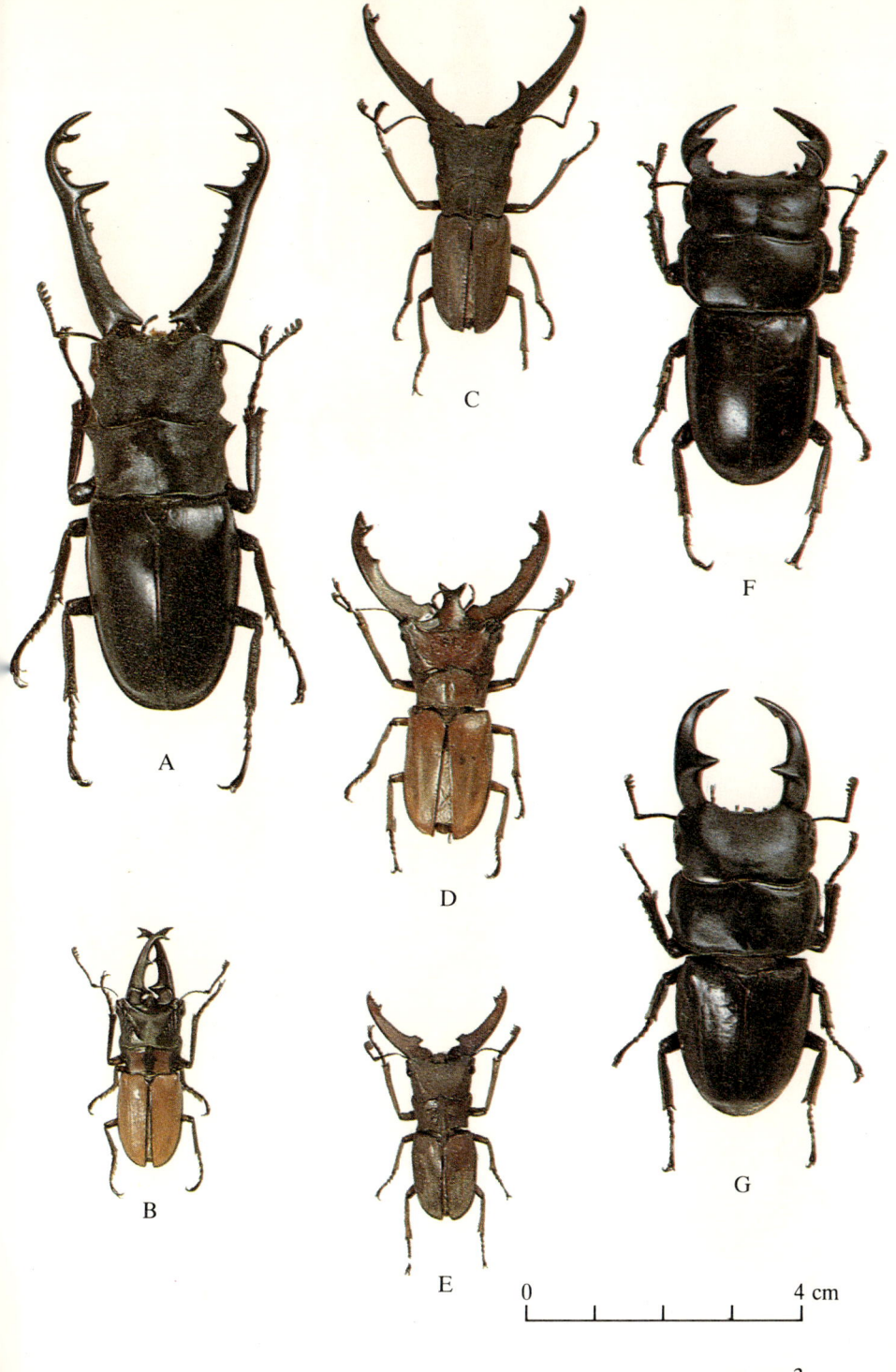

PLATE 3

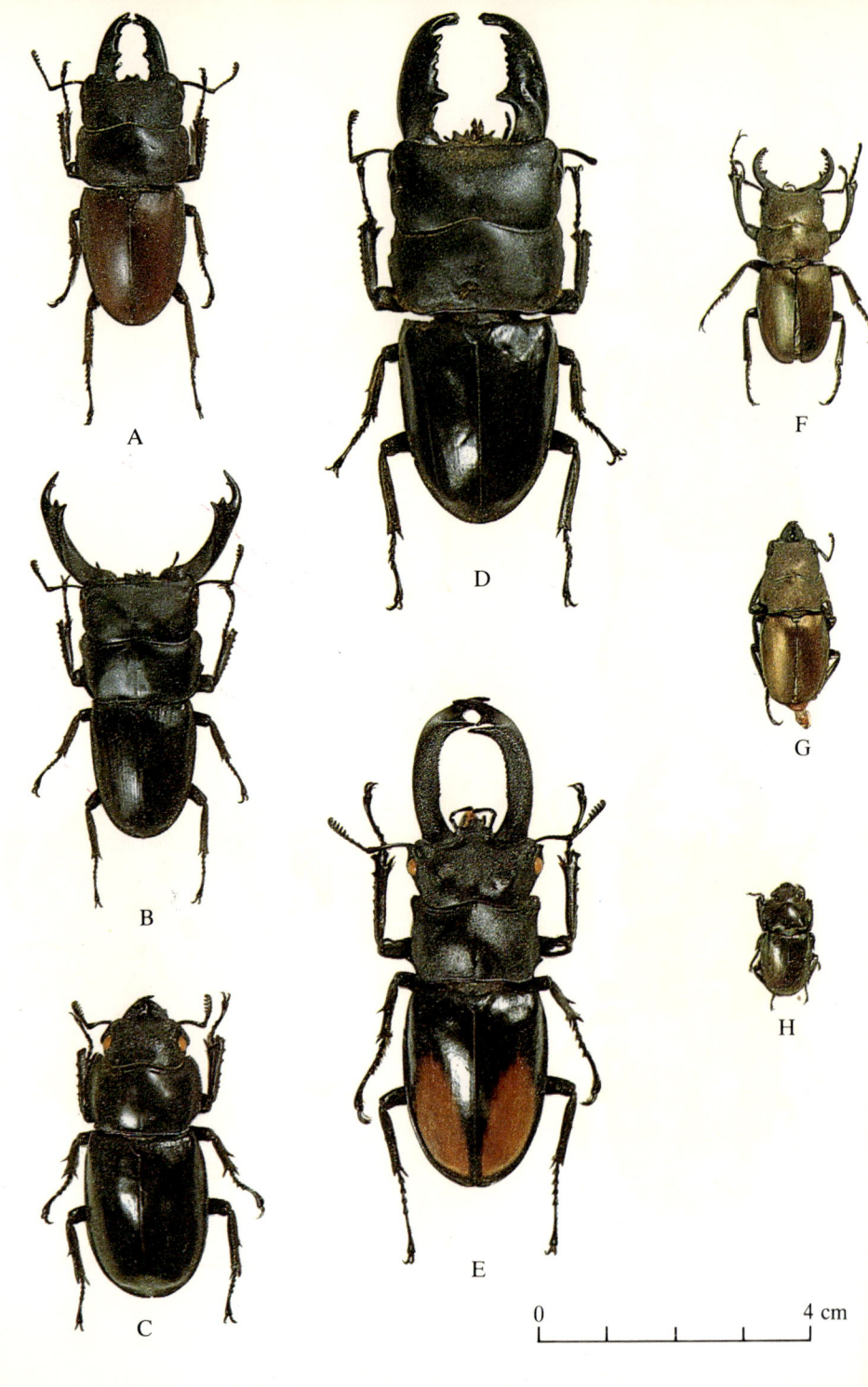

PLATE 4

0   4 cm

A

B

C

D

E

F

0   4 cm

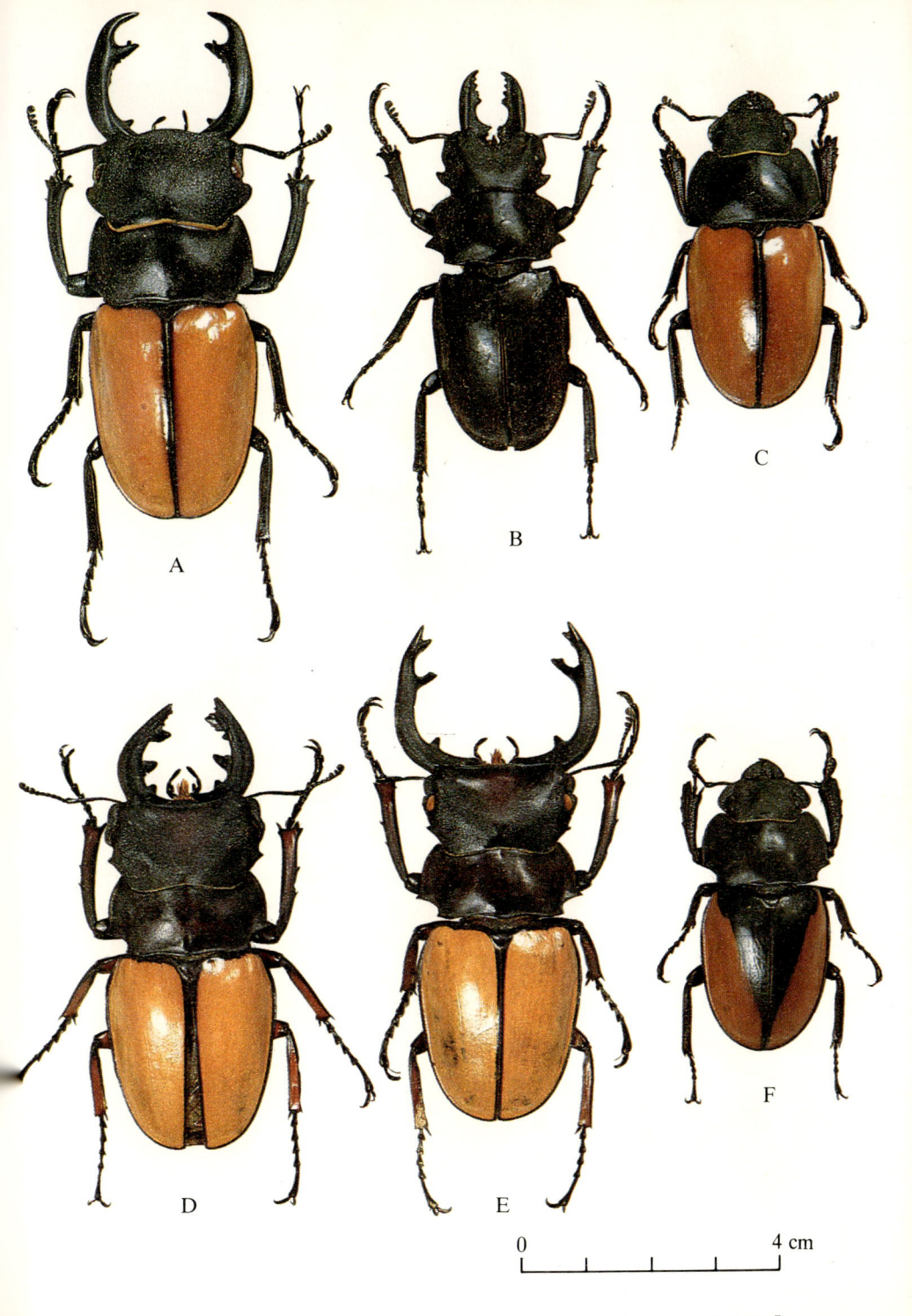

PLATE 5

PLATE 6

0 4 cm

0 |----|----|----|----| 4 cm

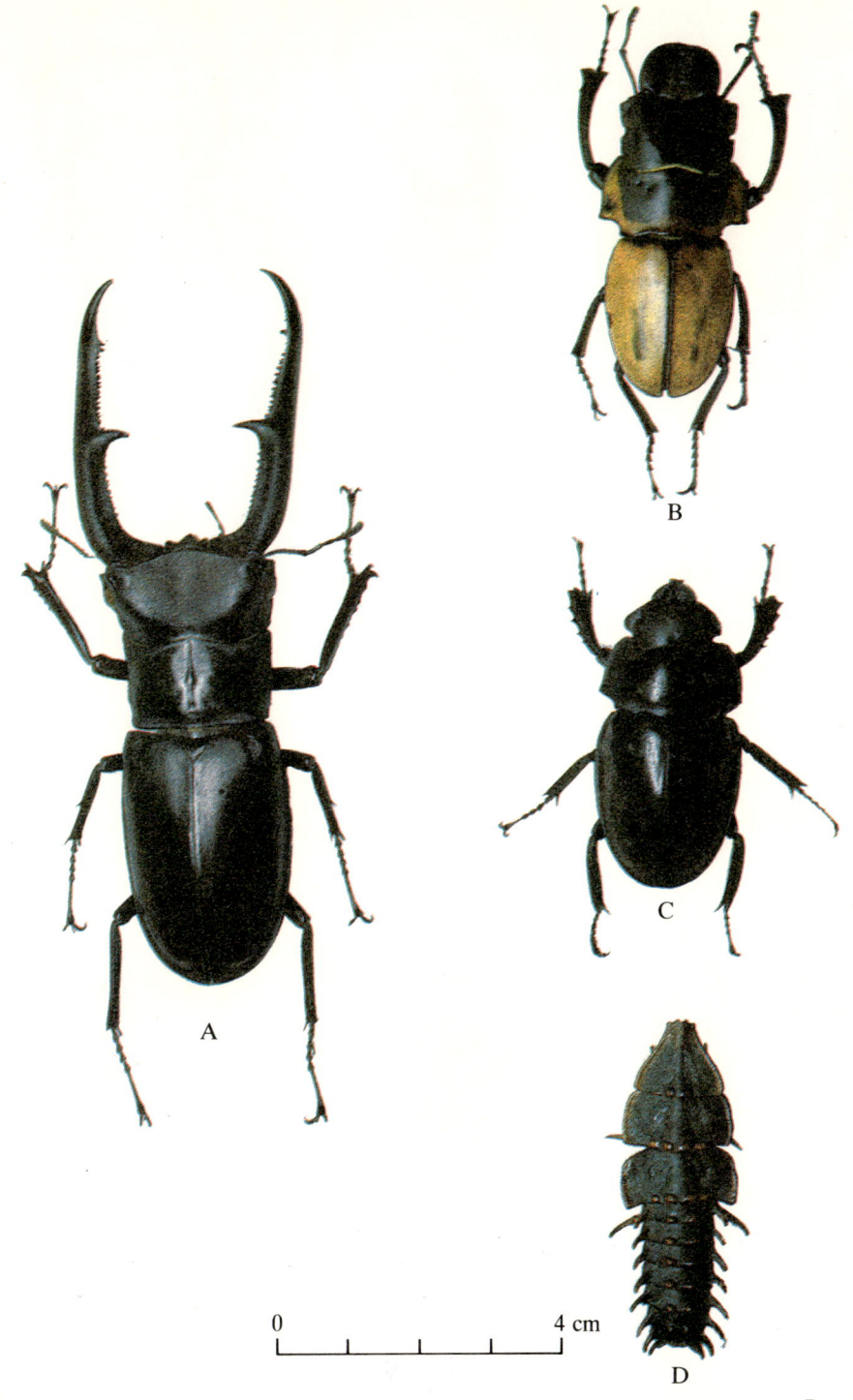

PLATE 7

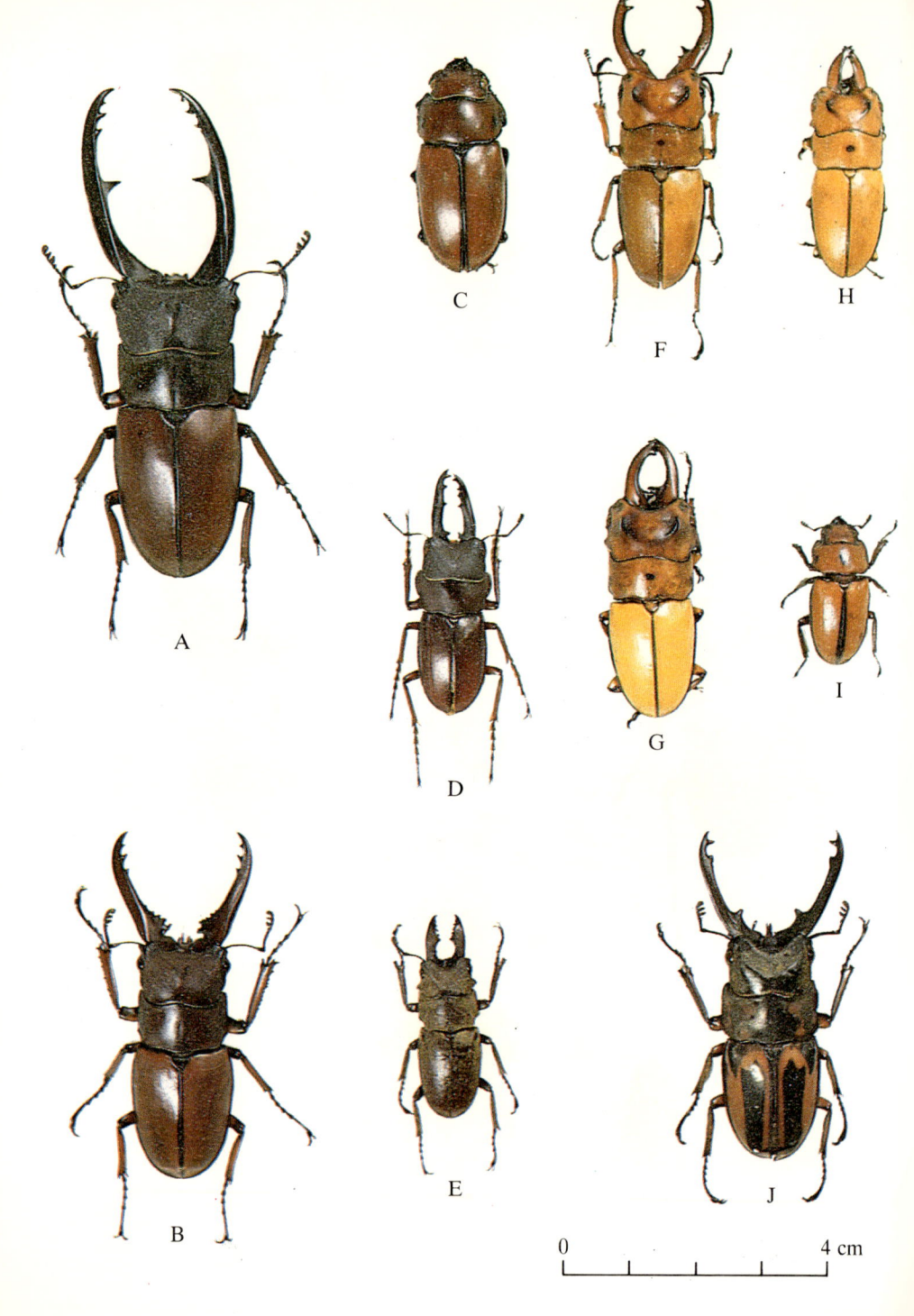

PLATE 8

A

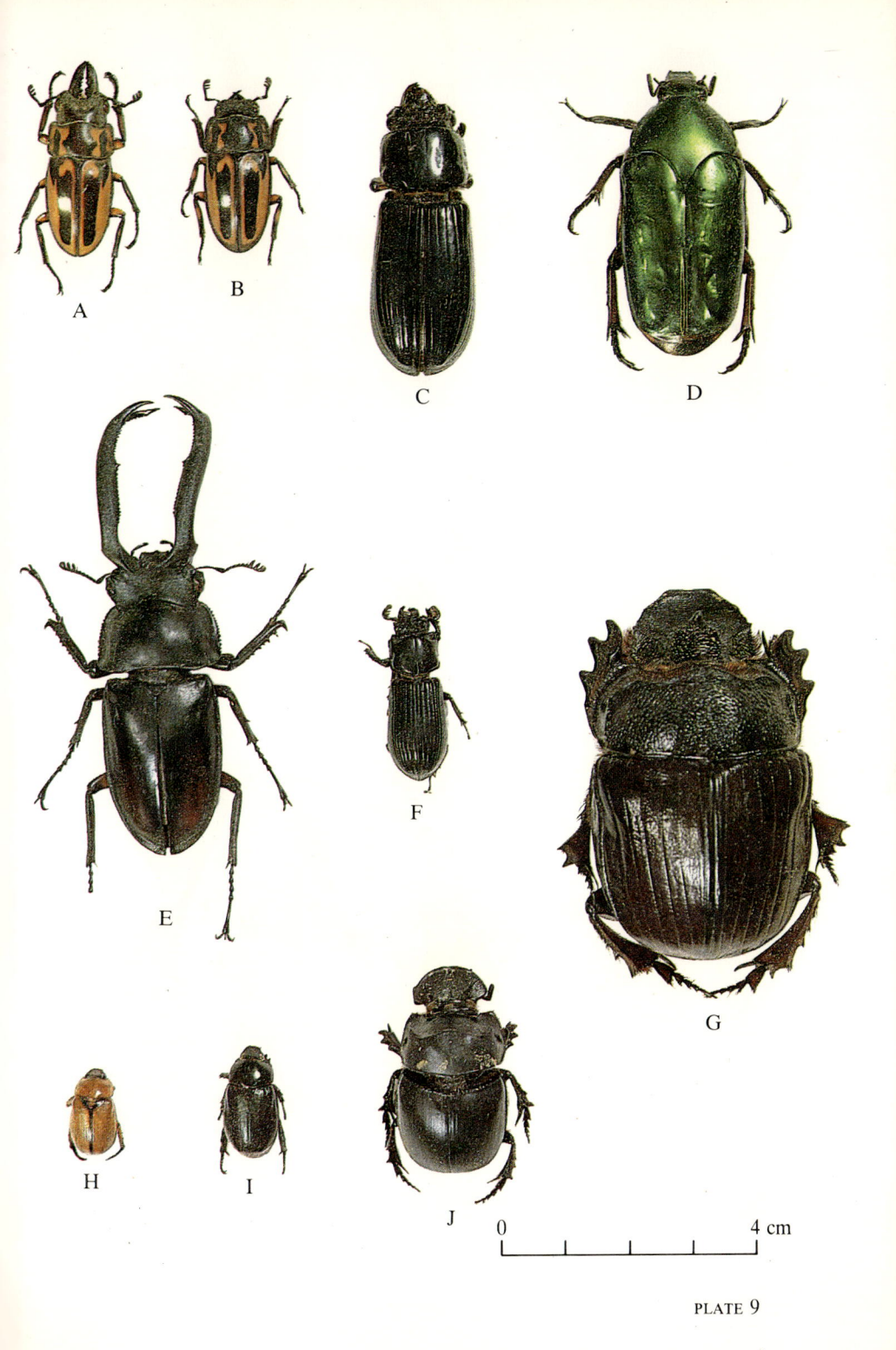

B

C

D

E

F

G

H

I

J

0   4 cm

PLATE 9

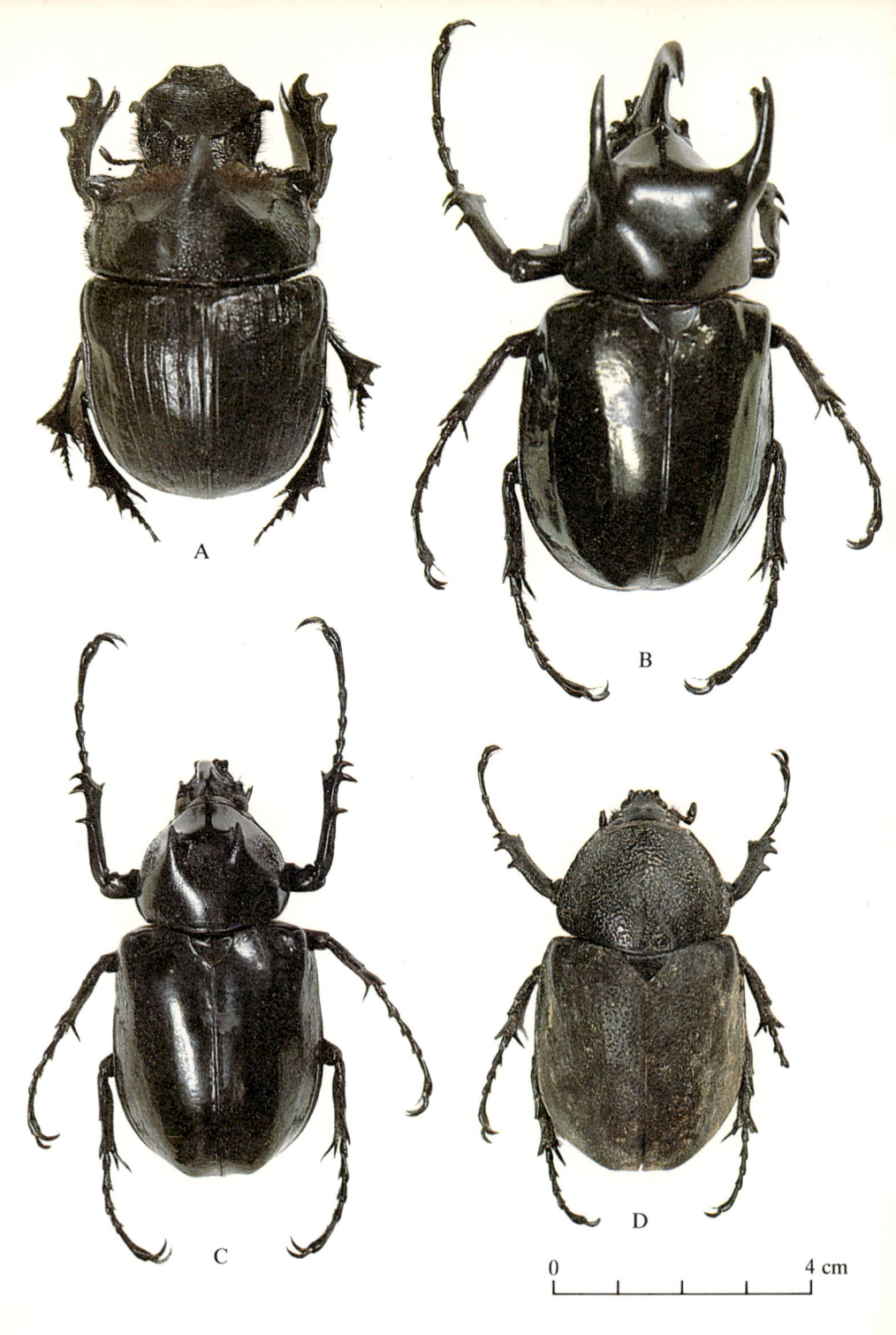

PLATE 10

A

0   4 cm

A

B

0　　　　　　　　4 cm

PLATE 12

A   B

0 ⊢——⊢——⊢——⊣ 4 cm

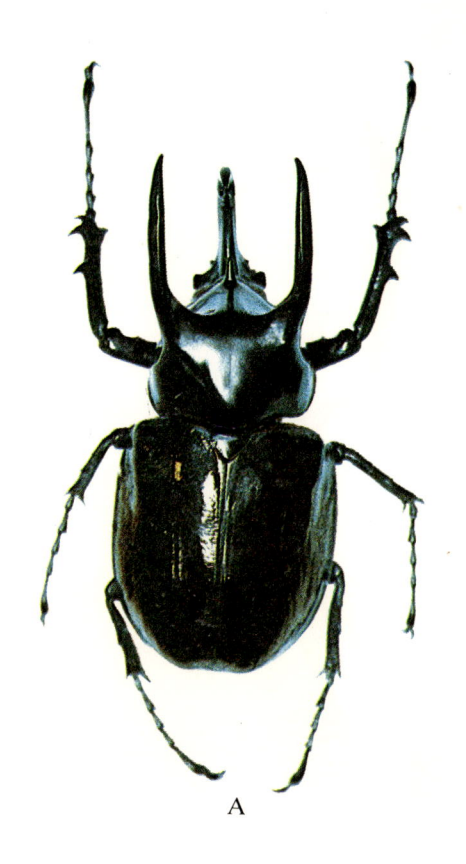

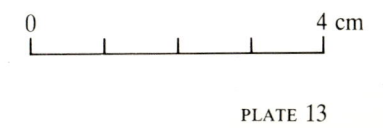

PLATE 13

A

B

C

0   4 cm

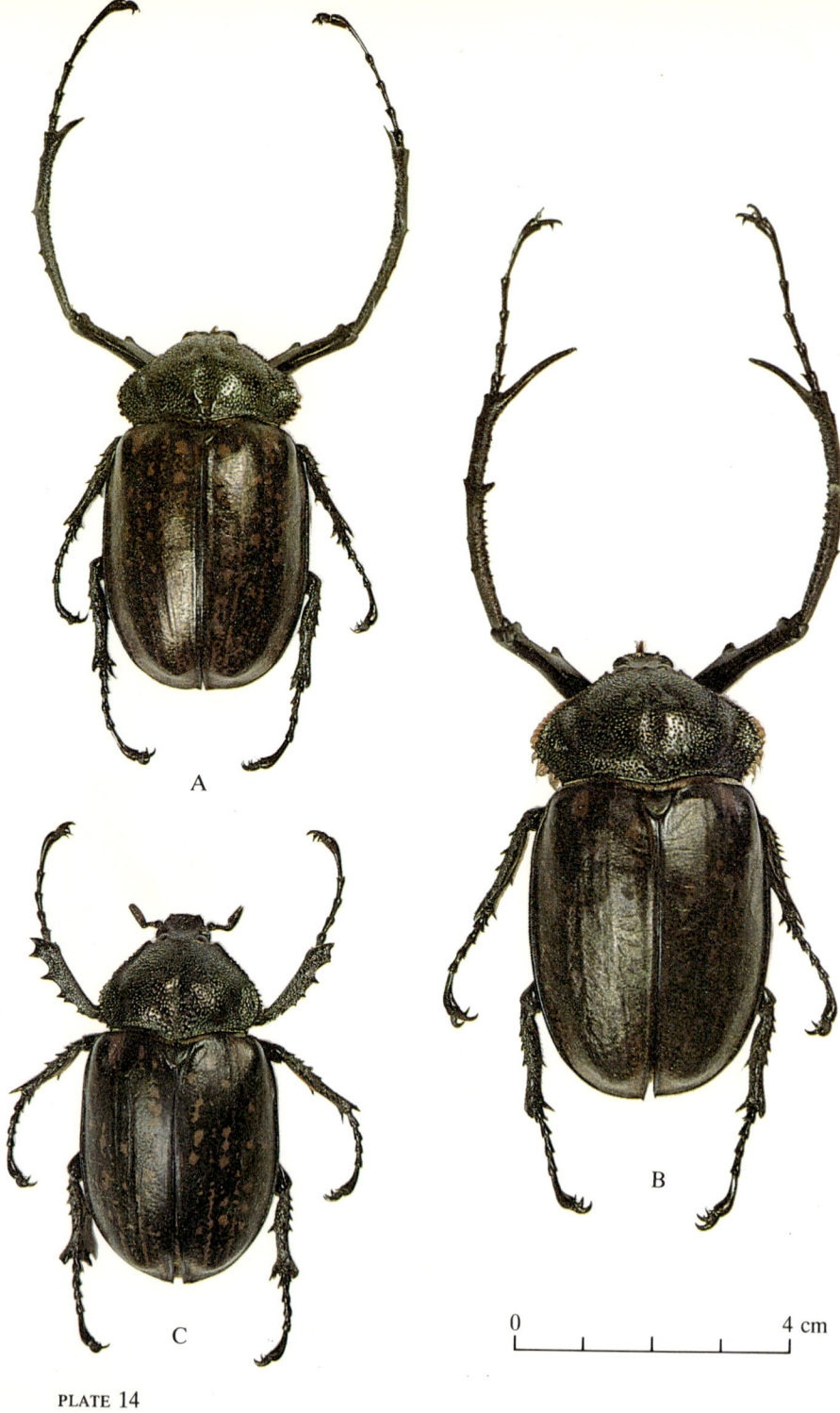

PLATE 14

PLATE 15

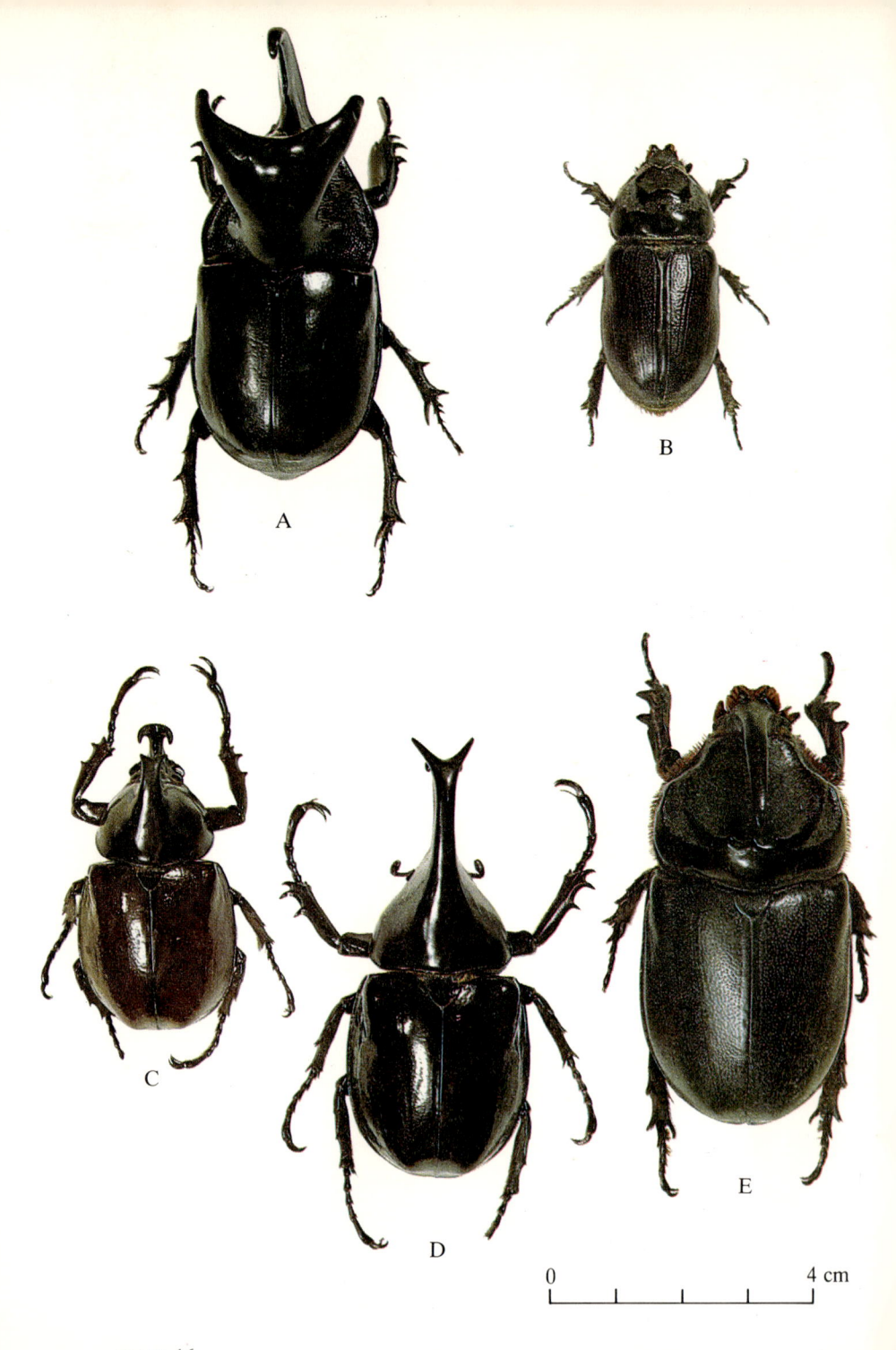

PLATE 16

A

B

C

D

E

F

G

H

I

J

K

L

0　　　　　　　　　　4 cm

PLATE 17

PLATE 18

PLATE 19

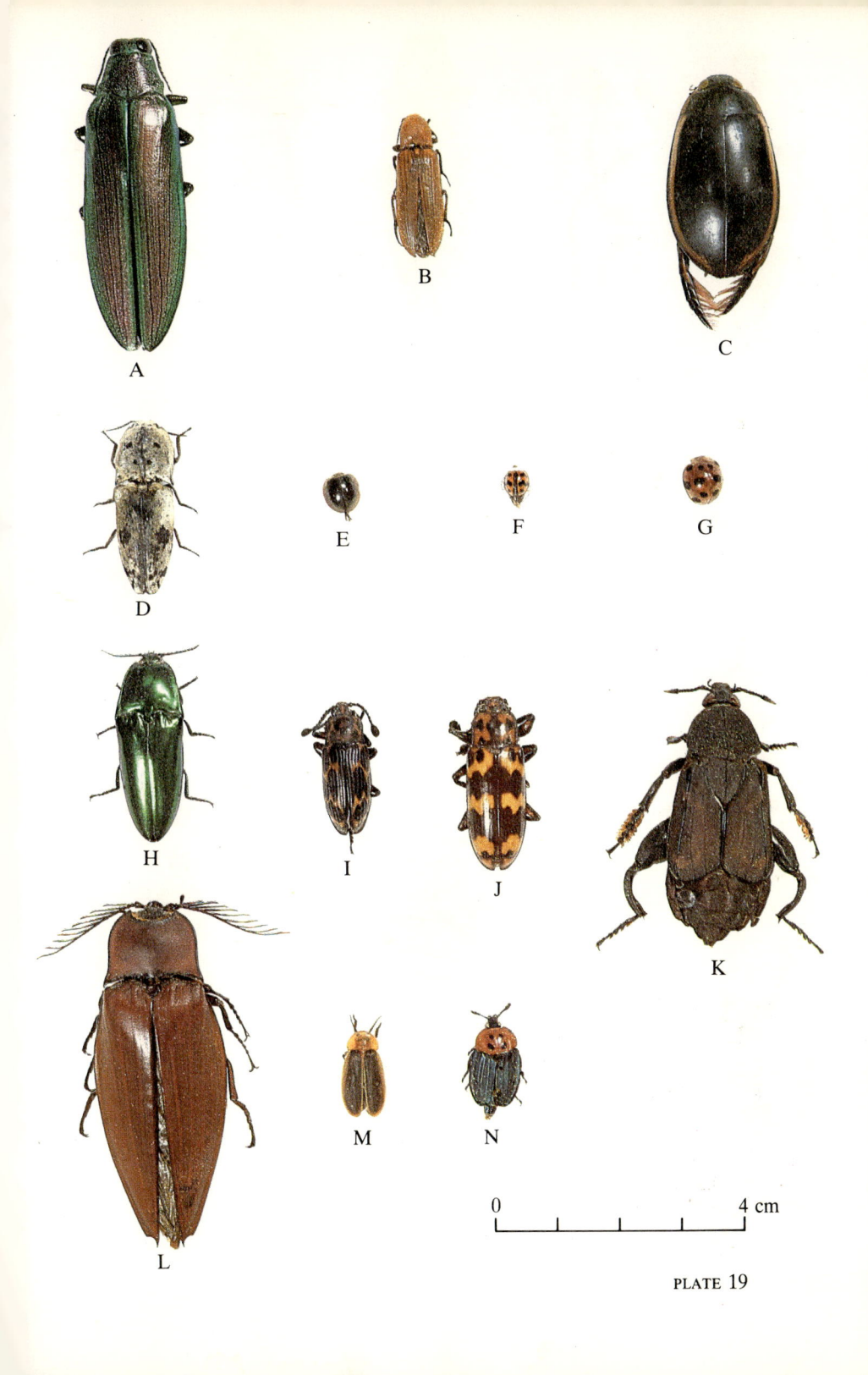

PLATE 20

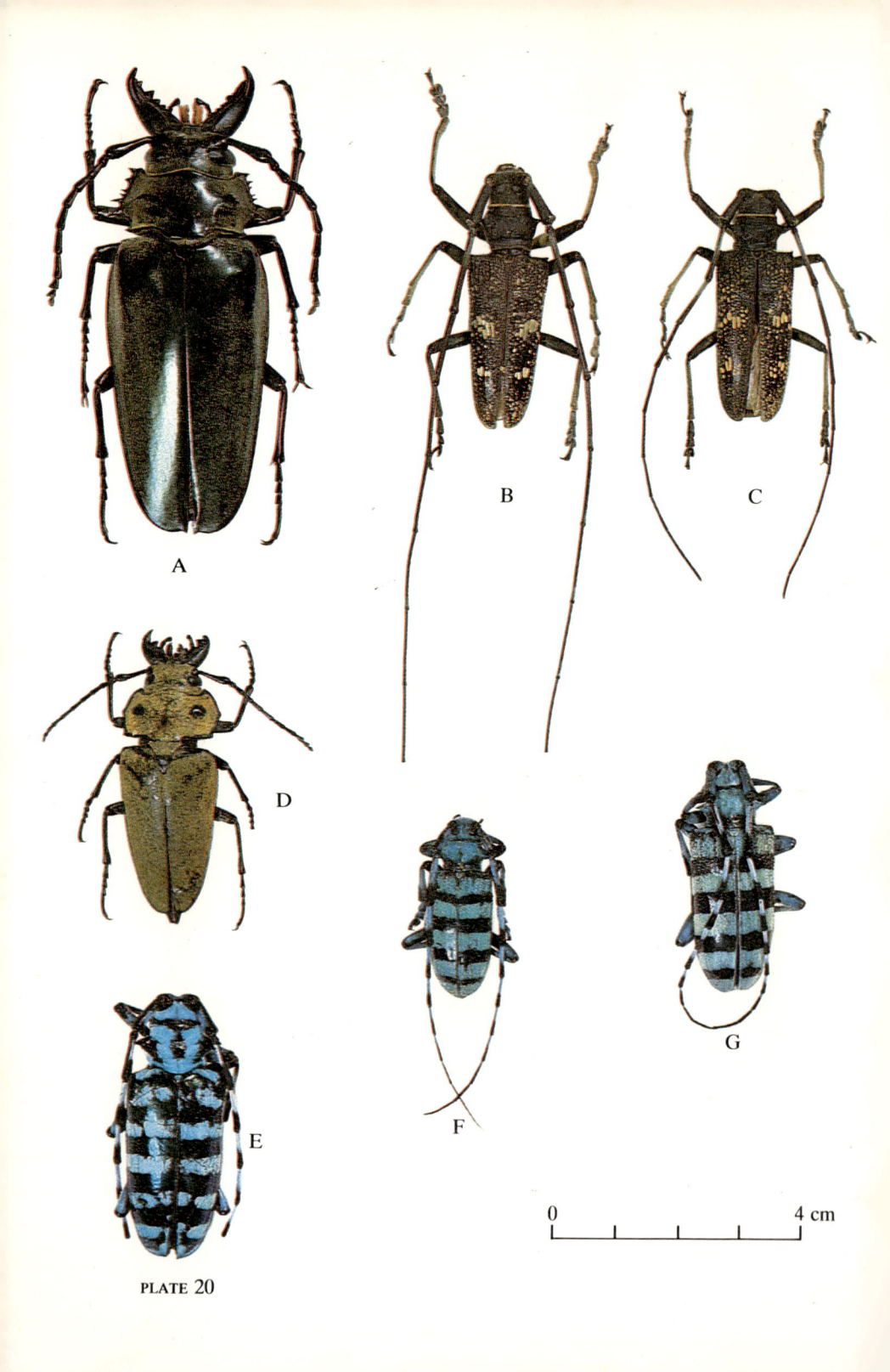

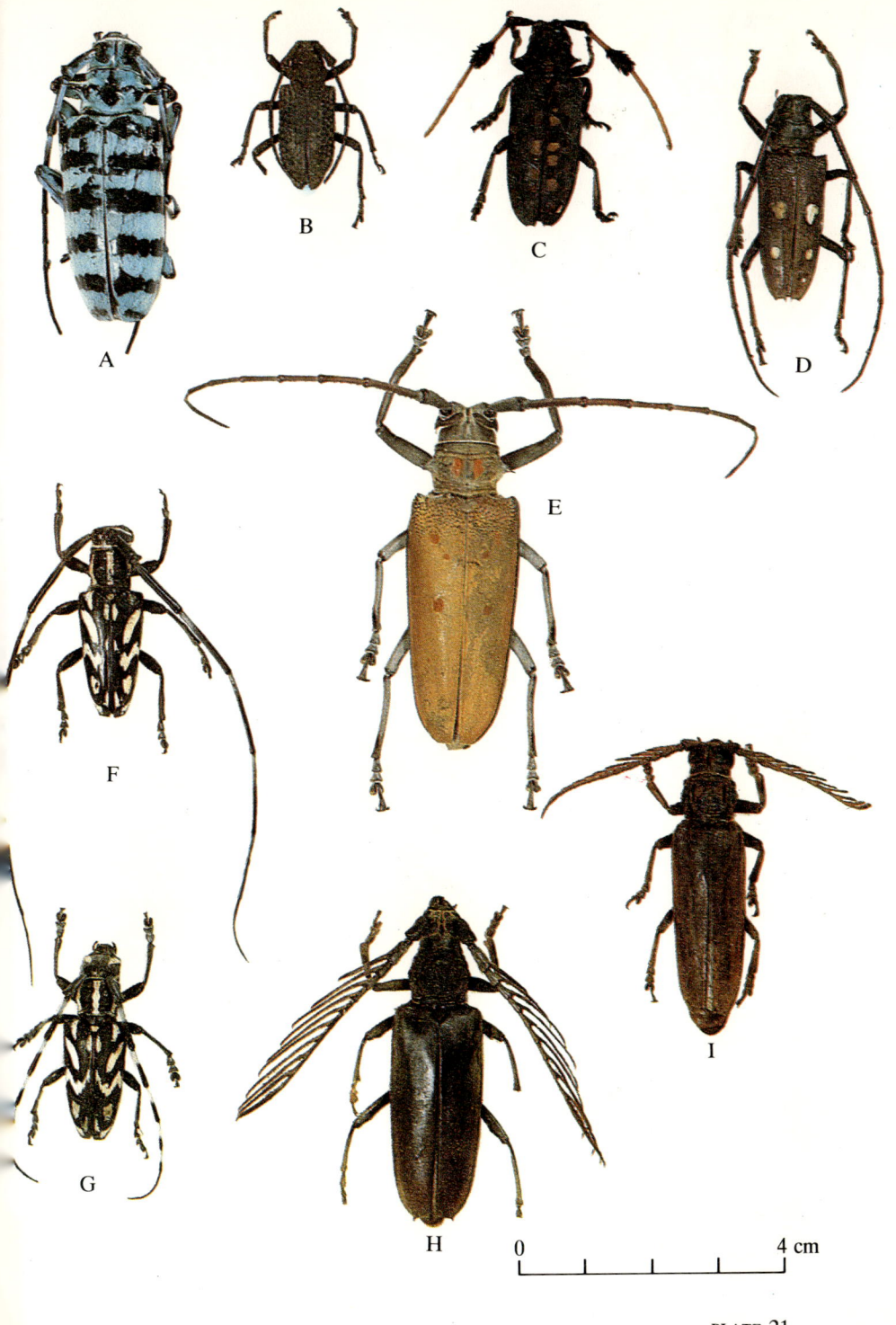

PLATE 21

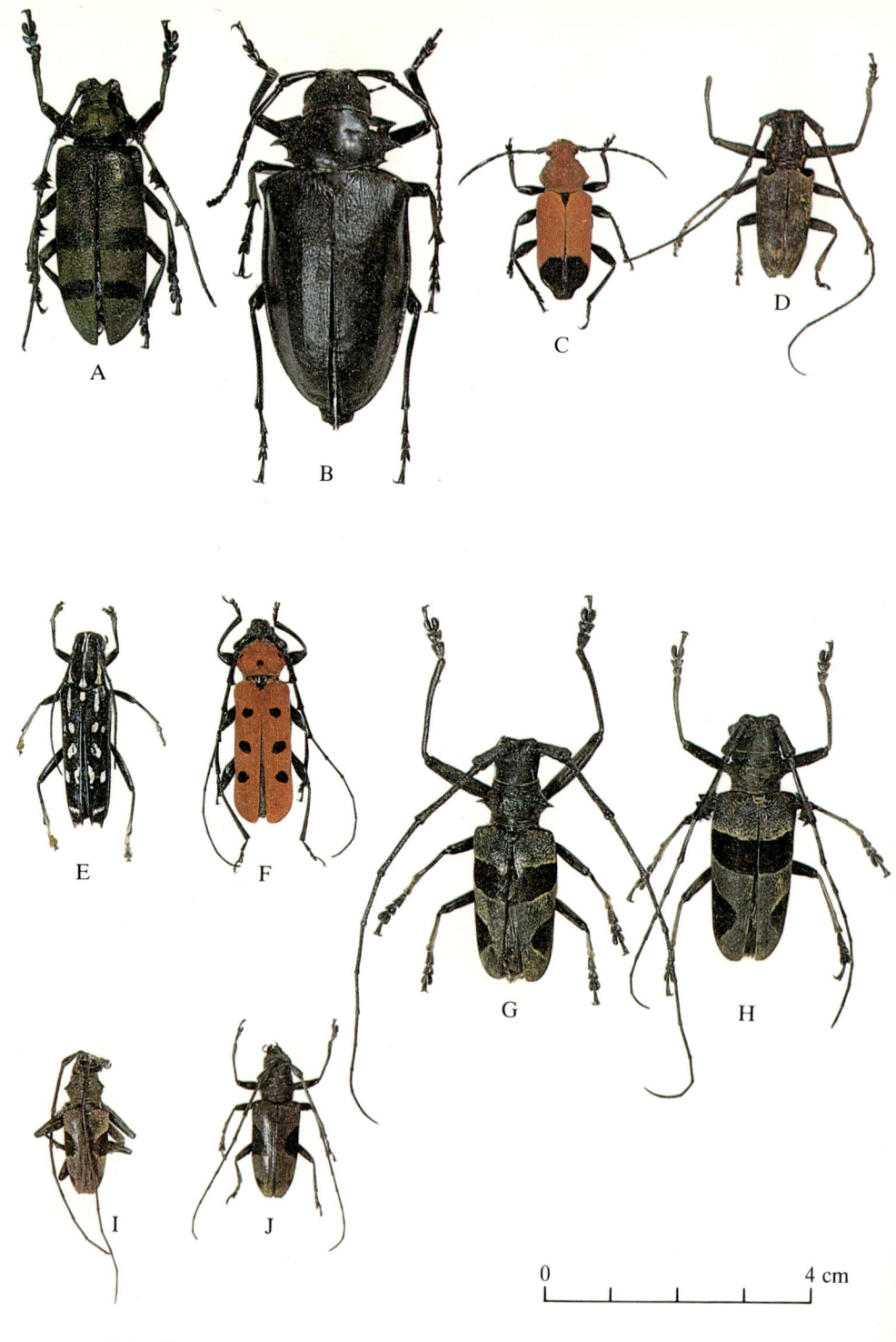

PLATE 22

A

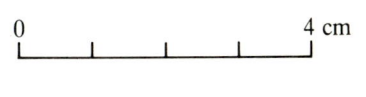

0   4 cm

PLATE 23

A

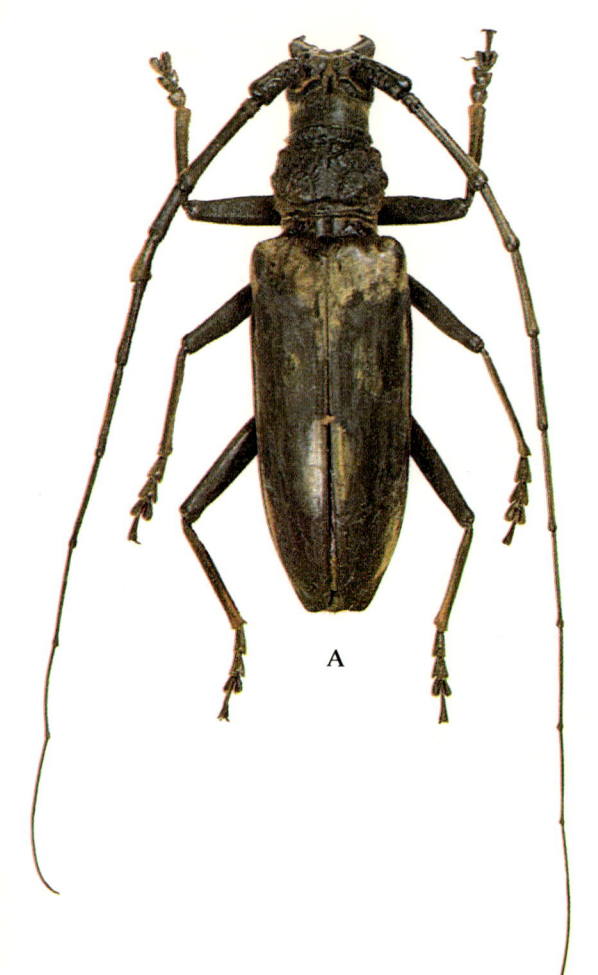

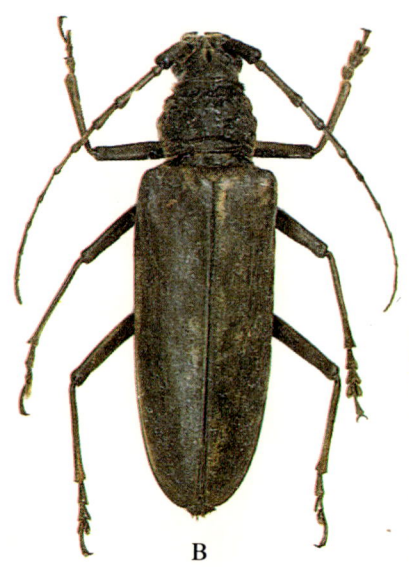

B

0　　　　　　　4 cm

PLATE 24

A

B

C

D

0   4 cm

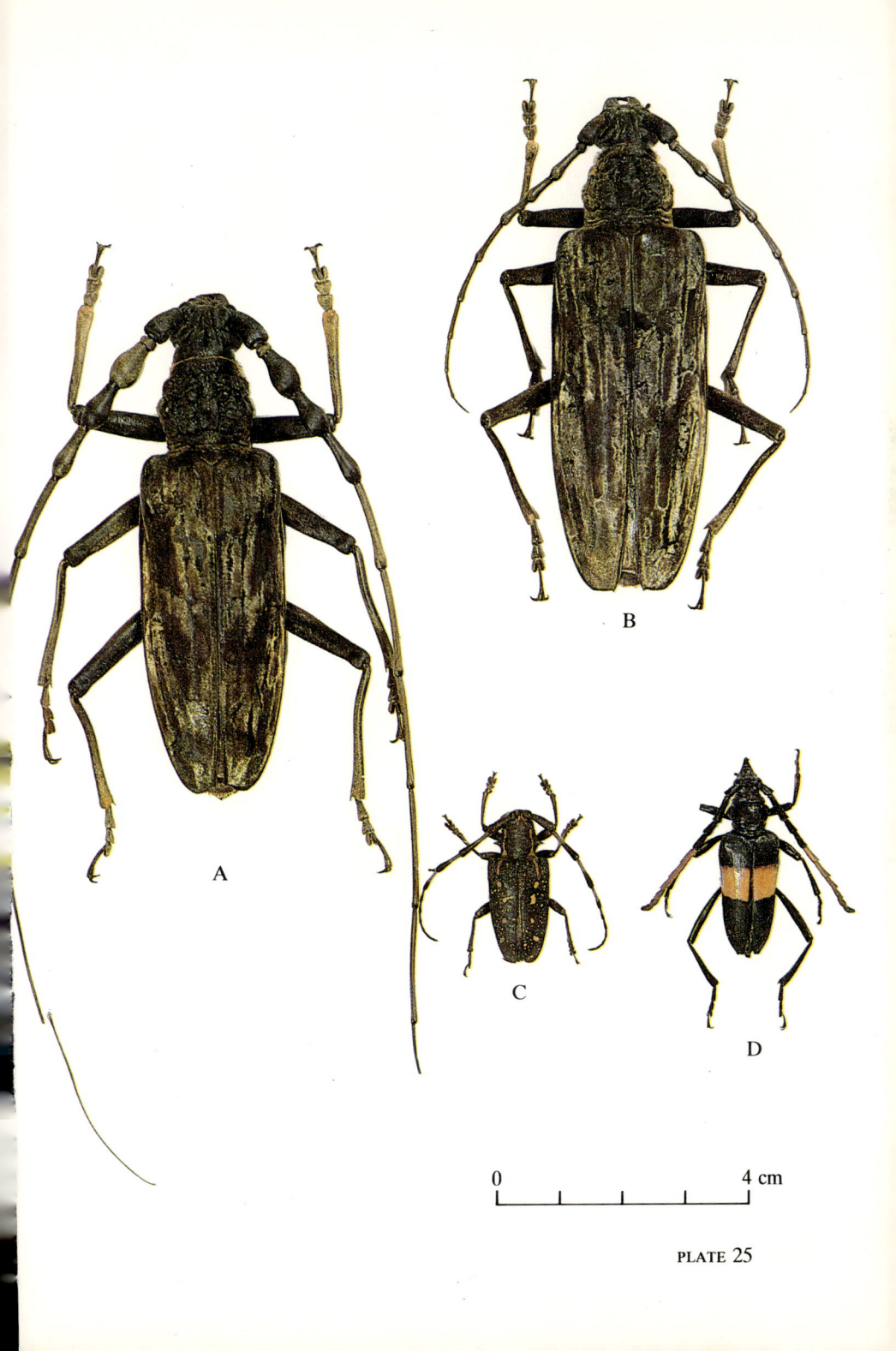

PLATE 25

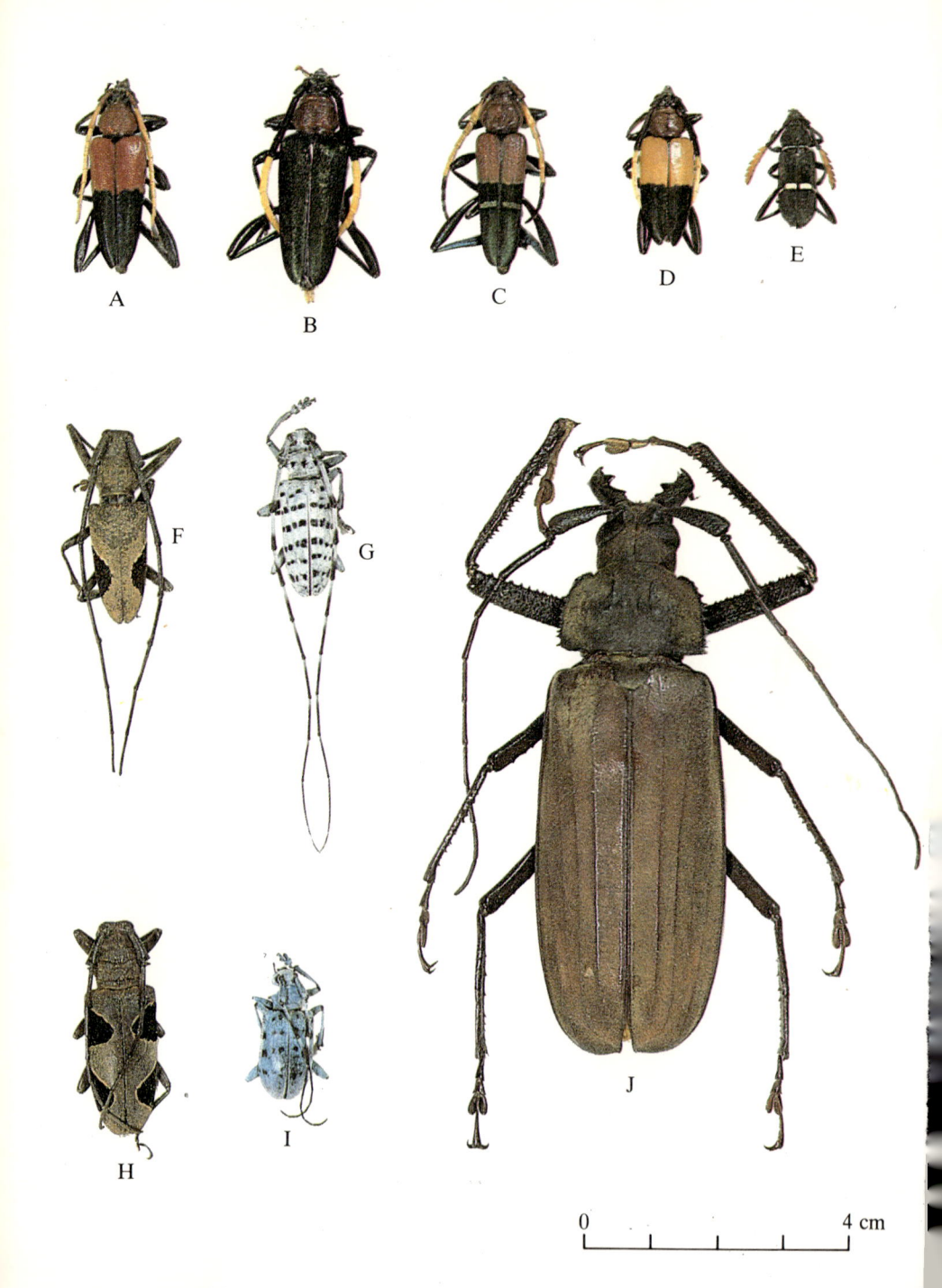

PLATE 26

0   4 cm

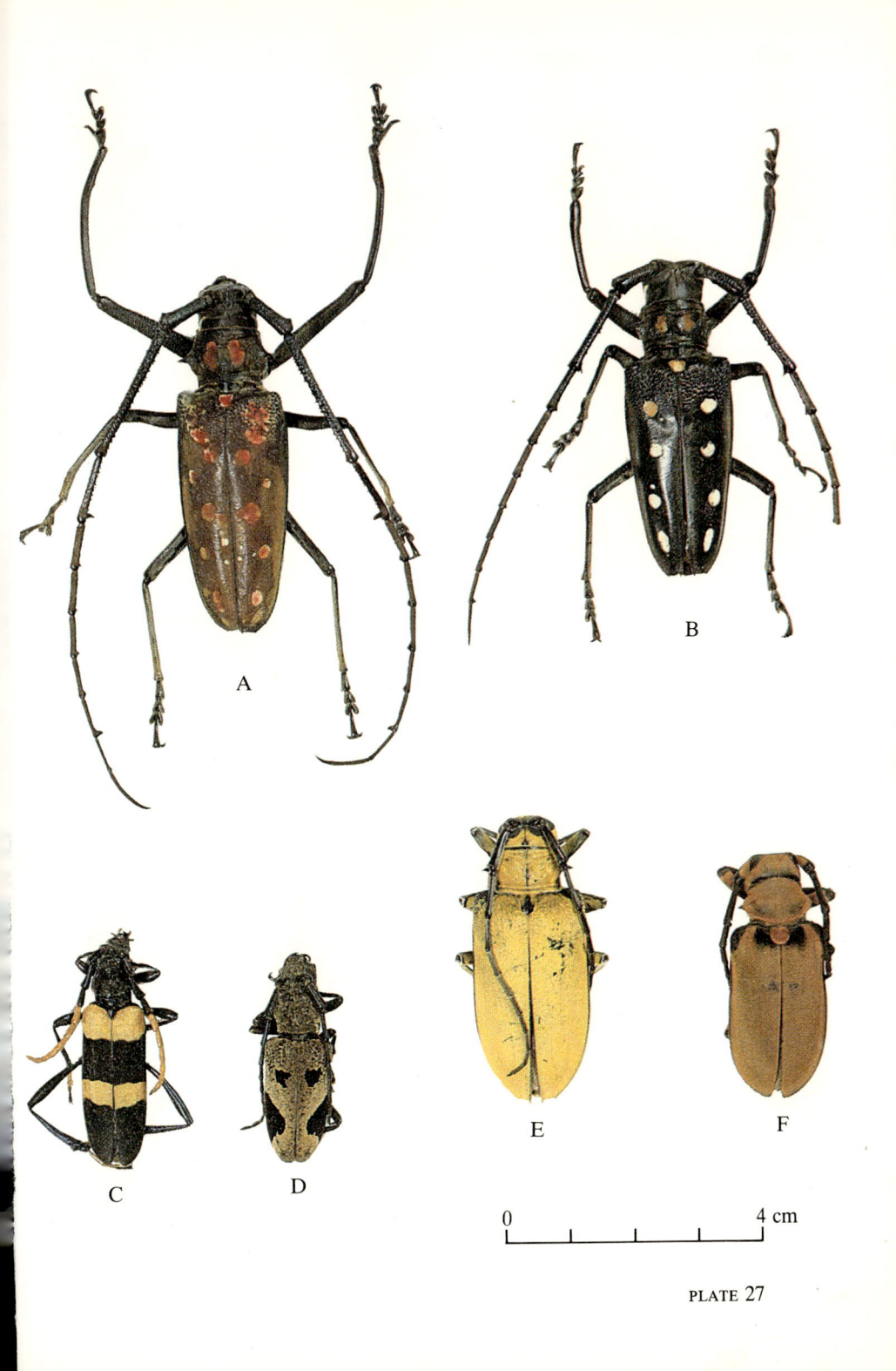

PLATE 27

PLATE 28

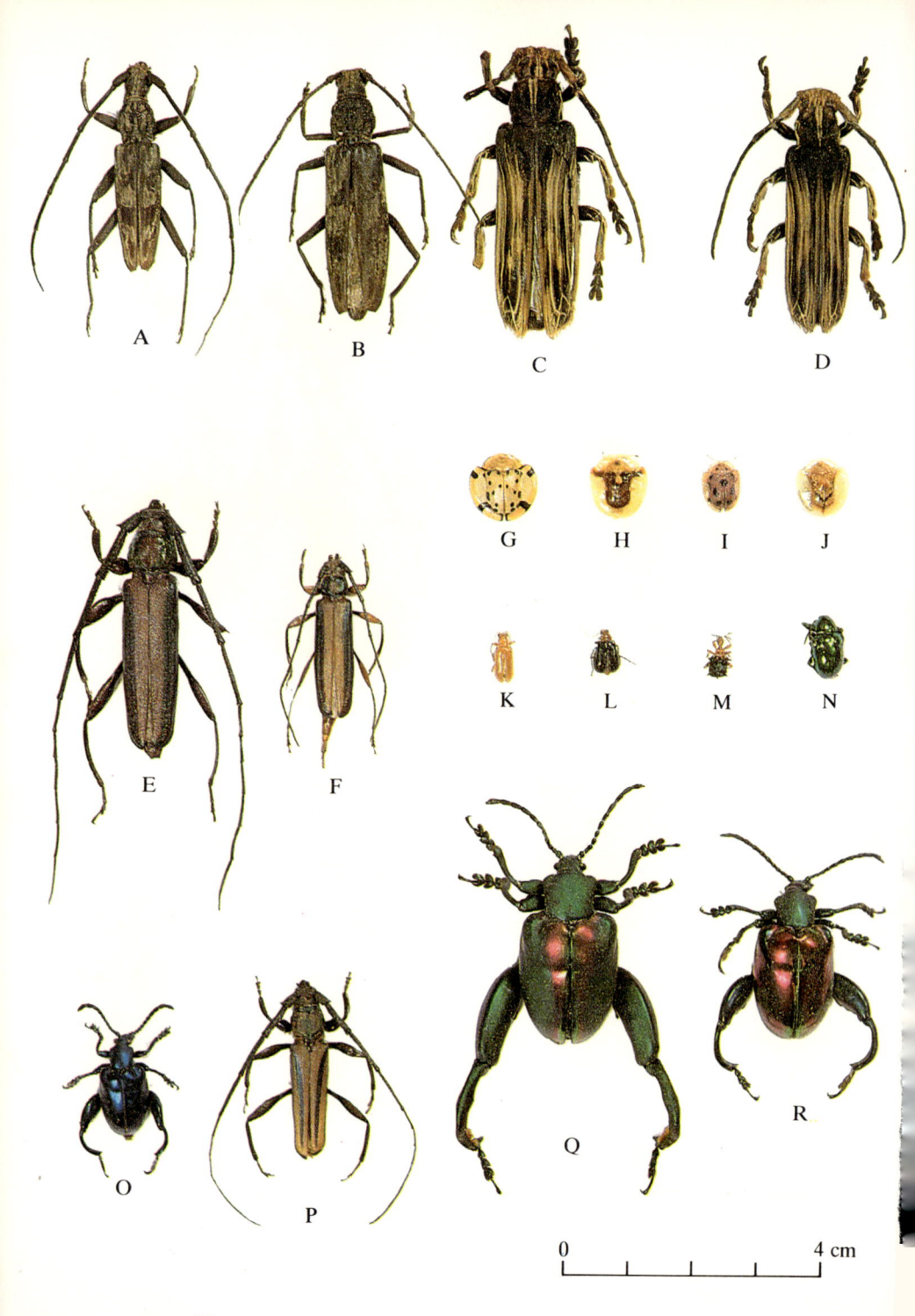

PLATE 29

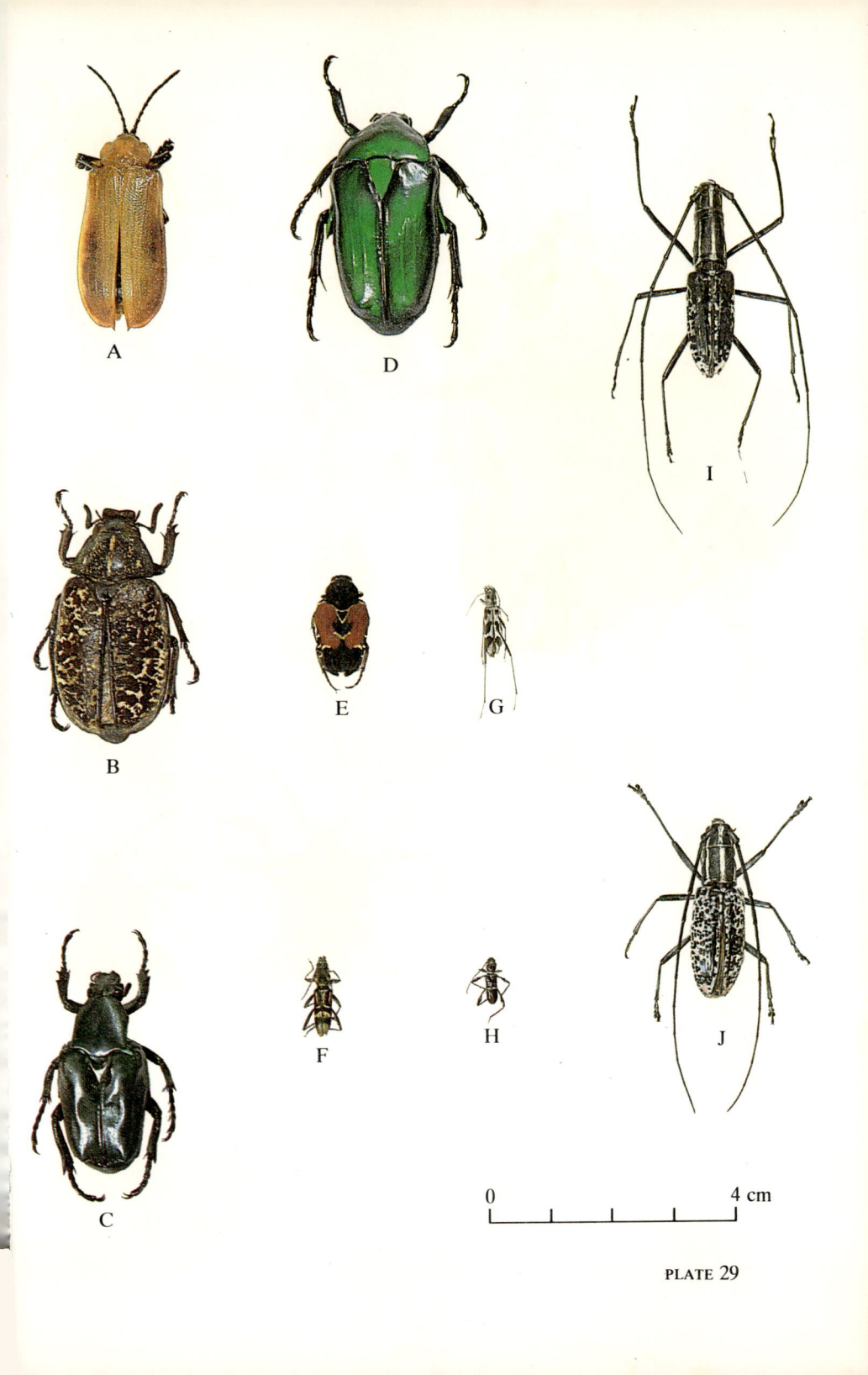

A

B

C

D

E

F

0   4 cm

PLATE 30

A

B

C

D

E

F

0   2 cm

PLATE 31

PLATE 32